REMAKING
RUSSIA

REMAKING
RUSSIA

Edited by

HEYWARD
ISHAM

INSTITUTE FOR EASTWEST STUDIES

PRAGUE BUDAPEST WARSAW NEW YORK ATLANTA
MOSCOW BARDEJOV DEBRECE KROSNO LVIV UZHGOROD

M.E. Sharpe

Armonk, New York
London, England

Library of Congress Cataloging-in-Publication Data

Remaking Russia : voices from within / [edited by] Heyward Isham.
p.   cm.
Translated from Russian.
Includes bibliographical references and index.
ISBN 1–56324–435–7.—ISBN 1–56324–436–5 (pbk.)
1. Soviet Union—History.
2. Russia (Federation)—History—1991–
3. National characteristics, Russian.
I. Isham, Heyward.
DK510.34.R46   1995
947—dc20
94–38420
CIP

Printed in the United States of America

The paper used in this publication meets the minimum requirements of
American National Standard for Information Sciences—
Permanence of Paper for Printed Library Materials,
ANSI Z 39.48-1984.

∞

| BM (c) | 10 | 9 | 8 | 7 | 6 | 5 | 4 | 3 | 2 | 1 |
| BM (p) | 10 | 9 | 8 | 7 | 6 | 5 | 4 | 3 | 2 | 1 |

To the memory of Ambassador Charles E. (Chip) Bohlen,
who enjoyed peeling the layers from what he liked to call the
Soviet "Onion" and whose indomitable leadership and
wise counsel inspired and guided a generation of
Foreign Service specialists on Russia

The Answer

But, I tell you, no past years have been spent in vain,
No unnecessary paths taken,
No things possessed without purpose,
No worlds unperceived,
No gifts left unacknowledged,
And no love given in vain. . . .
And it's never too late to start life all over again,
Start down the entire path,
So that no word or sigh from the past need be canceled out.

Ol'ga Berggol'ts
1952, 1960

Institute for EastWest Studies

The Institute for EastWest Studies (IEWS), founded in 1981 as a trans-Atlantic partnership, serves as a catalyst to build sustainable democratic market societies in Central and Eastern Europe and to facilitate their achieving peaceful and productive interstate relations together with full integration into the community of open societies.

The primary goal of the IEWS is to develop and apply global knowledge to help make the societies of post-Communist Europe more productive, just, and responsible at the local, national, and international levels. To this end, the IEWS conducts programs of public policy research and analysis and serves as an action vehicle for achieving practical results in the transformation to civil societies. The IEWS emphasizes wider citizen participation in political and economic life, the enhancement of local community self-reliance and self-government, and the development of leadership in parliamentary bodies and grass-roots organizations.

The IEWS operates through a network of centers, including New York, Prague, Warsaw, and Budapest, and collaborates with individuals and institutions in order to link Central and Eastern Europe and the Newly Independent States with Western Europe and the United States.

Contents

About the Editor
and the Contributors

Heyward Isham, born in New York City in 1926, graduated from Yale University in 1947 and pursued Russian language and area studies at Columbia University and later at the U.S. Army Language School at Regensburg, Germany (now the George C. Marshall Center at Garmisch). Entering the Foreign Service in 1950, he served as a political and economic officer at U.S. missions in Berlin, Moscow, Hong Kong, and Paris, where he was Deputy Chief of the U.S. Delegation to the Vietnam Peace Talks. He has also served as U.S. ambassador to Haiti, senior foreign service inspector, and faculty adviser at the National Defense University. Since retiring from the Foreign Service, Isham has worked as a consulting editor at Doubleday, where he acquired and edited a number of books dealing with contemporary Russia, and in his present position as vice-president of the Institute for EastWest Studies, where he has developed and implemented projects on postcommunist reconstruction for East Central Europe and Russia. He is the editor, with Maurice Friedberg, of *Soviet Society Under Gorbachev: Current Trends and the Prospects for Reform* (M.E. Sharpe, 1987).

Richard Pipes, born in Cieszyn, Poland, July 11, 1923, came to the United States in 1940 and was naturalized in 1943. Pipes received an A.B. from Cornell University in 1945 and a Ph.D. from Harvard University in 1950. Since 1950 he has been a member of the Harvard University faculty, where he is the Frank B. Baird Jr. Professor of History and Walter Channing Fellow in the Humanities. He has served as director of the Russian Research Center, Harvard University; as senior consultant at the Stanford Research Institute; and as director of East European and Soviet Affairs, National Security Council. Among his many books are *The Formation of the Soviet Union* (rev. ed., 1964), *Russia Observed* (1989), and *The Russian Revolution* (1990). His most recent work is *Russia Under the Bolshevik Regime* (1994).

Ales (Aleksandr Mikhailovich) Adamovich (1927–1994) fought as a teenager in a partisan detachment in Belarus, and his stirring wartime prose gained him renown in later years. An author, political commentator, screenwriter, member of the Belorussian Academy of Sciences, and professor of philology, Adamovich became a prominent critic of Stalinism and an advocate of political democracy who made his views known through television debates, novellas, articles, and speeches on the floor of the USSR Congress of People's Deputies, in which he served as a deputy (1989–91). His many writings included *Guerillas*, which appeared in two volumes in the early 1960s, a documentary history of the German siege of Leningrad (now St. Petersburg), which he wrote with Daniil Granin, and *Out of the Fire*, which he wrote with Ianka Bryl' and Vladimir Kolesnik. Adamovich also wrote the screenplay for the film *Come and See*, directed by Elem Klimov. Until his untimely death of a heart attack on January 26, 1994, he was director of the Film Research Institute in Moscow, and a month earlier had been elected to the council of a new organization, the Russian Antifascist movement.

Iurii Afanas'ev, born in 1934, is a historian, former director of the State Archives, and currently rector of the Russian State University for the Humanities. A leader of the democratic movement in the former Soviet Union, Afanas'ev, together with Andrei Sakharov and Boris Yeltsin, founded the Interregional Deputies' Group, a democratic opposition bloc in the USSR Congress of People's Deputies. He also served as a member of the parliamentary commission on opening the KGB Archives and is a founding member of Memorial, the anti-Stalinist human rights organization. He speaks fluent French and is the author of numerous books on Russian contemporary history. He edited and contributed to the collection of reformist essays published in 1988 under the title *There Is No Other Way*.

Konstantin Azadovskii, born in Leningrad in 1941, graduated from Leningrad State University and Herzen Pedagogical Institute. Like his father, Mark Azadovskii (d. 1954), a noted literary historian specializing in Russian and German folklore, Konstantin Azadovskii fell victim to the perennial KGB hostility to independent-minded and outspoken intellectuals. When in 1969 he refused to be a witness against a fellow professor in a trumped-up narcotics charge, he was banished to a teaching position in Petrozavodsk. Following his return to Leningrad in 1974, Azadovskii directed the foreign languages section of a higher educational institution. In 1980 the KGB arrested him on fabricated narcotics charges, and he served a two-year prison sentence at a labor camp in Magadan. After 1985, renouncing earlier intentions to emigrate, Azadovskii intensified efforts for his rehabilitation and, publicly supported by leading Moscow and Leningrad intellectuals, was finally able, in 1989, to have the criminal sentence annulled for lack of evidence. A specialist in German literature, Azadovskii has published more than two hundred articles, monographs, and translations, including edited volumes of the correspondence of Rainer Maria Rilke, Marina Tsvetaeva, and Boris Pasternak, and numerous works on the Russian Silver Age. His many international awards and honors include the Friedrich-Gundolf Prize and the Prize of the Austrian Ministry of Culture and the Arts.

Leonid Batkin's major field of study is the history and theory of culture. He is head research fellow at the Institute of World History of the Russian Academy of Sciences and the Institute of Advanced Humanities Research of the Russian State University for the Humanities. Several of Batkin's books on the Italian Renaissance have been published in the West, among them *Die italienische Renaissance: Versuch einer Charakterisierung eines Kulturtyps* (1981); *Leonardo da Vinci* (1989); *Gli umanisti italiani: Stile di vita e di pensiero* (1990); and *L'idea di individualità nel Rinascimento italiano* (1992). He was awarded the Prize of the Council of Ministers of the Italian Republic in 1989. Batkin was also a contributor to the unauthorized collection of essays *Metropol* (1979). His recent publications on Russia include *Renewal of History* (1990) and *Political Mirages of Present-Day Russia* (forthcoming). A founder (and subsequently a representative) of the Moscow Tribune, a political club formed in 1988 with the support of Andrei Sakharov, Batkin became a leader of the Democratic Russia movement in January 1991. He left that organization a year later, together with Iurii Afanas'ev and Iurii Burtin, and he is today a member of the group Independent Civic Initiative.

Vitalii Borovoi, protopresbyter of the Russian Orthodox Church (Moscow Patriarchate), was born on January 18, 1916, to a peasant family in the Vitebsk region of Belarus. He is married and has one son. Father Borovoi was educated at Vilnius Theological Seminary and the Warsaw University Department of Theology. He served as inspector and teacher at Minsk Theological Academy from 1945 to 1954 and as a professor at the Theological Academy in Leningrad (now St. Petersburg) from 1954 to 1962. He was the Russian Orthodox representative to the World Council of Churches and a member of its staff from 1962 to 1985. He also served as an observer for the Russian Orthodox Church at the Second Vatican Council and was a professor at Moscow Theological Academy (1972–78, 1984–92). He is currently deputy representative of the Department of External Church Relations of the Moscow Patriarchate. He is a professor and doctor of theology of Moscow Theological Academy, of St. Vladimir's Seminary in New York, of the Department of Theology at Charles University in Prague, and of Pravoslávna Bohoslovecká Faculta v Prešove (Slovakia).

Denis Dragunskii was born in 1950 and graduated from Moscow State University. After receiving an M.A. in classics from Moscow State University in 1973, he taught modern Greek at the USSR Ministry of Foreign Affairs Diplomatic Academy for several years. Dragunskii then began a career as a freelance journalist, playwright, and screenwriter. Dragunskii's eighty publications have contributed to the public debate in Russian about postcommunist statehood, regional ethnic diversity, the conflict of political values and attitudes, and the moral crisis of Russian society. He is the author of one of the longest continuously running plays in Moscow. Since the late 1980s he has focused his writing and research activities on the issue of interethnic relations and ethnic conflicts in the former USSR. Dragunskii is a frequent contributor to several influential Moscow journals. In September 1994 he became a resident fellow at the United States Institute of Peace, Washington, D.C.

Sergei Filatov, born in 1951, studied psychology and history at Moscow State University. From 1973 to 1981 he served as research fellow at the Institute of Sociology of the Academy of Sciences. In 1981 Filatov became a senior research fellow at the USA/Canada Institute, and since 1991 he has also served as director of the Center for Sociological Research of the Russian Scientific Foundation, where he has led several multiethnic sociological studies. Filatov is the author of several dozen works on the history and sociology of religion in Russia, the United States, and Canada, including *Catholicism in the USA* (1993). During the Gorbachev years he was an active member of the the the Church and Perestroika movement founded by Father Gleb Yakunin.

Daniil Granin was born in 1918, graduated from Leningrad Polytechnical Institute in 1940, and spent nearly two and one-half years of the siege of Leningrad (now St. Petersburg) on the front lines outside the city. He worked as an engineer until 1950 and had his first major success as a writer in 1955 with the novel *Those Who Seek*. His other works include *After the Wedding, Challenge the Storm, The Picture, The Bison* (New York: Doubleday, 1989), and *Our Dear Roman Avdeevich*; many essays and short stories, including the anthology *This Strange Life* and *A Book of the Blockade* (with Ales Adamovich). Granin is a former people's deputy of the USSR and serves as director of the St. Petersburg board of the International Foundation Cultural Initiative.

Fazil Iskander was born in the Black Sea port city of Sukhumi on March 6, 1929. He completed Russian secondary school, studied in Moscow at the Library and Literary Institutes, and graduated from the latter. He has worked on local newspapers in Briansk and Kursk but began his writing career with poems and continues to write them. Iskander spends most of his time on prose fiction, although he occasionally writes essays and articles. He notes:

> My novel *Sandro from Chegema* is the most voluminous of my works—I hope in a spiritual as well as a physical sense. A sense of humor is a decoration awarded us for the offenses inflicted on us by stupidity. When a person gazes upon a child, he involuntarily smiles. The more helpless the child, the wider the smile. Humor is an experiment in pure form, in anticipation of the good. We have no other proofs of

the anticipation of the good. Humor will save the world, provided we do not lose our sense of humor at the very moment of its salvation.

Iskander is a vice-president of the Russian PEN Center and has been awarded the Malaparte Literary Prize (Italy), the USSR State Prize (1989), and the Töpfer Foundation Pushkin Prize (Germany, 1992). His novel *Sandro from Chegema* has been translated into English, French, and German and published in the United States, England, France, Germany, Sweden, and many other countries.

Vyacheslav Ivanov is a scholar and a writer. He has published poems; verse translations from various languages (among them poems by Lord Byron, Rudyard Kipling, and James Joyce); memoirs; essays; articles; and books on Russian and world literature, folklore and mythology, linguistics, and semiotics. The son of the well-known writer Vsevolod Ivanov, Vyacheslav Ivanov was born in 1929 and graduated from Moscow State University, where he lectured until 1958, when he was dismissed because of his friendship with Boris Pasternak, then the target of political persecution after winning the Nobel Prize. For thirty years Ivanov was refused permission to travel to the West. He worked at the Institute of Slavic and Balkan Studies and was one of the founders of the Moscow-Tartu school of semiotics. In 1989 he was again invited to Moscow State University as chairman of the new Department of the History and Theory of World Culture; he is now a director of the Institute of World Culture at this university. He then became director general of the M. Rudomino Russian Library of Foreign Literature, where he served until 1993; since that time he has chaired the library's International Advisory Board. A former people's deputy of the USSR representing the Academy of Sciences, Ivanov is currently a professor at the Slavic Department, University of California, Los Angeles. He is a corresponding fellow of the British Academy and a fellow of the American Academy of Arts and Sciences, a member of the Russian Academy of Natural Sciences, and an honorary member of the American Linguistic Society. He has received several Russian government awards for his scholarly research.

Dmitrii Likhachev was born in St. Petersburg in 1906. He is an academician and a professor at the Institute of Russian Literature of the Russian Academy of Sciences. He graduated from Leningrad State University in 1928 and was arrested in February of that year during a roundup of university students and other "academics" who participated in the discussion circles that flourished at the time. After nine months in a Leningrad jail, he served a five-year sentence in the Solovetski Islands penal colony and as a railway dispatcher on the construction of the White Sea–Baltic Canal. Likhachev defended his candidate's degree in 1941 and his doctoral thesis in 1947. Considered Russia's foremost expert in Old Russian literature, Likhachev has promoted medieval Russian studies through his own scholarly works on the formal, theoretical, and historical aspects of this period as well as through many editors of Old Russian masterpieces for scholarly and general audiences. Some of his most influential works include *Poetics of Old Russian Literature, Development of Russian Literature from the Tenth to the Seventeenth Century, Epochs and Styles; History of Russian Literature from the Tenth to the Seventeenth Century* (produced under his general editorship); and *Textology: On the Material of Russian Literature from the Tenth to the Seventeenth Century.* He was awarded the USSR State Prize for the second edited volume of the series *History of the Culture of Ancient Russia.* Likhachev, a former people's deputy, also served as president of the USSR Cultural Fund.

Emil Payin, born in 1948, holds a Ph.D. degree in history. He is the author of more than sixty scholarly works and several dozen newspaper articles on the problems of interethnic and political processes in the regions of the former USSR. After defending his dissertation at the Institute of Ethnography of the USSR Academy of Sciences in 1983, Payin worked in various academic institutions in Moscow. From 1989 to 1991 he served as an expert on the USSR Supreme Soviet's Commission on Problems of Deported Peoples, was a member of the Government Commission on the Problem of the Crimean Tatars, and worked as a consultant to the Russian Federation Supreme Soviet's Council on Nationalities. From 1991 to 1993, Payin was director of the Center for Ethnopolitical and Regional Studies. In February 1993 he joined Boris Yeltsin's Presidential Council, and in June 1993 he assumed his present position as director of the council's Working Group on Nationalities Problems.

Anatolii Pristavkin was born in the environs of Moscow in 1931. He graduated from the Gorky Institute of Literature in 1959, and in the same year a number of his stories were published under the title *A*

Difficult Childhood. This theme, drawing on his personal impressions, was developed further in the novels *The Soldier and the Boy* (1971), *A Golden Cloud Spent the Night* (1981), and *Kukushata* (1989). *A Golden Cloud Spent the Night* was awarded the USSR State Prize in 1988 and has been translated into more than thirty languages, including English, French, German, Swedish, Spanish, and Greek. In 1991 his novel *Kukushata* was awarded a German literary prize. Pristavkin is currently a professor at Gorky Institute of Literature and chairman of the Presidential Commission on Pardons of the Russian Federation. He is married and has three children.

Nikolai Shmelev, born in 1936, graduated from Moscow State University in 1958, holds a Ph.D. in economics, and is a professor of economics affiliated with the Institute of Europe, Moscow. Shmelev's devastating critique of the Soviet economy published in the monthly journal *Novyi mir* in 1987 brought him national and international attention. Some consider this article the starting point for all modern discussion in Russia about the transition to a market economy. In 1989 Shmelev was elected to the USSR Congress of People's Deputies. From 1990 to 1992 he served as a member of the Presidential Consultative Council. He is the author (or co-author) of more than sixty books on international economic relations and on the economic problems of the USSR and Russia, including *The Turning Point: Revitalizing the Soviet Economy* (New York: Doubleday, 1989). A collection of his short stories was published in Moscow in 1988.

Galina Starovoitova was born in Cheliabinsk and received her Master of Science degree from Leningrad State University and her Ph.D. from the Institute of Ethnography of the USSR Academy of Sciences. Starovoitova has done extensive fieldwork in the Caucasus region, notably in the areas of Karabakh and Abkhazia. She was elected as a representative of an Armenian constituency to the USSR Congress of People's Deputies in 1989, where she supported the reformist efforts of Mikhail Gorbachev. In June 1990 she was elected to the parliament of the Russian Federation representing Leningrad (now St. Petersburg). She served as Boris Yeltsin's spokesperson during his campaign for the presidency of the Russian Federation in 1991 and as his adviser on interethnic issues until the end of 1992. A longtime advocate of human rights,

Starovoitova is a member of the Moscow Helsinki group. She is currently head of the Center for Ethnopolitical Studies at the Institute for the Economy in Transition and serves as editor-in-chief of the newspaper *Evropeets* (The European), published in Moscow. Starovoitova has just completed a year as Peace Fellow, Jennings Randolph Program for International Peace at the United States Institute of Peace, Washington, D.C., and assumed duties as Thomas J. Watson Distinguished Visiting Professor at Brown University in September 1994.

Arkadii Vaksberg was born in Siberia in 1933. He received a doctorate of law degree from Moscow State University and worked as a lawyer for twenty years before becoming a journalist and a writer. He has been a columnist for *Literaturnaia gazeta* since 1971 and is nationally known for his exposés of abuses of power and corruption at the highest levels of the Party nomenklatura under Leonid Brezhnev. Vaksberg is the author of more than thirty books published in various languages. Two of his works, *The Prosecutor and the Prey: Vyshinskii and the 1930's Moscow Show Trials* (1990) and *The Soviet Mafia* (1991), were published by Weidenfeld and Nicolson; *Stalin Against the Jews* was published by Knopf in 1994. Vaksberg is vice-president of the Russian PEN Center.

Liudmila Vorontsova, born in 1954, graduated from Moscow State University and is a candidate of history. She is head research fellow at the Sergeev-Posad Museum Complex. Vorontsova is the author of a series of illustrated volumes on Russian medieval art and has published articles on Russian utopian communities in the Middle Ages. Since 1991 she has been deputy director of the Center for Sociological Research of the Russian Scientific Foundation. She is the author of several works on the Russians' attitudes toward the world and themselves since perestroika.

Andrei Voznesenskii, born in Moscow in 1933, graduated in 1957 from Moscow Architectural Institute and, encouraged by Boris Pasternak, turned to writing. In 1959, with the appearance of his poems "Masters" and "Goya," he first received critical attention, and his first two volumes, *Parabola* and *Mosaic* (1960), were followed by *40 Lyric Digressions from the Poem "Triangular Pear"* (1962). Like Evgenii Evtushenko, Voznesenskii was considered an outstanding representative of the post-Stalinist "young poetry," and his readings, often held in sports stadiums, attracted thousands. In 1963, Nikita Khrushchev publicly denounced him as a "bourgeois formalist," shouting, "Out of the country! You are slandering the Party and Soviet authorities. The minister of the KGB will get you a passport!" The threat of exile was not pursued, however, and Voznesenskii continued to publish his work, including *Antiworlds* (1964), *Heart of Achilles* (1966), *Shadow of Sound* (1970), *A Look* (1972), *Master of Stained Glass Windows* (1976), and *Temptation* (1978). In 1979 he won the USSR State Prize for Poetry. He contributed to the unauthorized collection of essays and prose *Metropol* (1979) and wrote the lyrics for the rock opera *Iunona i Avos*. His work in the videopoetry genre has been exhibited in New York, Paris, and Moscow. He has been a leader in the rehabilitation of Pasternak and in the establishment of the museum in Pasternak's dacha at Peredelkino, serving as chairman of the Commission for the Heritage of Pasternak.

Alexander M. Yakovlev is a professor and a doctor of law. A 1952 graduate of Moscow Juridical Institute, he was senior research fellow at the Institutes of Law, successively, of the USSR Ministry of Internal Affairs, the Procuracy, and the Ministry of Justice (1957–75) and since 1975 has been head of the Criminal Law and Criminology Department of the Institute of State and Law, USSR/Russian Academy of Sciences. In 1989 he was elected to the USSR Congress of People's Deputies and served as a member of the USSR Supreme Soviet's Standing Committee on Legislation. In 1993 he coordinated the work of drafting the new Constitution, and since 1994 he has been the president's representative to both chambers of the new parliament. He is a member of the Board of Directors of the International Society of Social Defense in Paris and of the Institute of Sociology of Law for Europe. Yakovlev has held several visiting professorships in the United States and Canada (1990–93) and in 1991 was awarded an honorary doctorate of law by the University of Alberta. He is the author of ten books, including *The Bear That Wouldn't Dance: Failed Attempts to Reform the Constitution of the Former Soviet Union* (with Dale Gibson, 1992) and *Striving for Law in a Lawless Land: Building a Law-Based State in Russia* (M. E. Sharpe, forthcoming).

Acknowledgments

Many friends and colleagues have had a hand in the making of this book. At the Institute for EastWest Studies, under the aegis of which the project was initiated, John Mroz and Stephen Heintz have supported me from the outset; at the Harriman Institute of Columbia University, Marshall Shulman, Bob Legvold, and Rick Ericson have shared their wisdom generously; at Harvard University, Dick Pipes, Adam Ulam, Tim Colton, and Marshall Goldman have offered constructive counsel (and Professor Pipes, of course, also agreed to write the introduction); at the Library of Congress, Jim Billington has been a source of inestimable encouragement; and Senator Claiborne Pell has over the years been a perceptive interlocutor.

A special word of appreciation should go to S. Frederick Starr, president of the Aspen Institute, who reminded me of the *Vekhi* (Landmarks) essays and suggested that a contemporary variation on the theme would serve my purposes. Another early supporter was Klaus Segbers of the *Stiftung Wissenschaft und Politik* at Ebenhausen.

Apart from the contributors themselves, a number of whom—notably Daniil Granin, Nikolai Shmelev, Vyacheslav Ivanov, and Andrei Voznesenskii—have given valuable advice, I should like to mention, among Russian colleagues: Viktor Sukhodrev, whom I first met when he was interpreter for Politburo member Frol Kozlov during the latter's ground-breaking visit to the United States in 1958, and whose wife Inga helped me monitor the Russian press in 1992 and 1993; Vladimir Petrovsky, one of Russia's most accomplished diplomats, now head of the United Nations European Office, who with his wife Mira provided valuable suggestions; Nina Katerli and Misha Efros in St. Petersburg, who introduced me to one of our authors, Konstantin Azadovskii, in 1987; and Aleksandr Avelichev of Progress Publishers, Moscow, with whom I worked on book projects for Doubleday. Aleksandr Vladislavlev, Konstantin Borovoi, Igor Safarian, and Mikhail Yuriev shared their insights about Russia's business climate, even if they could not be among the book's contributors. My indefatigable liaison representatives in St. Petersburg and Moscow were Irina Barkman, Elena Dvorets, and Marina Pristavkina. To Marina, in particular, fell the task of shepherding the final batch of manuscripts from Moscow to New York, which she accomplished with unfailing good humor and, as the authors will attest, equally unfailing persistence.

I have a special debt of gratitude to my talented team of translators— Catherine A. Fitzpatrick (who translated seven of the chapters), Jonathan Edwards, Jamey Gambrell, and Antonina W. Bouis. Their literary gifts and sensitivity to context were invaluable. The staff of the Federal News Service in Moscow and Washington, D.C., worked diligently to achieve high standards of accuracy.

For the book's epigraph I an indebted to Arkady Volsky. In the interview he gave a correspondent of the weekly newspaper *Argumenty i fakty* (No. 28, July 1994), Volsky, leader of the Civic Union, summed up his view of Russia's prospects by citing the lines of the distinguished Russian poet Ol'ga Berggol'ts (1910–1975). The translation is my own. The verse was written in the early 1950s and may be found in her *Sobranie sochinenii v trekh tomakh* (Leningrad: Khudozhestvennaia literatura, Leningradskoe otdelenie, 1988, Vol. 2, pp. 120–21).

Throughout the eighteen-month editorial process, which included providing staff support on two field trips to Russia in 1993, preparing and checking drafts, compiling biographical notes, conducting liaison with the translators, the publisher, and the designer, my assistant, Lisa Petter, has rendered exemplary service.

And to my wife, Sheila, who with my sons Christopher and Ralph and my daughter Sandra has been my indispensable bulwark of support over the years, go my profound thanks.

Preface

The idea of bringing together in one volume a group of distinguished Russians to share their observations about the future of their country goes back to two conclusions I reached many years ago about the time-honored craft of what used to be called "Kremlinology." The first is that Western observers in and out of government tend to neglect the study of the domestic roots of Russia's foreign policy, overlooking the fundamental traits of the Russian character as shaped by history, language, and culture and as reflected in the word—spoken, written, or sung. From tsarist times until the present day, what Russian historians, philosophers, novelists, poets, publicists, bards, and scientists have articulated about their society has had an unmistakable bearing on the way the country's political leaders act in relation to other governments and the international community of nations.

The second conclusion, deriving from my tour as second secretary and political officer in the U.S. Embassy in Moscow in the mid-1950s, was that Western stereotypes about the efficiency of communist totalitarian controls were highly misleading. The political sophistication of the average Russian, his ability to spot the absurdity, hypocrisy, ineptness, and cruelty of the system, his skill in circumventing, deceiving, or robbing those in authority, could be observed whenever one fell into conversation with Russians encountered in the parks and the markets, at the museums or the theaters of large cities and provincial centers, or while visiting factories and collective farms.

But measuring the attitudes of either influential political elites or ordinary Russians was no simple matter in those years. At that time any foreign observer seeking to understand Soviet politics had to navigate through a minefield: censorship of the media, KGB surveillance, public fear of associating with foreigners, habits of secretiveness affecting all levels of society, and strict controls over internal travel by foreigners. Whenever one could break through by luck or happy circumstance to make friends with Russians—and this was always a very relative term in that informant-ridden society—one was astonished and enormously cheered by the generosity of spirit, intellectual curiosity, and conversational ebullience manifested during convivial evening meals around kitchen tables or on the porches of country bungalows. When one heard these frank and earthy commentaries about the bosses (the *nachal'stvo*), the Kremlin leadership (the *verkhushka*), commentaries laced with an irreverence toward the authorities that contrasted with the outward show of subservience and conformity, one felt the extraordinary, enduring strength of this people. One sensed a remarkable capacity, often hidden from external view, to adapt, to persevere, to put on an artful act of dissimulation while preserving, at least within the close circle of family and friends, a sense of individual integrity, a code of ethics quite immune to whatever false doctrines the Communist Party might seek to inculcate.

Beginning with Nikita Khrushchev's Secret Speech of February 1956, which destroyed major elements of the Stalin myth, the painful process of coming to terms with the realities of the Stalinist legacy gained momentum, and here the intelligentsia made effective common cause with the population. The men and women who produced the bold, unflinching, and stirring poems, memoirs, novels, films, and folksongs of the 1960s and 1970s galvanized the youth, opened the eyes of an older generation reluctant to face its past, and, together with the underground *samizdat* authors and the reformists within the Central Committee and the associated think tanks, set the stage for perestroika.

But in the subsequent rush to destroy myths, idols, political structures, and inherited assumptions, a reverse phenomenon occurred that, paradoxically, has complicated the task of foreign observers seeking to understand this new, stormy, decentralized Russia: information overload. Just as Soviet citizens have been submerged by the avalanche of revelations to the point of exhaustion, so foreign observers have found themselves inundated with a torrent of highly diverse and contradictory information. Although Russians now have almost unlimited opportunities to interact with foreigners and express their views in the independent press or in a wide range of international business or professional contacts, the picture that emerges is so multifarious as to defy coherent analysis. Could we not ask the Russians themselves to "look beyond the horizon?"

With the help of friends and colleagues in Russia and the West, and aided by no small amount of good luck, I was able to secure the participation in our dialogue (around the kitchen table, so to speak) of some twenty intellectuals—distinctive in age, background, accomplishments. These contemporary representatives of the postcommunist intelligentsia in Russia are no radical maximalists or irreconcilable oppositionists: they are socially committed pragmatists ready to work with President Yeltsin to solve such burning issues as proliferation of neo-fascist publications, rampant corruption among government officials, especially at the local level, and impoverishment, especially among the elderly (many of whom cannot affort their own funeral expenses). They see public apathy and cynicism as direct threats to democracy. But they see enormous reserves of moral strength as well—reserves that the West, in their view, should help both regional and national leaders mobilize.

For anyone concerned with assisting Russia's unprecedented effort of reconstruction, healing, and reintegration with the West, for anyone who respects and admires the Russian people for what they have contributed to our common cultural values and security interests, the essays in this volume should prove stimulating, sobering, and, in the end, reassuring.

With the exception of the notes prepared by Vyacheslav Ivanov and Catherine A. Fitzpatrick, which are marked by the initials V.I. and C.A.F. respectively, the rest of the notes have been prepared by the editor, Lisa Petter, his assistant, and Irina Gazaryants, his press monitor.

HEYWARD ISHAM

REMAKING
RUSSIA

Richard Pipes

Introduction

Every reader of newspapers is aware of the crisis that has afflicted Russia since the fall of communism, a crisis that seems to defy resolution and threatens to plunge the country, alternately, into civil war or a new totalitarian morass. Among the causes of the crisis, the most glaring is the collapse of the economy. A rate of inflation that, aggravated by unemployment, has wiped out savings and placed essential consumer goods beyond the reach of ordinary citizens has brought hardship to millions. The crisis has found expression in the surprisingly strong showing of the antidemocratic, antimarket parties in the parliamentary elections of December 1993. The dismissal by President Boris Yeltsin of the leading advocates of economic reform from his cabinet attests to the gravity with which his government views the matter.

And yet it can be argued that Russia's gravest problems are not economic. In the remarkable collection of essays written for this volume by some of Russia's leading publicists and scholars, economic issues receive their due, but the emphasis lies elsewhere. The principal theme running through these contributions is that communism's most ruinous legacy lies in the moral and psychological sphere: economic failures appear as a consequence rather than cause of Russia's current predicament.

The word that recurs in these essays is "identity," a term rarely heard in classical Russian and imported from abroad to describe a novel condition. In the nineteenth century, Russian intellectuals were likely to ask, "Who is guilty?" and "What is to be done?" as Alexander Herzen and Nikolai Chernyshevskii, respectively, named their books. The over-riding question today seems to be "Who are we?"—the title of the essay by Fazil Iskander, and a question raised also by Iurii Afanas'ev and Galina Starovoitova. One cannot appreciate the depth of the malaise currently afflicting Russia without taking into account this pervasive sense of bewilderment and disorientation.

In October 1917 a small body of radical fanatics who seized power over Russia launched the nation on a course that had no precedent in human experience: a course, they assured their subjects, which placed them in the vanguard of history. Nothing was left standing: every insti-tution, every value, every custom was put on its head. The new regime abolished private property, virtually forbade religious practices, sub-jected all publications to an ubiquitous censorship, and reduced law to a branch of administration. Three-quarters of a century later, when the experiment had to be abandoned, Russians, surveying the wreckage, realized that they were not marching in the forefront of humanity at all but had been shunted to a siding leading nowhere. In every respect but the military they had been left far behind not only by the West but also by some advanced Third World countries. Eager to rejoin humankind, they cannot figure out how they found themselves in their plight and where to turn to extricate themselves from it. Are they Europeans? Are they Asians? Or perhaps a unique breed of Eurasians?

The postcommunist states of Eastern Europe had an easier time digging themselves out from under the rubble because they enjoyed the benefit of a well-developed sense of nationhood and statehood. For the Poles or Czechs, the forty-five years of communist rule were a period of foreign occupation that followed on the heels of the wartime occupa-tion by Nazi Germany. Once the alien invaders had been gotten rid of, Poland and Czechoslovakia quickly reverted to the status of national states. In Russia, the situation is far more complicated because of the confusion of nationhood, statehood, and empire; it is further exacer-bated by the fact that communism was indigenous rather than imposed from abroad. The dissolution of the Soviet Union and the loss of imper-ial possessions has left a mental and psychological vacuum that Russians have great difficulty filling.

The Russian national state developed coterminously with the Russian empire: the processes of state building and empire building were distin-guishable neither historically nor geographically. For Russians, national identity was, therefore, indissolubly coupled to the notion of a boundless state—already in the seventeenth century, the largest in the world—ruling "younger brothers" (the Ukrainians and Belorussians) along with a multitude of "lesser breeds." The loss of these possessions amounted to an amputation. The Bolsheviks realized the connection between state building and empire building soon after coming to power: ignoring their slogan of "national self-determination" and abandoning the ideology of anti-imperialism, they reverted to the imperialist traditions of tsarism. The frenetic expansionism of the Soviet state, especially after World War II, may have been anachronistic and ultimately futile, but it undoubtedly gained the authorities considerable support among the population, which had little use for communism.

When Britain gave up its empire half a century ago, the English people experienced no crisis of identity because their "Englishness" was distinct from the colonial possessions: the latter were a source of a pride, but they did not define their nationhood, which derived, among other sources, from the traditions of parliamentary democracy and individual rights. Russia's case is different. The dissolution of the empire has dealt a heavy blow not only to the self-esteem of Russians but also to their ethnic self-perception. Poorer than Westerners and less cultured, lacking in political traditions of which they can be proud, isolated by their religion and ideology from most of the world, Russians gloried in the fact they had the world's largest state and an army that inspired fear among foreigners. This sense of vastness and might compensated them for the inferiority they felt when comparing Russia with the West. As several of the authors note, Russian national self-consciousness was to a large extent great power consciousness. What, then, remains of this consciousness when the country ceases to be a great power?

To feel truly and proudly Russian, Russians, therefore, instinctively strive toward expansion and its corollary, militarism. It is striking that today even some of the most committed Russian democrats yearn for the restoration of the empire, although restoration can be accomplished only by force and at considerable peril to the cause of democracy.

The problem is compounded by the fact that Russians have much greater difficulty reestablishing links with precommunist Russia than do other Europeans freed from totalitarianism. There is, to be sure, Russian culture: the great novels and the poetry of the Golden and Silver Ages, the arts, and the sciences. But the legacy of "high culture" in

Russia, as elsewhere, carries meaning only for the educated elite. It is depressing how quickly Russian cultural life has collapsed in the 1990s following the withdrawal of state subsidies and the advent of mass entertainment. True, economic difficulties bear much responsibility for this situation: people who can barely afford necessities have little left over for culture. But how to explain that Moscow bookstores and street stalls, which no longer carry serious publications, find a ready market for cheap escapist literature? What does it tell of Russia's vaunted literary tastes that Agatha Christie is the country's best-selling author? Serious books, once brought out in editions of 100,000 and more, now, if published at all, rarely exceed printings of 10,000. The most popular television program is a Mexican soap opera. The "high culture" sponsored by the defunct regime appears to have been a hothouse plant that flourished because, except for sports, it had no diversions to compete with it.

Two additional factors aggravate the problem Russians face in trying to determine their national identity: the native roots of communism and the unsettled condition of the world they would like to rejoin.

Russian nationalists have long if unconvincingly argued that communist ideology and practices were entirely foreign in origin, without any links to Russia's past—a kind of plague imported from the West. But this concept of a "foreign invasion" of Russia has carried no more conviction than the attempt of Austrians to depict themselves as the earliest victims of Nazi aggression. Austria jubilantly welcomed the *Anschluss*, just as Russia provided the original home to communism. Russians cannot shake off the communist legacy as readily as the Poles or the others whom Moscow had conquered and subjugated. Russians must confront the sources of communism in their own past and ascertain why and how this particular ideology first struck root in their country. This is a difficult task under the most favorable circumstances, as shown by the experience of post-Nazi Germany. It is doubly so in a country, which, as Íurii Afanas'ev points out, has been systematically robbed of the knowledge of its own past.

Another formidable difficulty Russians face in trying to overcome their "identity crisis" is the absence of ready models abroad. To the extent that Russians identify with a foreign civilization, it is with the West: some might accept the nebulous status of "Eurasians," but all feel offended by the suggestion they are Asians. Unfortunately, the contemporary West no longer offers the kind of ideal that it had provided in the past century. The present-day West—racked by doubts about its past, its traditional culture dissolving in Third World cultures and destructive subcultures of domestic origin—is losing the sense of its own identity. Where, then, are the Russians to turn? Perhaps the answer is in the transnational, hedonistic, consumer-oriented culture, emanating from the United States, which is sweeping the world and submerging ethnic cultures. I believe most Russians would find this prospect highly unattractive. The problem, then, remains.

A characteristic feature of postcommunist intellectual life in Russia is the luxuriant flourishing of ideas—ideas that branch out in every conceivable direction but have little in common with each other. The reason for this development, so contrary to what one has come to expect of a country held for decades in the tight grip of thought control, is that even in the worst days of Stalinism Russians did not cease to hold private opinions. The educated learned to cope with the stifling atmosphere of uniformity by developing something akin to intellectual schizophrenia, conforming outwardly to the official line of the day and keeping their own thoughts to themselves. As soon as the authorities unshackled speech—this happened gradually after Stalin's death and very rapidly after 1985—the country experienced a veritable explosion of ideas. The restraints on the expression of independent thought imposed since 1918 produced the contrary result: unable to articulate their opinions openly, Russians gave freest rein to their imaginations. Their thought, precisely because it had so long been silenced, knew no bounds. As a result, it knew nothing of "political correctness" by means of which opinion makers in the West, especially the United States, inhibit freedom of speech.

But Russian thought also knew nothing of the moderation that clips the wings of irresponsible ideas exposed in the public forum: Russian debates tend to be monologues rather than dialogues, as people speak past each other in their eagerness to articulate pent-up ideas. There is really nothing resembling public opinion in Russia: there are only myriad independent opinions, cultivated in the sheltered hothouses of the secluded private world. The result is an intellectual jungle that makes it very difficult to create a national consensus, and without such consensus there can be no national policy.

The two propositions on which most of the contributors to this vol-

ume agree are that the communist system has been destroyed beyond
the possibility of repair and that Russia finds itself in a transitional—or
even the final—stage of the revolution (against communism), characterized by the emergence of a new class of entrepreneurs and
general fatigue on the part of the rest of the population. The process
is irreversible: the revolution has triumphed. In the words of Leonid
Batkin:

> The current post-October [1993] stage, however, involves not only
> the dismantling of Soviet power but the setting of conditions for a
> whole new era in Russia's existence. An era of transition, yes, but the
> change will be much deeper, longer lasting, and more fundamental
> in nature than the term "transition" suggests.

The belief rests in good measure on the findings of public opinion
polls. According to Sergei Filatov and Liudmila Vorontsova, polls indicate that the communist ideal has the support of at most 5–10 percent
of the urban population and that less than 10 percent of Russians want
a restoration of the planned economy; more than one-third qualify
as "adamant anticommunists." By general agreement, anticommunist
sentiments are strongest among the young. The procommunist sentiment corresponds, roughly, to the proportion of Russians (with their
dependents) who before 1991 had been members of the Communist
Party, who had benefited the most from communism and lost the
most from its collapse: in other words, the privileged clientele of the
defunct regime. The moderate optimism of many Russian intellectuals derives from the feeling that, obstacles and setbacks notwithstanding, the momentum lies with the forces of reform. The specific traits
of the "Soviet man" have been increasingly marginalized, the public
opinion polls indicate, shifting toward older and less-educated sections, the inhabitants of small towns and villages who are used to
depressed living standards and have long ceased to aspire to anything more.

Nikolai Shmelev agrees that people's ways of thinking are changing,
especially among the young, and that "all the diverse forces and interests in Russian society are still moving in a distinctly positive direction—
toward democracy and the market."

This optimism (balanced by what Leonid Batkin calls his own "resigned pessimism") seems contradicted by the parliamentary elections

of December 1993, which gave the party of a neo-Nazi demagogue nearly one-quarter of the vote and the combined forces of the "Red-Brown" coalition close to one-half of the seats in the State Duma.

This vote is best explained by the political inexperience of the Russian population and its depolitization. It is not as alarming as it appears at first sight and as it would be in a country with stronger traditions of statehood, as, for example, Germany.

The citizens of a democracy learn to make frequent choices at all levels of the political structure: municipal or communal, provincial, national. Party allegiances are fairly firm, usually running in families. People vote for parties and politicians whose past they know and whose platforms carry for them concrete meaning. As a rule, the major parties enjoy a hard-core following, and elections are decided by relatively small shifts of voter sentiment.

Lacking in democratic experience, confronting a multitude of freshly baked parties with contrived names and improvised platforms, Russians vote their grievances and hopes rather than their interests. Now, as in the past, when given a chance to express their political preferences, they have shown themselves to be exceedingly volatile: a country that one day is overwhelmingly tsarist turns the next day equally overwhelmingly against the tsar, entrusting its fate to democratic socialists; when the democratic socialists disappoint its expectations, it abandons them to their fate allowing the Bolsheviks to take power, only to turn six months later against the same Bolsheviks.

Such inconstancy should not be attributed to national character. Rather, it is due to the fact that throughout Russian history the average person has had no sense that either the system of government or the people running it in any way affected his personal destiny. In normal times, Russians have been politically uninvolved; in times of crisis they looked for saviors able miraculously to solve all their problems. Dmitrii Likhachev rightly stresses the "credulity" of Russians, their willingness to trust those who promise to deliver the most in the shortest time. The recent successes of Zhirinovskii fall in this category: did he not promise to solve all of the country's problems in seventy-two hours? The chances are that he will be forgotten as soon as other magicians appear on the scene to outbid him with even more outrageous promises. And it is reasonable to expect that as they acquire the habits of democracy, Russians will learn to distinguish better politics from demagoguery and form more durable political constituencies than has hitherto been the case.

Several essays in this collection voice anxiety about current political trends. Some authors (for example, Alexander Yakovlev and Leonid Batkin) fret that the new constitution may vest too many powers in the president; others (for example, Denis Dragunskii) are more troubled by the weakness of the democratic government. And, of course, economic problems are never far out of sight. But the prevailing tone is one of guarded optimism: certainly more so than might seem warranted to Western observers who, fed a steady diet of alarming news from the East, see catastrophe looming. The difference in assessment may be due to the fact that Westerners worry how far Russians have left to go, whereas the Russians take comfort in knowing how far they have come.

WHO
ARE
WE?

1

Anatolii Pristavkin

By Candlelight, Near My Beloved

The Russian writer Vassily Aksyonov, my contemporary, once wrote a short story the title of which I cannot recall. He wrote it when he was young, and I read it when I was young. The story went like this: Once upon a time, in a little village, there lived two fellows who were neighbors. One of them was energetic, or, as they say nowadays, "socially active," and had gone to fight for freedom in the Revolution, and spent many years battling for it. Then he returned home and went to see his neighbor. His neighbor had sat at home during all those terrible years—and not even at home but in his shed, where he sat and pondered and invented things for so long that he was covered over with moss.

When the veteran soldier came to visit, a man tired but happy that his life had turned out as it had, the inventor took him into his little shed. The soldier asked what his neighbor had been doing all this time, and the inventor pushed some buttons and a machine sprung to life. And that was the whole story. Who could judge what was later more important for history and for humankind itself, the mythical freedom attained through bloodshed in the Civil War, or this strange, fantastic machine that transformed life for the better in the twinkling of an eye and, in its own way, helps humankind to survive?

People will say this is fiction, but I can also tell you a story from real life. While digging through Siberian archives on the history of the Angara River, I once found mention of a hydrological station that, despite that same Civil War, had managed to survive for many years in a place remote from the rest of humanity and had yielded results later used by scientists to build hydroelectric stations, cities, and factories. There was something that made a modest young man from the capital, who had just graduated from the institute, come and watch this little-studied, wild river of the taiga. He kept watching and wrote down all his observations in a little notebook—the speed of the current, the floods, the composition of the water, the time of the freezing over, and so on. He made his home in a *zimnik*, a little Russian wooden cabin banked about by earth, and lived for years, forgotten by everyone, not even paid a salary. People say he survived by catching fish, picking berries and mushrooms, and digging his own garden.

Wars roared past—World War I, the Russian Revolution, and the Civil War. The Whites came by hunting the Reds, and the Reds, the Whites, but the man kept writing and writing, forgotten by everyone, and then vanished, nowhere to be found. Perhaps Soviet rule crushed him, as it had many others it could not understand, but the little notebook remained. And it came in very handy fifty years later, when builders came to this territory.

My reflections are in a way not about art, or literature, with which I have been involved my whole life, yet about them all the same, since by virtue of the peculiarities of literary creativity, a writer has a fierce need, greater than anyone else, for a little cabin all his own, a *zimnik* on the bank of a distant river, where far away from all the politicians and society, and sometimes even his family and friends, he can invent his miracle machine, scribble his thoughts and observations in a modest little notebook, all of which he believes will bring salvation to the world at the proper time.

And he certainly has no need of any power, except for one, main source of power, a force most ruthless and exhausting, but which enables you to sense yourself a creator, almost God—the power of the *word*.

The world began with the *word* and only the *word*, which depends on no one, serves no one, and can nonetheless preserve and save this world—as it has already done many times. And perhaps it can even make the world better. In the final chapter of Mikhail Bulgakov's famous novel *The Master and Margarita*, the only thing that the Master asks from the all-powerful Volanda—Satan—is for a little house, located beyond time and space, almost like our hydrologist's little cabin, where by candlelight, near his beloved woman, the Master can write his life's work about the life of Christ.

But the paradox is that the ideal creative life depicted in Bulgakov's novel remained beyond the author's reach in real life (meaning our actual Soviet life), just as for many other writers. Our government could not permit such creativity so far away from it, not under its control, not subject to it or governed by it. Perhaps this need for control is a feature of governments in general; I have not had the opportunity to compare. In Bulgakov's story, the Master is writing a novel about the life of Christ, a book as far removed as Christ's teaching itself from politics or ideology. From the authorities' perspective, though, this novel is undeniably a grave sin. In the novel, the Master is thrown into a madhouse. And that fate is not the worst version of a finale when an artist tries to exercise his inalienable right to freedom of creativity. Our generation does not have to be told what it means to be a dependent writer, much less a writer dependent on the government by his own will. During the Soviet era we produced a whole school of literature called "socialist realism," defined by its own adherents—not without some humor—as the depiction of the party-state in the form most accessible to it. But all joking aside, *sotsrealizm* demonstrated convincingly that writers can and will unite under the principle of mental servitude in literary collective farms under the aegis of the KGB, where they may collectively praise the slave regime under which they have found complete happiness.

This kind of work was handsomely paid for out of the state's treasury; everything depended on the degree of groveling and servility. Konstantin Simonov, a socialist-realist writer, even a classic one, recounted in his memoirs a conversation with Josef Stalin. "We don't mind paying the money," said Stalin, smiling and speaking in his Georgian accent. "But we should ... establish four categories of ratings, rankings in literature. The first category would be for an excellent work, the second for a good work. . . . What do you think?" And of course the Soviet writers answered in unison that they thought this ranking would be correct. Then Stalin asked what themes the writers were developing at the time and then suggested one of them himself—a topic that would presumably make it into the first category: "Now there's one theme that is very important," said Comrade Stalin. "Writers should take an interest in it." And they will take an interest; the leader need not worry. The writers were prepared to throw themselves into fulfilling the sacred order. But what was it—what was the topic? Don't keep us in suspense! "It is the topic of Soviet patriotism. If you take our average members of the intelligentsia—professors, doctors—their sense of Soviet patriotism has not been sufficiently and precisely [what a word!] cultivated. They have an unwarranted adoration of foreign culture."

Thus the word had been dropped. Now catch it! And hurry, for 1937 is coming, and very soon, oh, very soon they will nail to the pillar of shame all those whose patriotism has not been "cultivated" sufficiently or precisely—Anna Akhmatova, Mikhail Zoshchenko, Sergei Prokofiev, and Dmitri Shostakovich. Clearly they will not make it even into the "mediocre" category of art, and will have themselves largely to blame.

An artist who got an "F" from some potentate was not simply forced to starve—that would be only half the trouble—but would be expelled from the professional union, just as if he were expelled from life itself. And without anyone or anything to defend him, he could be locked in a loony bin or prison, or, like Aleksandr Solzhenitsyn, he could be forcibly exiled from his native country. The same fate would befall an artist's family and relatives.

Solzhenitsyn wrote a book called *The Oak and the Calf*. Drawing on his own life, he explores the relationship of the artist to the power of the state, comparing this power to a strong oak and himself to a naive calf butting its head against the tree. We know the outcome of such a collision. But not everything is so unambiguous. One of our most prominent and venerable playwrights, Viktor Rozov, wrote quite persuasively in *Literaturnaia gazeta* that a totalitarian state which maintains complete power over an artist has, in a sense, helped him by setting his creative energies in motion. The freedom that, in Rozov's words, no one can ever take away from the writer seems even more precious, the more pressure the authorities exert on him. In fact, the literary and artistic productivity of those recent years was far higher than it is today, at a time of freedom and absence of censorship. Surely, argues Rozov, that proves the point!

I am not an adherent of such a theory, from which we can conclude that it is best to do your creative work in prison. But behind that proposition we can very easily detect nostalgia for a strong state authority that would bring to our life and our souls the stability, peace, and quiet that are so necessary for the creative person. Some people, indeed, enjoyed these conditions in the past—for example, the secretaries of the Writers' Union, who lived in the dacha village at Peredelkino. (By the way, Bulgakov ironically calls this writers' colony "Perelygin.")[1] Of course by barricading themselves off from the world, shutting their ears and closing their eyes to boot, these secretaries would not have to notice how Boris Pasternak was being persecuted and tormented, how the poet Joseph Brodsky was being pilloried, how the writers Lev Kopelev, Georgii Vladimirov, and many others were being hounded out of the country. Did Viktor Rozov make any protest at the time? Or was he able, despite state coercion (not against him, of course), to preserve his peace and quiet and create imperishable works, in which the young heroes have long discussions about conscience and honor? Why, one of the theoreticians of *sotsrealizm* even told us in the press that a writer embodies his morality in his works and it does not seem to be needed in life!

I am not condemning anyone. You can serve God in various ways. You can lead your people across the desert in search of the promised land, or you can sit in an ivory tower and write a poem about nightingales and roses. But if people start killing a child at your doorstep, even if it is the doorstep to the room where you are writing your wonderful verses, if you do not put down your pen and defend the child, no justifications to your conscience (which, after all, is the chief judge of your actions) will save you.

And here I advocate consistency between your heroes' actions and your own. If you are preaching goodness and kindness and the noble soul, then be so good as to order the horses to be hitched to your carriage, grab a thermos of tea from home, and, like Anton Chekhov, head off for some place like Sakhalin, a Russian place of exile, so as to help the unfortunate convict laborers in person. Or be like the storyteller Janusz Korczak, who voluntarily lived in a Jewish ghetto and followed his little children into the gas chamber so as to mitigate their final sufferings at the cost of his own life.

During the attack on Vilnius by Moscow's troops in 1991, I recall how, with Mikhail Gorbachev's knowledge, young people were killed with tanks and sappers' shovels on the square in front of the television station. I happened at the time to be at the House of Writers in Latvia, where we were expecting a repetition of these events any day, only this time in Riga.

The writers behaved in various ways during those days. Some immediately packed their things and scurried back to Moscow; others, just to be on the safe side, stopped saying hello to me (what if the tanks came and the authorities started asking whom you talked with and whom you supported and why?); and still others seemed to remain in place but pretended that nothing except their own manuscripts interested them.

Those in the last group had still not lost their shame. They were troubled, and they were particularly aggressive in reproaching others for getting mixed up with politics when it was a writer's task to create the imperishable. Freedom, they said, will be defended even without us, but nobody can write books for us.

But I am not accusing them of anything. They were far more practical than I. By getting entangled in events where you had to stand watch at the barricades and appear on television or simply speak at street rallies, I put myself and my family in danger. My wife and I and our small child remained all alone on an entire floor and built our own "barricades" for a time, pushing a desk up against the door. Had they wanted to, the soldiers could have easily broken in, and we already knew by then that if trouble began, no one would hear our cries. There were threats over the telephone and in writing all the time. I can recite those terrible little messages by heart even now.

They did not make good on the threats and did not touch my child, but they did destroy the manuscript of stories on my desk, a whole book of fairy tales I had written for my daughter.

Now I think that perhaps these fables might have lived a longer life than my speeches for freedom. But it is also possible to think that by appealing to soldiers not to shed blood, I saved more than one life. Of course, the price was not small—those fairy tales I'll never be able to write again. But tell me, where is the line between honor and dishonor? When we cross that line without realizing it, we end up beyond good and evil and cease to acknowledge even our lies to ourselves, the worst of all kinds of deception, leading to degradation both of the individual and of his art.

And tell me, would I not have cursed myself in a moment of lucidity, if something terrible had happened? Would I not have destroyed those fairy tales with my own hands, if I had saved them instead of saving people's lives?

That is the question I pondered in agony when I fell ill after all those events, and that is what continues to torment me to this day.

In 1993, the diaries of Thomas Mann were published for the first time in the Russian language, in particular the pages devoted to the first years of his life in emigration after leaving fascist Germany in 1933. Mann speaks candidly of the spiritual distress he experienced after leaving his home in Munich, "a marvelous house with all the furnishings, which will be impossible to save." Of course one's home cannot be saved if a writer charged with disloyalty to the state is stripped of his citizenship. But losing the home that was our fortress, refuge, and protection was by no means the worst thing. The manuscript of Mann's long-awaited book *Joseph and His Brothers* had already been typeset at the Fischer Verlag and was ready to be published, if the writer would publicly renounce his participation in the antifascist émigré community. That would have been the right time to shout: "Freedom will be defended even without us, but no one can write books without us!" Or publish them. And even the great Thomas Mann flinched when he experienced, in his words, the tormented dissension within himself. "An onerous discussion," he wrote, "on the impossibility of right behavior, of having to give in to brutality. About the need for spiritual freedom and peace of mind."

Oh, how hard it was (even for him!) to combine these two things, not to yield, yet to keep one's peace of mind! We so need that peace, without which there is neither creativity nor sleep nor normal life. But just what can one do about this very "brutality," which as Mann could not help but know was only the beginning, the foretaste of all the rest of the brutalities of fascism. Still, Mann makes up his mind, not immediately, but firmly, and pushing aside the concerns about his home and his book, he throws down the gauntlet to fascism, and acts, in his own phrase, "as my conscience and deep convictions required."

It is worth noting that alongside the word "convictions," forged in such tribulation, stands the word "conscience." Not only through his heroes does the author express his morality; he establishes it at the cost of his whole life.

I am grateful to fate for granting us (and preserving for us) those Thomas Mann diaries. Although they seem to be from a different day, they help us understand ourselves. Indeed, the diaries seem quite relevant, because once again the brown fascist plague is forming into ranks of combatants; it has acquired a faint reddish tinge from its alliance with the Bolsheviks, but the hour is near when they will burn down the Reichstag . . . or at least the Ostankino television station! They will erect new concentration camps and gulags (or restore them, since they already exist and are awaiting their hour). No wonder the first "decree" of the self-styled "president" from the White House said in black and white, "actions . . . committed by an official are punishable . . . by the death penalty" (Art. 64.1 of the Penal Code). This document was signed on September 22, 1993, by Aleksandr Rutskoi personally. The murders committed recently on the streets of Moscow are only the beginning. Bloodshed will not stop them; on the contrary, that is their accustomed element.

> *It will pass through the country like an iron hand*
> *And drown it in blood!*

Aleksandr Galich, the wonderful contemporary poet and bard who died in exile, wrote these prophetic lyrics about the impending Bolshevik fascism. Once again, members of the intelligentsia are faced with the fundamental question: Who do they stand with today? Will they give up this present wretched, depressed democracy (such as it is) to be eaten alive by those louts awaiting their hour?

First those thugs will devour the democrats, and then each other. There are no other options. Although we have studied it so poorly, that is the logic of history.

There was one man who seemed to be a "member of the intelligentsia" (but I am putting the phrase in quotes just in case). He provoked the wrath of other intellectuals by accusing them, during the days of the October 1993 rebellion, of displaying "the loathsome sentiments of loyal subjects." The intelligentsia, he said, acted this way "exclusively out of its bile, servility, and toadyism."

This accusation recalls the history of our Russian intelligentsia reflected in a collection of articles entitled *Vekhi* (Landmarks) published in 1909. In his article Petr Struve wrote: "The intelligentsia is a totally unique factor in Russian political development, its historical significance stemming from its attitude to both the idea and the actuality of the state."

How is this attitude expressed? As Struve wrote,

> The Russian intelligentsia's ideological form is its *dissociation*, i.e., its alienation from the state and hostility to it. . . . Consequently, in a certain sense Marxism, with its doctrines of the class struggle and of the state as the organization of class domination, was the most intense and complete embodiment of the intelligentsia's antistate dissociation.[2]

Landmarks contained an even harsher accusation: the pure and honest intelligentsia, raised on the teachings of the best people, had lowered itself "to bestial unruliness"—down to the level of Leninism at least.

The outcome is well known: the intelligentsia supported the Bolsheviks and was itself destroyed. But not all of its members followed the Marxists. A fairly large number, in the expression of Georgii Fedotov, did not even contemplate revolution, among them Vasilii Rozanov, Leo Tolstoy, Fyodor Dostoevsky, Vladimir Solov'ev, Nikolai Leskov, Aleksandr Ostrovskii, and Vasilii Kliuchevskii.

Despite the enormous break in the spiritual tradition, we, the weak shoots of a once-powerful tree, are grappling with the very same problems, not so much political as moral, and our solutions will to some extent, more so than in the past, determine where we are headed and the future of our unfortunate country. Will we speak decisively and firmly, as we are expected to do, about the "conscience and deep convictions" that will not allow us to stand apart from the people of Russia, if we do not wish her misfortune?

We will be saved if—and I believe this—I immediately throw in the trash all the newspaper articles in which I called upon people to defend themselves from the Red-Browns, and if I throw out what I am writing now, and if I go away somewhere, perhaps to the Seliger Lake in the Tver province, where in a log cabin by candlelight, near my beloved woman, I will sit up late writing some historical novel or something eternal about God, love, flowers, or children, and as the long twilight pours through the little window, I will painstakingly trace out the words and revel in their sounds. And I will have no need of any government, even the most obliging, even the most precious.

Translated by Catharine A. Fitzpatrick

Notes

1. "Peredelkino" apparently comes from the roots for the prefix *pere*, "before," and *delianka*, "plot of woodland." *Pere* also means "repeated," and *lygin* appears to have been coined from *lgat'*, "to lie," in other words, to tell falsehoods.—C.A.F.

2. Petr Struve, "The Intelligentsia and Revolution," in *Vekhi (Landmarks): A Collection of Essays on the Russian Intelligentsia, 1909*, trans. and ed. Marshall S. Shatz and Judith E. Zimmerman (Armonk, N.Y.: M.E. Sharpe, 1994), p. 118.

2

Vyacheslav Ivanov

In My Beginning Is My End

Traditional Values in Russian Social Life and Thought

Geographical Space and Cyclical Time

What is amazing about Russia, when we look at a map, is its size. Even now, after the breakup of the Soviet Union (which, geographically, was roughly equivalent to the former Russian empire minus Poland and Finland but with some Asian areas added), the space occupied by Russia proper is enormous. It encompasses the northern parts of Eastern Europe and Asia and some neighboring areas to the south of them. This spatial aspect is the predominant one.

Since the publication of Petr Chaadaev's *Philosophical Letters*, it has been assumed that the Russian indifference to time is compensated for by the importance of space. We are consumed with geography, and we have no real history. From the standpoint of time, Russian history is very long: more than one thousand years since the coming of Christianity. Nonetheless, the same pattern of events is repeated constantly. For instance, many details of the present-day situation in Russia, such as the lack of basic foodstuffs at affordable prices, political instability verging on chaos, the diversity of small political parties having no great popular support, and the growth of abstract intellectual interests among the young, are almost identical with conditions in 1917.

There are also many points of similarity with how the tsars (Peter the Great, Alexander II) or political leaders (Stolypin, Lenin, Gorbachev) carried out previous Russian reforms. In spite of ideological differences, the technique of "revolution from above" was identical. It was not a mass movement or a popular decision but a decree of the ruler that launched political change. Citizens who did not agree to obey the new order immediately could be punished severely and often cruelly (Asian parallels such as Kemal Ataturk's reforms in Turkey come to mind). The principles of political persuasion and compromise played a lesser role than open, violent suppression of opponents. The cyclical (nonlinear) character of history, characterized by the recurrence of similar events ("eternal return"), is common to Russia and to other large countries of Eurasia, such as India and China. It is by no means accidental that at the beginning of this century, great Russian writers such as Velemir Khlebnikov and scientists such as Aleksandr Chizhevskii were seriously discussing the role of cycles or recurrences in world history, pointing to this idea in the philosophical and religious systems of Asia, especially in India and in the traditions of Buddhism as a whole.

The way important political events repeat themselves makes it possible to venture rough predictions. I remember that when I was elected a USSR people's deputy in 1989, some specialists in Russian history predicted to me that our congress would be dissolved just as the first State Duma (parliament) had been. Almost every attempt in this century to create an independent instrument of legislative power in Russia has ended with the more or less violent dissolution of these bodies. After the unsuccessful coup of August 1991, the congress to which I belonged was replaced by the last USSR Supreme Soviet (of which I was also a member), a body that had practically no time to work until the USSR itself ceased to exist in December of that year.

The Russian parliament that was elected a year later was doomed in October 1993 to repeat the same historical pattern, reminding one of the dissolution of the Constituent Assembly early in 1918.

Another historical cycle that may repeat itself is the probability that postcommunist Russia will be reborn in its largest geographical extension, following a period when many regions split off and separate, as occurred during and after the Civil War in our country. The Russian army, which had been rebuilt during the four years after the Revolution, was instrumental in carrying out this consolidation process. In Russia today, a modern army and certain other institutions similar to it or connected with it have remained intact. Their presence makes possible the rebirth of the entire complex of the republics of the former Soviet Union, perhaps as a system of loosely associated independent states that for all practical purposes would be dominions of a single commonwealth. The relics of the economic network that had united all parts of the disintegrated empire, as well as the nature of the existing ethnic conflicts, might contribute to this restoration of the whole system.

To understand not only Russia's present but its future, one needs a deep knowledge of its past. For lack of this knowledge, most of the so-called Kremlinologists in the West (the United States included) failed to predict Mikhail Gorbachev's reforms and other important events of recent years. The scope of the present article permits one to give only a few examples of problems, which can be better understood if we examine the ways they have been solved traditionally.

Russia Between East and West

It is not so much Russia's geographical position as the ideological implications and consequences of its position that are particularly important. At different periods of Russian history, the choice between an orientation toward the West (Europe) and, conversely, attempts to find a Russian identity outside the West European context became a matter of fierce debate.

Without dwelling on the choice between these two different credos, as described in the Old Russian Primary Chronicle and in later episodes of the struggle against the Mongols and Tatars, one might simply mention the main ideological schism at the time of Peter the Great, who has remained the most controversial tsar of Russia. In Russian culture there are two contradictory images of the tsar himself and of his Westernizing efforts. In the mainstream of the literary tradition, starting with Lomonosov and continuing with Aleksandr Pushkin, Peter draws praise. The so-called Petersburg myth centers on the tsar as Pushkin's "Bronze Horseman." This heroic theme has been developed and discussed by many Russian writers and thinkers who follow Pushkin's line of depicting the Great Westernizer.

Their approach contrasts with an entirely different image of Peter the Great in Russian thought, in which he is represented as a kind of devil, a reincarnation of the Antichrist, as the Old Believers called him.

Rethinking the problem of Peter the Great in the light of our historical experience, we may say that he was the first to introduce mainly those aspects of Western modern technology that were important for Russia as a military power (he had been especially interested in modernizing the Russian fleet, much as the Russian government was in the years immediately preceding Gorbachev). To achieve this modernization, however, Peter had to begin the enormous task of creating an entirely new framework for science in Russia, and this effort in turn led to the establishment of the Academy of Sciences, the emergence of Lomonosov to international prominence, and the reforms of the educational system.

The need to create conditions for a modern national technology had equally ambivalent results in the Soviet Union during the postwar years. The gifted scientists who were essential for the development of new military technology might become dangerous for the regime, as Andrei Sakharov did. Peter the Great's immediate pragmatic aims make him more akin to the Bolshevik reformers (who also spoke about the need to utilize Western technological achievements, while remaining hostile to foreign ideology) than to Alexander II or Gorbachev. Scientific and technological innovation may well interfere with political institutions that differ from Western models (modern Chinese experience might also be instructive on this point).

In the Russian intellectual world of the nineteenth century, the Westernizers who thought it was necessary to follow the European route toward economic development were opposed by the Slavophiles, who argued for an original Russian path of development. In these debates, one may see again the importance of geographical (spatial) reasoning. The historical (temporal) problem of the path of development to be chosen was seen as a purely geographical one: shall we go with the East or with the West?

Paradoxically, Marxist ideas about Russia's economic development as expressed at the beginning of the twentieth century were conceptually akin to the policy of introducing a market-oriented economy in Russia. Although the aims are, of course, radically different, what is common to both trends of thought is the assumption that the West European model is universal and should be repeated by Russia. The Slavophiles, as well as the contemporary Russian populists (ending with the great economist Nikolai Kondrat'ev, whom Stalin executed in the beginning of his rule), did not think it was necessary to repeat the experience of the West.

In one of history's ironies, Russian scholars have recently discovered a letter Marx wrote to one of the early Russian populists in which he agreed with the idea that Russia could chart a distinctive, non-European, and noncapitalist path of development. Marx's position was, of course, not known to those Marxists who were later active in transforming Russia into a typical European country with a system of state monopolistic capitalism that they called socialism.

The first wave of emigration from Russia after the Revolution included an influential group of thinkers who insisted on the need to forge close links between the culture and self-awareness of Russia and that of the other Eurasian (in the past mainly nomadic or steppe) peoples. To this group of "Eurasianists" belonged the great émigré linguist Prince Nikolai Trubetskoi. In his works of the 1920s and early 1930s (only recently collected and translated into English), Trubetskoi argued that the legacy of Genghis Khan was still valid for Russia. Stalin's despotic rule seemed to confirm Trubetskoi's thesis. In general, most of the Slavophiles' favorite projects were realized in the Soviet empire. For instance, the area of Soviet expansion and influence in the time after Stalin's death roughly coincided with that described in Fedor Tiutchev's poem "Russian Geography," written in 1829, describing a Russian empire that would reach

From the Nile to the Neva, from the Elbe to China,
From the Volga to the Euphrates, from the Ganges to the Danube.[1]

But to Trubetskoi, as to many other followers of the Eurasianists' ideas, links with the nomadic peoples of the steppe would not necessarily signify atrocities of the kind we find in Stalin's regime. What was important to them was the possibility of a specifically Russian historical path of development that might be different from that taken by the rest of Europe. Eurasianists such as Trubetskoi contended that an original Russian course of development was definitely possible—one that differed from the one chosen by Latin or Germanic peoples (that is, by

France, Italy, England, Germany, the Scandinavian countries, the United States, and Canada).

Through the writings of Lev Gumilev, the recently deceased Russian ethnologist (who was the son of the famous poet Nikolai Gumilev, executed in V.I. Lenin's time), the ideas of Eurasianists have become widely known and popular in modern Russia. To present-day Russian society, Russia's relationship to Europe and to Asia may be the most urgent problem. The issue has lost its theoretical aspect and has become the main topic of vigorous debate. Eurasianist ideas are being widely discussed in the light of the effects of the government's economic reforms, based as they are on the pattern of the developed countries of Western Europe and North America. The cultural impact of these reforms is being violently criticized by many journalists and politicians who are connected with the so-called village school of literature. These critics stress the importance of the ancient peasant way of life, which remains their ideal, as it was for the Slavophiles and populists in the nineteenth century. Their views might be compared to those of the Islamic fundamentalists.

The reappearance within the Russian Orthodox Church of a hostile attitude toward the ecumenical movement might be ascribed to the same trend. The Orthodox Church, to which the government has made overtures, is rapidly becoming a possible substitute for the Communist Party, reversing the postrevolutionary development of the Party as a substitute for the church. One of the most dangerous scenarios of the Russian future, therefore, is that of a theocracy of the Byzantine type. The geopolitical aspect of the East-West problem has recently become evident in the opposition expressed by Russia's senior military leadership to plans for expanding membership in the North Atlantic Treaty Organization to include some Central and East European nations.

Intellectual Elite, the Power and the People

The concept of an original path of Russian historical development is linked with the traditionally archaic culture of the people of Russia, as opposed to the culture of an intellectual elite that is usually oriented toward innovative ideas (leaving aside a fundamentalist group of intellectuals that seeks to move closer to the views held by the majority of the population). The difference between the advanced culture of the intellectual elite and the more conservative character of popular culture is easy to observe: the latter, for example, remains oriented toward the cult of Lenin and other symbolic legacies of the Soviet system.

A similar difference might be seen if one studies how, after the Bolshevik Revolution, the atheistic views of a large number of intellectuals co-existed with the traditional religious beliefs of the majority of the population. Earlier, after the acceptance of Christianity, this kind of "dual-faith" (*dvoeverie*) was manifest in the parallel use of Christian beliefs that were introduced by the elitist layers of Old Russian society (the priests, the princes with their families and their guards), and the vestiges of ancient paganism that hid below the surface of the new faith.

To understand the changes produced by the Revolution, it is important not to exaggerate the degree to which Christian beliefs had spread. Insofar as images of the Christian Orthodox Trinity and Saint Sophia (God's Wisdom personified in a Gnostic way) became objects of veneration, Christian beliefs were authentic. By the fourteenth century, Russian peasants were so intimately connected with the new religion that they were called *krest'iane* (the distorted form of *khristiane*, "Christians"). Faith in the principal Christian images, however, co-existed with a whole web of superstitions surrounding lesser mythological creatures. From Russian folklore and from anthropological studies of the Russian villages of the nineteenth and early twentieth centuries, one may see that traces of paganism have survived for almost a thousand years. In the beginning of this century the great Russian poet Aleksandr Blok wrote a thesis on Russian folk spells and incantations that revealed the rich tradition of pagan magical poetry. The great Russian thinker and scholar of our century Mikhail Bakhtin discovered the difference between official and unofficial culture as found, for instance, in Nikolai Gogol's literary work. That difference has always existed in the Russian cultural tradition.

At the beginning of Peter the Great's reforms, which were transforming Russia into a Westernized country, only the elitist part of society participated in the movement. The gap between the people and the intelligentsia (the intellectuals as a social class), which was vividly described in Blok's essays, was already evident before the Bolshevik Revolution. But the majority of intellectuals (such as the populists) tried to build a bridge between themselves and the people. Their utopian aims envisaged a unified society without social inequalities.

Traditionally, the intellectuals who worked to advance the interests of the people were opposed to the state, or were at least independent of it. To control the activity of the intellectuals the government used an elaborate system of secret police, which had approximately the same functions under different successor regimes. The existence of the secret services and their growing influence at court seriously damaged the relations between the government and the intellectuals. One of the main obstacles to reforms from above (such as those of Alexander II or Gorbachev) was the refusal of most politically active intellectuals to cooperate with the government. People like Sakharov joined the opposition even when the government was, in part at least, carrying out their own program. In his memoirs, Count Sergei Witte recalls that the undeviating opposition on the part of the intelligentsia was one of the main obstacles to his attempts to introduce reforms in the period following the 1905 Revolution.

Inherent in the Russian tradition is an affinity for anarchy. This affinity is evident, not only in the writings of Mikhail Bakunin and Prince Petr Kropotkin, but also in the teachings of Tolstoy, who held that military conscription was unlawful.

In any conflict between the Russian state and the people, the army and its senior commanders usually supported the authorities, as may be clearly seen in cases in which celebrated Russian military commanders waged war against their own people (Aleksandr Suvorov crushing Emilian Pugachev's revolt in the eighteenth century or Mikhail Tukhachevskii putting down A.S. Antonov's peasant revolt after the Civil War). With the exception of the Decembrists, Russian army officers did not usually oppose the power of the state. Elements of the army might be used in organizing military coups, as occurred several times in the eighteenth century, but these plots aimed at minor changes in the existing system and had nothing to do with radical political reform. Intellectuals who were involved with scientific and technological research of a military character (Dmitrii Mendeleev helping the Russian intelligence service, Sergei Korolev working on rockets, the young Sakharov inventing the Russian version of the hydrogen bomb) never refused to do this work, no matter what their political views were.

In his last prophetic verses, the great philosopher and poet of the second half of the nineteenth century, Vladimir Solov'ev, asked Russia, "What kind of East do you want to be? Do you want to be the East of

Xerxes or that of Christ?" The Asian military despotism of the Persian emperor Xerxes (or later of Stalin) is opposed to the utopian ideal of the country that personifies Christ's aims. In Byzantium, as well as later in Russia, both principles were realized. According to the great Russian philosopher Nikolai Fedorov, the political and state system of the Grand Duchy of Muscovy could be defined as an absolute monarchy that was restricted by the institution of "God's fool." From the point of view of modern psychiatric research, the latter phenomenon might seem clearly abnormal. But God's fools played an important role in the whole structure of values of Russian society. One needs only to recall the scene in Aleksandr Pushkin's play *Boris Godunov* or in Modest Mussorgsky's opera based on it, in which God's fool damns the tsar.

We see from this example that the national culture also determines such features of the personality and psyche as are thought to belong to the sphere of psychology and medicine; the history of madness in Russia differs from what we see in Western Europe. *Woe from Wit; or, The Misfortune of Being Clever*, to borrow the title of Aleksandr Griboedov's play, becomes a traditional recurring topic of Russian cultural life. Chaadaev was officially declared insane after publishing his *Philosophical Letters*. The fate of many Soviet dissidents who were thrown into mental institutions in recent times is widely known, but in Russian literature such a fate was known much earlier, to Tolstoy, for example, as well as to Griboedov before him.

In his late years, Sakharov, in whose life different Russian cultural traditions intersect, played the role of the "blessed fool" in the sense Fedorov described it. Many Russian dissidents represented a continuation of the intellectual type described in Russian classic prose as the "superfluous person" (*lishnii chelovek*).

The highly abstract character of both ideals and goals is a prominent feature of such heroes and of Russian culture in general. But these abstract ideas are often realized in a very practical way. As an example one might cite the prehistory of Russian space rocketry. The idea of conquering space originated in connection with the proposition that the dead can literally be resurrected, as suggested by Fedorov. His former student Konstantin Tsiolkovskii began his theoretical work on space ship travel because Fedorov was concerned about the consequences of the physical resurrection of the dead. The existing space on earth would not suffice in the event of the resurrection of all the generations that had lived on the planet. Thus, while the West was amazed at the success of the Russian sputnik, nobody realized that the project had originated with Fedorov's concern over how to deal with the physical resurrection of the dead. This concern should be common to all modern science, according to his thinking, and Fedorov's contemporaries, such as Fyodor Dostoevsky and Vladimir Solov'ev, took his views very seriously.

The abstract ideas put forward by Russian intellectuals are to be realized in an aesthetically perfect form. Since the story of Saint Vladimir's choice of the Christian faith, this aesthetic aspect seems to have been of utmost importance. According to Dostoevsky's celebrated formula, "Beauty will save the world." Thus, literature, visual arts, theater, music, and later cinema became the most important parts of the whole culture, competing with philosophy as well as with governmental institutions and partly substituting for them. From this point of view, the present-day revival of freedom in the arts may have most significant social results. The cultural and educational consequences of the recent economic reforms may become even more important than all other aspects of the changes. The serious economic difficulties that Russian cultural institutions are suffering, however, can sharply reduce their social impact.

The Church and the Intelligentsia's Beliefs: Ethics and the Market

The importance to a Russian of his personal mystical emotions stands in an inverse relationship to the relatively modest role of the Orthodox Church itself, which seems to be dominated by the government and the state. This subordinate tendency had long been apparent, but it became particularly strong with the schism in the church and the creation under Peter the Great of a special governmental institution, the Synod, that was in charge of religious activities. Since then, beginning in the eighteenth century, individual mystical aspirations found their semi-institutionalized way through different sects, which spread with particular speed among the peasants and the middle class. A body of unofficial spiritual literature was developed, mostly through manuscripts that were disseminated clandestinely, just as the dissident *samizdat* writings of the 1960s and 1970s were circulated. Mystical sects like the "flagellants" (*khlysty*) have modern counterparts, as we have recently seen in the White Brotherhood cult organized in Ukraine. Although the White Brotherhood reflected the influence of similar phenomena in American and Western religious mass culture, the main pseudo-Gnostic aspect of the beliefs of this sect, particularly the veneration of a woman claiming to be the female incarnation of the Holy Spirit, resembles the mystical movements of the previous two centuries. Among the majority of the population, such sects serve to express individual emotions, just as aesthetic religious images do in Russian art and literature.

As the eminent Russian historian Vasilii Kliuchevskii put it, in Russia there was God without a church, as distinguished from Europe, where many Russians saw a church without God. The important change that began in the middle of the nineteenth century consisted in the creation of an intellectual substitute for a creed. The well-known modern writer Vladimir Makanin, speaking about communism, recently coined the term "pseudoreligion" to designate the phenomenon. This pseudoreligion consisted of a set of philosophical and moral beliefs in which one saw the essence of rational knowledge. Some of these beliefs that still are valid for a large part of the intelligentsia can be considered direct continuations of Christian Orthodox values, but without the religious basis of the latter.

A typical Russian intellectual is not supposed to have any material interest in life. This negative attitude toward money and other worldly values may be traced back to similar religious ideas. They were first developed by the "non-acquiring-property" movement (*nestiazhatel'stvo*). The representatives of the latter did not succeed in their attempt to get rid of all the wealth collected by the church. But in the later history of the Orthodox Church, those who approached closest to the strictly ascetic ideal were the ones most venerated. These "elders" (*startsy*) embodied true Christianity for many Russians belonging to different social classes. The Christian Orthodox ideal was that of a truly wise man who had lost all interest in worldly matters. This ideal seems quite close to that seen in Buddhism and some other Oriental philosophical and religious traditions (their early influence on the Old Russian world outlook is possible).

But what is really astonishing is the close correspondence of this popular Christian ideal to that of a Russian intellectual, who was usually either an atheist or had no pronounced religious convictions. It was considered that a typical representative of the Russian intelligentsia should be completely disinterested, just as the medieval ascetic monks and, later, the elders were.

If the most prestigious religious and secular figures of Russian society were so ill-disposed toward wealth, then one may find a new explanation for the whole problem of the delayed development of capitalism in Russia. Let us remember Max Weber's view of the role of the Protestant ethic for the growth of capitalism in Western Europe. In Russia, one may see the opposite attitude toward worldly success. The continuity of this ascetic monastic tradition seems particularly important, for it influenced the world outlook of Russian intellectuals. Since the middle of the nineteenth century, the ideal representative of the intelligentsia has been a person lacking any means on which to live. The lives of some famous authors such as Vissarion Belinskii and Nikolai Chernyshevskii helped perpetuate this image. The socialist view of the hero as described in the literature of the revolutionary period also reflected this perception.

A negative attitude toward wealth not only discouraged those who might have wanted to acquire it but possibly engendered actual hostility toward material possessions. The revolutionary slogan "Steal what has been stolen!" (*Grab' nagrablennoe!*) derived from the notion that rich people were thieves and wealth was to be plundered or pillaged. One of the negative results of this tradition is the immoral character of trade and the mixture of crime and business. The spread of corruption among officials was Russian tradition documented since the seventeenth century. If the Russian tradition reveals itself in the lack of a legal basis for power (both in its legislative and executive branches and in respect to the separation of powers), it also is seen in the absence of an ethical attitude toward trade and business. Merchants and capitalists (originally called "merchants") existed, but they were not supposed to have civil rights that would place them on the same level as military officers (being nobles) and government bureaucrats. The latter were encouraged to become rich at the expense of other social classes. This system was rebuilt immediately after the Revolution, and Communist Party officials became the most influential and richest class.

After the demise of the Communist Party, the system of bribery and other forms of official corruption have been continued according to the original governmental (nonparty) pattern. The present system of taxation that makes business activity particularly difficult for small enterprises, which are less closely connected to the establishment than larger ones, is linked to this pattern of official corruption.

It would be a mistake to believe that capitalism and the market did not exist in previous periods of Russian history, but they were given no legal status. The capitalists of the period immediately preceding the Russian Revolution were trying to improve their ties with intellectuals. Some of them supported revolutionary movements, among them the Bolsheviks. In the period of Lenin's New Economic Policy (NEP) after the Civil War, an attempt was made to combine the communist totalitarian regime and the existence of private business and the market. In a sense, the impressive results of NEP resembled what is being achieved now in China. During Stalin's period and after, the system of monopolistic state capitalism was built. Elements of the system (especially those connected to the military-industrial complex) are preserved in present-day Russia, but they co-exist with the new forms of private enterprise closely linked to the old party and governmental system. Elements of the corrupt illegal economy of the Soviet era are now considered legal: the contemporary market economy in Russia continues the illegal "black market" developed in the years before the reforms of Mikhail Gorbachev and Boris Yeltsin. But all this is very far removed from the developed economic systems of Western countries. In Russia, most private enterprises produce nothing; they only sell at higher prices products that were already manufactured or have been imported.

What is lacking above all is the legal, ethical, and psychological basis necessary to establish new market relations. Without fundamental change, the feeling of instability, giving rise to fraud and frustration, will persist. It is not enough to sign a "decree" about the land and private property; active young people must be encouraged to buy land and start farms, transforming the agricultural system of the country. Judging from the results of the fall 1993 election campaign, the large and socially influential mass of villagers still oppose private farms. Decrees have had no effect on this rural mind-set.

This chapter was written in English by the author

Note

1. Fedor Tiutchev, "Russian Geography," quoted in Richard Hare, *Pioneers of Russian Social Thought* (New York: Oxford University Press, 1951), p. 132.

3

Fazil Iskander

Who Are We?

Pity for a person. Pain on behalf of another. Pity is higher than justice, although justice endures longer. In recalling from a distance in time the moment we showed pity for someone, we may conclude that perhaps we went too far; that person did not merit such a degree of pity.

But when we recall a just decision we made with regard to someone, we cannot tell ourselves that we went too far.

Pity, I am certain, cannot be explained by any rational considerations. It comes to a person from above, from God.

Almost anyone at times of torment remembers incidents from his life when he should have shown pity and did not. What was the matter; where was our God in that moment? I think there were signals from above, but at that time we were so dehumanized that we could not pick them up. A person who is not morally insensitive, though, preserves an ethical memory, and in recalling the scene of his indifference he undergoes torments, repents, and thus cleanses his soul.

The first impulse toward a sense of justice may be pity for someone, but ultimately the feeling of justice is love for the truth. In life's difficult cases, however, a person who dispenses with pity may become so confused in the search for a formula to attain the good that he reaches the most ruthless and unjust conclusions.

Such was our socialism in practice. The original impulse of all socialist theories, without a doubt, was pity for the unfortunate. How could it turn out that a doctrine based on compassion could produce a most ruthless society? Indeed, Maxim Gorky's words became that society's slogan: Pity degrades a person. Besides the inveterate executioners, though, were there not some people among the revolutionaries who sincerely desired the good? Did they see no contradiction between the declared ideal of this state—love for the people—and the utterly ruthless treatment of those people in real life? Undoubtedly they did, but they justified their pitilessness on several quite serious grounds.

Let us imagine a passenger who is waiting for a train while sleeping at the station, holding a loaf of bread. He is a normal, kind man, not disposed to theorize about life. A hungry child comes toward him. (This scenario is becoming less hypothetical daily.)

"Mister, can you give me a piece of bread?" asks the child.

The man breaks off a hunk of the loaf and gives it to the child. Then another child comes up to him with the same request. He breaks off a piece for him as well. Then a third, a fourth, a fifth. Finally, the loaf is all gone. Perhaps one more child or several children will have noticed that the man was giving away bread and come over to him. But no matter how painful it may be, he will be forced to throw up his hands and say, "There's nothing left. Try asking someone else."

But there's another possibility. Here the passenger with the loaf of bread is a fairly decent person, but he has an unfortunate tendency to theorize. A hungry child approaches. The man hands him a piece of the bread. Then a second, and a third. And suddenly the passenger realizes that he will not have enough bread for all the hungry children.

The problem has to be solved at its root. A final solution of the problem of hungry children must be proposed. Stirred by the magnitude and nobility of his task, the man hides the rest of the loaf in his briefcase, whips out a pen and notebook, and begins feverishly to calculate how to save all the hungry children from starvation. He is advancing his mission of helping children, but his inner drive has changed direction.

Now he no longer notices the children who approach him. He even pushes them away. And he feels neither pity nor shame because, after all, he is making an effort for their own good. Now the real children only interfere with his assistance to the theoretical children, with his design of a final and just solution to the question of children's hunger.

Of the two passengers in the station, who acted more correctly? I think, clearly, that it was the first passenger. As the saying goes, theory is dead, but the tree of life is eternally green.

The subtlety of the problem, though, is that the first passenger, for all his simplicity, is on a higher theoretical level than the second passenger, even if the second may be as celebrated as Karl Marx.

The theoretical superiority of the first over the second passenger, although probably unconscious, consists in this: he understands that the tragedy of existence is insurmountable and can only be mitigated. His partial consolation is in knowing that he fulfilled his duty: he gave away his bread to hungry children. And he accepts a priori the responsibility for having to look a hungry child straight in the eye and say, "I have no more bread. Try asking others."

Although we acknowledge fully the lofty motives of the second passenger and his effort to find a final solution for the question of children's hunger, we have the creeping suspicion that he was simultaneously motivated, probably unconsciously, by the desire to rid himself of the tragedy of existence, so that today he can look a hungry child in the eye in the calm certainty that tomorrow (or one hundred years hence), there will be no more hungry children, thanks to his efforts.

There are no formulas for good, and there never will be. If it could be theoretically imagined that science could discover such a formula, it would mean that conscience had been abolished. But clearly it is only conscience that accompanies a person through all the unfathomable twists and turns of his life. There is no hiding it: conscience is tiresome. The temptation to shrug off the tragedy of existence has always been part of human nature. But we must understand that each time we avoid a pang of conscience, it strikes someone else with additional pain. Thus the prodigal son, seeking the easy life, made the life of his parents additionally burdensome.

Revolutions in general, because of their express aim to change world history, and our revolution in particular, succumb to the temptation to banish the tragedy of existence.

A new era! Science has proved there would be a new era, and now it has arrived! Those who succumbed to the temptation of revolution, shrugging off the tragedy of existence, simultaneously dodged the sense of responsibility toward those around them. The diverse and complex nature of the sense of duty to specific persons was replaced by a single radiant obedience to an idea.

This obedience to an idea is invigorating and produces a certain lightness of being. And the more irreproachably a revolutionary carries out his single revolutionary duty, the freer he feels from the burden of any duty to specific persons around him; after all, for the sake of the future just life, he has gone further than others. In this way, he compensates for his revolutionary zeal and produces new (temporary) acts of oppression on the path to final justice.

But where has pity gone? We are not talking about inherent misanthropes and hypocrites, but about sincere people.

I remember that, as a little boy at the outbreak of war, I lived for quite a long time at my grandfather's house in Chegema in Abkhazia. Once, my sister came to visit us from the city, and she and I, together with several other fellow villagers, set off for another village. I walked along, prodding a mule loaded down with baggage and striking him on the back from time to time with a stick.

"What are you hitting him for? It hurts him," said my sister.

I was surprised at what she said. Somehow, I had completely forgotten that the mule could feel pain. I was doing the same thing that the local peasants did whenever they drove mules. It would never occur to me to strike the mule with a stick while he was grazing in the meadow. But when you are traveling, a mule keeps trying to stop, chewing the green branches above the path, slowing down his gait. Thus, like all the peasants, I drove the mule along. But in the eye of my sister, a city girl, this was an unpleasant spectacle (although, of course, I had not hit the mule very hard). By the way, an even more incomprehensible sight for a city person would be that of the same peasant, climbing with a loaded mule up a very steep hill, and suddenly removing the packs from the animal and shouldering all or part of the load himself. The peasant takes pity on his animal and knows just the right moment to show it.

From the example of the peasant and the mule, we can see that pity is sometimes related to an understanding of the essence of the matter. We are sometimes amazed by rulers who lack this understanding. Although they have thousands of mechanisms to enable them to get at the essence, they make no use of them, in order to have the right not to show pity.

A person's ability to adapt to life, even to a harsh life, is enormous. From experience a person knows that sometimes pitilessness must be shown to another for his own good. Thus a teacher is remorseless when he keeps a slack student in class after school, a parent when he punishes a mischievous child, a surgeon when he cuts into a living human being.

The clever mechanism of adaptability eclipses reason. The revolutionary who condones the shedding of blood eagerly compares himself to the surgeon, usually forgetting that the surgeon sheds a person's blood precisely in order to save that individual. But the revolutionary sheds the blood of another person in order to preserve his loyalty to an idea whose validity is unproven.

Yet so great was the temptation to throw off the burden of the tragedy of existence, to solve the problem finally, to escape to the kingdom of freedom, that pity toward a person was replaced by pity toward a fairy tale understood as the new truth.

Perhaps it is our Asiatic dreaminess, a casual attitude toward life's practical values, that facilitated this process. In principle, however, under the right historical circumstances, this loyalty to an idea could have happened to any nation. Casting off the burden of tragic consciousness, or at least shouting "The hell with everything!" is characteristic of people everywhere.

The Russian writer Andrei Platonov has a wonderful description of this process in his novel *Chevengur.* All the communists in this story are completely sincere people, and they theorize endlessly about where and how to implant communism. They are half-children and half-madmen. They speculate tenderly about communism, interpreting every flash of their insane fantasy as communism and killing anyone who seems to them an enemy. They do not know what communism is, but they do know only too well that communism has already emancipated them from any oppressive feelings of responsibility for what happens around them.

Our revolution was the most total in history. The hierarchy of human values was utterly destroyed. The top became the bottom; the bottom became the top. The Russian poet Joseph Brodsky has written:

> *All forms of life are but adaptations*
> *including an upward glance at the ceiling.*[1]

The glance downward at one's own plate and upward at the sky are two forms of adaptation to life. But it turns out that there is an enormous difference between the two. If in the balance sheet of one's life the downward glance at the plate prevails over the upward glance at the ceiling, then at some point the plate will end up empty, no matter how much you look at it. And an idiotic gaze toward the ceiling will also gain you nothing.

Thus a church that is turned into a grain depot finally ceases to serve even as a warehouse, because one fine day it turns out that there is no grain to store.

There is something tragi-comical about a former communist shown on television standing in a church before a priest and holding a candle in his hand.

If only the priest with a gesture of his hand would push him back into the crowd of parishioners, as if to say that it is too early for the communist to be showing his face there! Instead, the priest blesses him with amusing caution, as if he is surprised and a bit unsure about the communist's sudden reconciliation. It is not an appetizing spectacle.

The Russian writer Konstantin Leont'ev was a brilliant stylist and romantic misanthrope who loved history like a rare steak. And that was typical. The lifelessness of the aesthete is fatefully counterbalanced with brutality as the highest manifestation of liveliness. Nietzsche was like this. He, too, was a brilliant stylist.

Ethical corrections to the sense of beauty can be surprising. Once when I went into my kitchen I saw a torchlight procession on television. My first impression was that it was beautiful and magnificent. And suddenly from the narrator's words I learned that this was a film about German fascism. What had seemed beautiful a moment before became dark and sinister, the torches notwithstanding.

Our famous military parades on Red Square were the same. At first glance there was beauty expressing the might and solidity of your fatherland. But when you realized that this power had turned millions of your fellow citizens into slaves, you began to notice the automatism, the inhumane stupidity of this orderly mass. But if you did not think about all that, the parade was beautiful.

Romanticizing the past is a false judgment about the past coupled with a false conclusion: life was more interesting and more harmonious then. Romanticism of the future is a false judgment about the future coupled with a false conclusion: life will be more interesting and harmonious. Despite its inaccuracy, romanticizing the past cannot do too much damage. A false estimate of the past is one that does not require us to pay a price. We will pay with our hides and those of our children, however, for a false calculation about the future. And we are already paying.

A compass that lies about the road ahead is much more dangerous than a compass that lies about the road already traversed.

The Russian philosopher Nikolai Berdiaev wrote that the sense of history, at least in the European world, was introduced by Christianity. That sounds like the truth. For Christianity, the meeting with God is in the future. Thus the life of an individual, and of many generations, falls into a purposeful pattern, and the scribes who believed in this purpose described the events of life and concentrated their gaze on the quality of change in life, emphasizing the enthusiasm of movement.

When a fairly large number of examples of changes in life appeared, introduced by the force of the human mind and the power of invention, a much more promising, much more visible, and shorter parallel to the Christian trajectory toward a goal appeared: the philosophy of progress. Even without God, the course of history could lead to world harmony.

Both the Christian faith and faith in historical progress are based on expectation. Expectation long deferred cannot but cause attacks of historical impatience and even historical despair in those who were waiting. An ancient Greek who might have happened to visit our train station with the hungry children would understand it all except for one thing: why were people worried about a train being late? The Greek would have thought that life has no other purpose beyond simply living. And in that he was beautiful.

Bouts of despair over one's faith in historical progress produce the philosophy and practice of revolution. Attacks of historical despair in the great Christian artists meant looking as deeply as possible into a person's soul, trying to fathom him to the end, to understand whether he was ready for a higher purpose and capable of it. Of course, a great artist may consider himself a nonbeliever, but living within Christian culture, he reflects its intense curiosity about the human soul, and the force of his talent alone may whip up his faith.

Was it not that same energy of historical despair that moved the brush of Rembrandt when he painted *The Prodigal Son*, the lyrical power of which exceeds the biblical narrative a hundred times over? It should not have been so, but the prodigal son keeps losing his way!

As the Russian émigre poet Naum Korzhavin has written:

The horses keep jumping and jumping
And the cabins keep burning and burning.

So has the human being grown better or worse since the times of the ancient Greeks? I would put it this way: people have become no better or worse in comparison to the ancient Greeks, but they have become more disgusting. More disgusting by comparison with what? In comparison with what we expected. But, the ancient Greek would ask in surprise, what were you expecting?

In the moral sense, the human being is eternally the student who is held back a year and shows greater and greater skill at using crib-notes. The one-sided technological development of the mind and a scheming way of thinking have strengthened in people the technology of self-justification in an immoral situation.

But the negative experience of humankind is so great that the question can be answered in another way. By comparison with the ancient Greeks, the best of our contemporaries have become even better, taking into account the negative experience that they have overcome. But the worst of them have become even worse, taking into account the negative human experience they have not overcome. Yet the worst are the more numerous. Humankind has become strung out like a straggling army, and the farther it marches the more it straggles. The noise of those at the rear may drown out the words of those in front, but the aesthetic power of Andrei Sakharov in no way cedes to the aesthetic power of Socrates.

A person in a crowd. . . . A person can blush from shame while alone. His conscience is the only witness. Conscience makes life difficult in order to make the meeting with God easier. Let us hope so. The workings of conscience are an endless rehearsal for that meeting. Human self-confidence nonetheless declares: even if there is something to this notion of conscience, I'll go on stage without a rehearsal!

A person may blush from shame in front of another. He may blush from shame in a crowd as well, but in his baseness he will stand accused alone. And in that is a hint that no references to collective blundering will save us.

A natural disposition toward the truth is a readiness to perceive shame in the event of a mistaken course of thought or action, and that requires solitude or the striving after solitude. A person pregnant with thought avoids others, and a person who hastens toward others has nothing to say.

That is why an association of conscientious, thoughtful persons is always relatively weak, whereas a league of scoundrels is solid and strong. A crowd caught in the basest act of treachery will never be ashamed. In a crowd a person may manifest courage he is incapable of showing as an individual. But in the crowd he becomes part of a collective body, and thus he gains a sense of greater personal invulnerability. In the same crowd a person may experience wild fear and panic to which he never gave in as an individual. Here, too, is the influence of the collective body.

A lesser individual strives hard to be part of a crowd and ruled by it. The more advanced an individual, the more offensive it is to be in a crowd and ruled by it, for the crowd always flattens and disfigures thought. This is the tragedy of collective and nationalist movements, and the tragedy of politics in general. Only that which has been discovered by solitary individuals is of enduring use.

The solitary thinker sends signals of solidarity above the heads of rulers and the crowd. He arouses the will to goodness by appealing to the individual. And this is the most honest means of communication with people, for each individual decides personally and of his own free will whether or not to receive these signals.

In a crowd, if a person listens to himself, he will hear how his individuality is being sucked out of him. It is an extremely unpleasant sensation. And if another person there actually feels full-blooded in a crowd, then it seems as though what was lacking in him is what was sucked out of the first person.

We could say that Christianity is to blame for human historical despair, if we did not know that, even without Christianity, sooner or later the philosophy of progress would have emerged.

The philosophy of progress, faith in a self-sustaining movement toward a goal, weakens the will to good in a person; the current itself carries you along. But in fact the current does not bear you anywhere because evil, changing its appearance, perhaps only slightly, floats right along with you. The will to good, even if it only creates the illusion of escaping evil, really does reinforce the moral muscles of a person. And that result alone is no small accomplishment.

Religion and culture are the will to good expressed in prayer and in image.

The idea of progress as a historical goal has exhausted itself. The technical refurbishment of life will continue, but no serious person will believe that technology will lead at any point to a moral breakthrough.

Do people need a historical purpose? Is it not better to live like the ancient Greeks, for the sake of life itself? Perhaps it would be better, but for us and for our country this is impossible.

The transition from a rather enduring totalitarian regime to democracy has brought unimaginable psychological difficulties along with it. Under a totalitarian regime, it was as if you were forced to live in the same room with a violently insane man. Thus you work out your habits of survival beside him. Say he demands that you play chess with him every morning. In order to survive, you play, and you are obliged to play fairly well and to lose just as carefully, but in such a way that he does not notice that you are deliberately letting him win. (Even so, it was nice to think to yourself: "What a great chess player is going to waste!")

The habit of concentrating your efforts on surviving beside a violently insane man made the tragedy of existence recede. It seems that when we live in the same room with such a madman and adapt ourselves to him, we perceive many of our obligations as a kind of luxury, and we do not fulfill them, or we only pretend to fulfill them.

But now the lunatic has disappeared, and life has set before us our unfulfilled, half-forgotten obligations, in all their unsightliness. (And it turns out we were even exaggerating our chess-playing skills.)

But what had been our most valuable acquisition, the thing on which we expended so much of our intellectual capacity—mastery of the cunning needed to survive beside a madman—now turns out to be useless garbage. It is too bad. There is not even a Byzantium to which we can travel bearing our patent on cunning. Having adapted to the prolonged dialogue with a violently insane man, we have failed to notice that we have forgotten how to speak normally. When we communicate, we can never understand who our interlocutor is—a lunatic pretending to be normal or a conniver taking us for a wild lunatic.

In this unvirtuous world, trust is a great virtue. The world easily dumps its poisonous effluence on the trusting person. But the trusting person holds fast to his beliefs without ceasing to be trusting. Like any gifted person, he is the last one to notice his gift and thinks that people are not talking about him but about somebody else.

Many people in Russia have been gripped by anguish, rage, and an all-encompassing suspiciousness. The south of the country is in flames, but there is no strength to stop this fire. Will it take exhaustion from bloodshed to sober up people who are shooting at each other? Or are they searching for new insane leaders in that bloody fog, so that once again they can make use of their clever experience in adapting to cohabitation with madmen?

The great bluff of communism is being replaced by the provincial bluff of nationalism. Nationalism is the competition of the noncompetitive. But it is their rulers who made the people this way, for many years hiding from the people, through bribes and flattery, their own non competitiveness.

The new bluff of nationalism is a weapon of revenge for their loss of power and constitutes the most reliable means of regaining it. We are traversing the path from the single sclerosis of communism to the diffuse sclerosis of nationalism.

Nationalists of all stripes have revived communism's flagging hatreds. The old banners are saturated with blood; the new, dry banners thirst for it.

When the appetite for life is lost, an appetite for the destruction of life appears.

Only the enthusiasm of creation can overwhelm and break down the walls of hatred being built up around us on all sides. We are a people who have lost our appetite for creation—the appetite for a precisely executed drawing, for earth neatly sliced by a plow, for freshly crushed grapes, for a passionately written page.

In our confused, dark time, who will restore our appetite for creation? Darkness can be opposed only by light and clarity. We need a natural authority with a clearly expressed will to good, with a clearly creative program, with clear laws that defend the work of those who create. But while bickering continues in the structures of power, while the representatives of national authority hang on one another like exhausted boxers, we cannot expect any creative energy. Hatred reigns.

When the earth becomes parched for lack of love, it is irrigated with blood. That is how our poor land is today. And exactly in accordance with climactic conditions, the land toward the south of the country is rapidly growing parched for lack of love, and there it is being irrigated with rivers of blood.

Love was the main thing in Christ's teaching. A person has thousands of temptations, but there is only one reliable bulwark, and that is love. Even the most inveterate criminal who has committed dozens of crimes still needs this love, still remembers its light and tattoos his body with the words *Ne zabudu mat' rodnuiu*: "I will never forget my mother." And although he has caused his mother the greatest anguish, he still remembers the light of her love and wears that tattoo, not realizing that it is the last sign that his soul is not completely dead.

When we love a child, a woman, an old man, a friend, when we love in general, we feel a sweet lightness of body. We feel the same physical relief when we dive into a warm sea on a hot day. We sense the same sweet physical relief when inspiration comes to us, because inspiration is being in love with unfolding truth.

At that moment a person casts aside all the weight of selfishness. If humankind as a whole were capable of being loved for one moment, then in that same moment all the accursed questions left unresolved by the ages would fall away. Alas, that is impossible. Only the rarest souls are capable of eternal love. But even the recollection of love invigorates us and, more important, illuminates the final task, which is still unattainable for most people—casting off the load of selfishness. The most zealous persons carry the heaviest baggage of selfishness.

"Live as freely as the birds of the air," said the Teacher. "My burden is not heavy," a person replies thoughtfully, and continues on his way.

Today, just as in 1917, we are once again being overwhelmed by insane hopes and gloomy disappointments. It is dangerous to expect too much; it is not easy to establish an equilibrium of mutual trust in our unbalanced society.

But a person always has one and the same task—a duty within the limits of his responsibility and a responsibility within the limits of his duty. When somebody says that the boundaries of duty and responsibility are not clear to him, he lies.

It is high time for us to resign ourselves to changing our slovenly universality to an honest particularity. Thus we will be closer to eternity.

Everyone must bear his cross. Quietly, with interludes now and then, but to the end. In doing so we must keep in mind that grumbling is never rewarded. But if grumbling makes the burden easier, then grumble.

It is not easy. Human vanity is boundless. Some take up a cross that is clearly too heavy for them. I forgot to warn that the weight of the cross must not deform our sense of humor. That would be dangerous. A person who takes up too heavy a cross must be stopped in time and ridiculed. Why? I will reply with an Abkhazian fable: A cow was so distracted as she grazed along some succulent grass that she wandered up a steep cliff. A mule down below saw her and began braying loudly in alarm.

"What difference is it to you?" the shepherd asked the mule. "What do you mean?" replied the mule. "If she falls off the cliff, I'm the one who will have to pull her out."

Our intelligentsia should not be ashamed of its role to serve as the warning voice of that mule, at a time when delight in cud-chewing lures our society, the cow, up a new cliff.

But where is the shepherd?

Translated by Catherine A. Fitzpatrick

Note

1. Joseph Brodsky, "Conversation with a Dweller of the Spheres." Translation courtesy of Joseph Brodsky.

4

Dmitrii Likhachev

I Object

What Constitutes the Tragedy of Russian History

In reading this essay, do not rush to any conclusions about the author's position. The essay does not promulgate nationalism, although it is written with sincere pain for my beloved native Russia. I ask simply that the reader hold no primitive prejudices about Russian history, prejudices with which general discussions of Russia abound at present. I support a normal view of Russia and Russian history. The reader will understand by the end of the essay (if he or she has the patience to read that far) just what this "normal view" is and which features of the Russian character contain the true reasons for the country's current tragic predicament.

Eurasia or Scandoslavia?

In my introductory remarks at the Byzantine Congress in Moscow in 1989, I discussed the fact that Russia's location between the North and South was of crucial importance, particularly in the first centuries of its historical existence, and that the designation of Russia as "Scandoslavia" was far more appropriate than "Eurasia" since, strange as it might seem, the country received very little from Asia.

If we leave aside the native, pagan culture of Rus, it was Byzantine and Scandinavian culture that played a decisive role in the development of Russian culture. The currents of these two vastly differing cultures extended throughout the entire, gigantic, multinational expanses of the East European plain. The South and the North, and not the East and the West—Byzantium and Scandinavia, not Asia and Europe—played the definitive role in the foundation of the culture of Rus.

Russian culture is usually characterized as falling somewhere between Europe and Asia, between the West and the East, but these boundaries are perceived only when looking at Rus from the West. In fact, the influence of nomadic Asiatic peoples was virtually nil. Byzantine culture gave Rus its spiritual-Christian character. Scandinavia gave Rus its military organization—the *druzhina*.

To deny the broad effects and significance of the Christianity brought from Byzantium and Bulgaria is to take an extreme position, that of vulgar historical materialism (all historical Marxism is vulgar, for that matter). It is not simply that under the influence of Christianity mores became more benign (our own experience has taught us how adversely the dominance of atheism as an official worldview has affected public morality); the patterns of historical life, the relations between principalities, and the unification of ancient Rus all felt the impact.

The tenets of Christian love not only affected the private life of ancient Rus, which cannot be fully known, but its political life as well. I will give only one example. Yaroslav the Wise begins his political will and testament to his sons with the following words:

> I am leaving this world, my sons: love one another, for you are brothers of one father and mother; and if you find love between you, God will be in you, and you will vanquish your enemies, and will live in peace; if you live in hate, in quarrels and enmity, then you yourselves will perish and will ravage the land of your fathers and grandfathers, who built it with their great labor; but live in peace, and brother listen to brother.

Far more complex than the spiritual influence of Byzantium from the South was the impact of the Scandinavian North on the state structure of Rus. V.I. Sergeevich argues that the political organization of Rus in the eleventh to thirteenth centuries combined the power of the princes with that of popular *veches*, or assemblies, which seriously limited the rights of the princes.[1] This dual structure of prince and *veche* married the northern German system of princely armies or *druzhinas* with the native Russian *veche*.

In considering the influence of Swedish governance on Rus, we must remember what the German historian Karl Lehmann has written:

> The Swedish system at the beginning of the thirteenth century [that is, three centuries after Riurik was called from Sweden] had not yet arrived at the legal concept of a "state." The *riki*, or *konungs riki*, of which the oldest writings of the West Gothic law speak in many places, is the sum of individual states, linked with one another only by the personality of the king. There is no other higher legal authority governing these "individual states" and "regions"; neither is there any independent entity or any entity proceeding from the regions through election or birth. The kings simply stand alongside each other. Every region has its own laws, its own administrative system. A person belonging to one of these regions is a foreigner in another region in the same sense as if he were someone belonging to another state.[2]

Riurik, Sineus, and Truvor—the *konungi* who were called from Sweden (if they did, in fact, exist)—could well have taught the Russians military affairs, the organization of the *druzhina*. The principality system in Rus was largely supported by its own governmental and social traditions; by the institution of the *veches*, and by landholding traditions. It was precisely these structures that were meaningful during the period of dependence on the Tatar conquerors, who attacked the princes and above all the institution of the principalities.

And so, in the North, in Scandinavia, the organization of the state lagged substantially behind that of Rus, where the relations between principalities had developed mainly under Vladimir Monomakh and his oldest son, Mstislav, and then continued to change under the influence of internal demands in the twelfth and thirteenth centuries.

When the invasion of Genghis Khan's grandson, Baty, in the thirteenth century destroyed the system of the principalities' armies (an event that was disastrous for Rus, despite what the Eurasianists, who subject facts to their own preconceived ideas, write about Baty Khan), the communal governmental system that regulated everyday life remained as the people's main support network—as the most eminent of the Ukrainian historians, M.S. Grushevskii, has described.

The Traditions of Statehood and the People

In addressing Scandinavia's contribution to the establishment of particular forms of state power in Rus, we face the question of "democratic traditions" in Russian historical life. It has become a cliché to assert that Russia had no democratic traditions, no normal state authority that in any way took the interests of the people into account. Here is yet another prejudice!

I will not go into all the facts contradicting this hackneyed opinion but will simply outline the case against this view.

The treaty of A.D. 945 between the Russians and the Greeks concludes with the words "and from all the princes and from all the peoples of the Russian land." The "peoples of the Russian land" are not only Slavs but include; on an equal basis, all the Finno-Ugric tribes.

The princes constantly gathered at conferences. The prince began his day with a meeting with the members of the senior *druzhina*—"the thinking *boyars*." The Duma was a permanent council attached to the prince, and the prince undertook no business "without informing the best men of my Duma," "without conferring with my men."

The existence of legislation—the Russian Law—must also be taken into account. The first legal code had been published by 1497, which is significantly earlier than the analogous acts of other peoples.

The Despotism of Power

It is a widespread conviction that the Russians did not resist the tyranny of Ivan the Terrible, just as later they did not resist the tyranny of Josef Stalin and his successors. First of all, it must be said that Ivan the Terrible and his despotism are not at all characteristic of Russia. In the first half of his reign, Ivan himself convened Assemblies of the Land (*Zemskie Sobori*), which made important decisions. In the second part of his reign, when all the signs of his mental illness had become apparent, it should not be forgotten that Ivan's predecessor on the European horizon was the "northern Nero"—the Danish King Kristern II, who ruled Denmark from 1513 to 1523 and whose mass executions of Swedish nobles, if one considers the relative sizes of Russia and Denmark, surpassed in scale those of Ivan. It is not surprising that we have few documents about resistance to Ivan the Terrible's tyranny, just as little is known about the behavior of those arrested and executed under Stalin. The most important fact, however, is known: the resistance that the church mounted and Ivan's punishment of its leader, the Metropolitan Filip.

And what about the many peasant uprisings under Stalin? Are these not sufficient to prove resistance? And what about the news that filtered out of the Stalinist torture chambers of the intelligentsia's resistance to cruel interrogations, when people were forced to sign confessions in a half-conscious state under the threat of harm to their families?

"Bartholomew's nights" were always sudden and always paralyzingly brutal.

The Theory of "Muscovite Imperialism": Moscow as the Third Rome

It is strange that it was an elder of the small Eleazarov Monastery in Pskov, a city not yet subordinate to Moscow, who invented the theory of aggressive Muscovite imperialism. For that matter, the meaning and source of the few words that the elder Filofei wrote about Moscow as the Third Rome were revealed some time ago, and the actual concept of the origin of the Muscovite princes' power has been discovered. It is "The Tale of the Vladimir Princes" and is, by the way, carved on the throne of the Muscovite ruler, which stands in the Uspenskii Cathedral in the Moscow Kremlin.

In the Byzantine view, the emperor was the protector of the church, the only protector in the world. It is clear that after the fall of Constantinople in 1453, given the lack of an emperor, another protector had to be found for the Russian church. The elder Filofei chose as that protector the person of the Muscovite ruler, Ivan III. There was no other Orthodox monarch in the world. The choice of Moscow as the successor to Constantinople, as the new Princely City, was a natural consequence of church views. Why, then, did it take another half-century to come to such a decision, and why did sixteenth-century Moscow not accept this idea, but instead commission an entirely different version from the retired Metropolitan Spiridon: "The Tale of the Vladimir Princes," whose heirs were the Moscow rulers?

The answer is simple. Constantinople had committed heresy by joining the Florentine Uniate with the Catholic Church, and Moscow, therefore, did not want to be seen as a second Constantinople. That is how the idea that the "Vladimir princes" traced their lineage directly from the first Rome and Augustus Caesar came into being.[3]

It was only in the seventeenth century that the idea of Moscow as the Third Rome began to have a broader significance, and later, in the nineteenth and twentieth centuries, these few phrases of Filofei to Ivan III acquired enormous importance. Many prominent people were hypnotized by the rather one-sided political and historical interpretation of the idea of Moscow as the Third Rome, including Nikolai Gogol, Konstantin Leont'ev, Nikolai Danilevskii, Viacheslav Ivanov, Nikolai Berdiaev, A.V. Kartashev, Sergei Bulgakov, Vladimir Solov'ev, Nikolai Fedorov, Georgii Florovskii, Iurii Samarin, and thousands upon thousands of others. The person who least realized the magnitude of the idea was its "author," the humble elder Filofei from the humble Eleazarov Monastery of independent Pskov.

The Orthodox peoples of Asia Minor and the Balkan peninsula, when under the rule of the Muslims, until the fall of Constantinople, recognized themselves as subjects of the emperor. This relationship was purely philosophical, but nonetheless it existed as long as the Byzantine emperor did. These ideas existed in Russia as well. They are studied in Platon Sokolov's marvelous work, *The Russian Church Hierarchy from Byzantium* (Kiev, 1913), a study that has remained little known because of the events following its publication.

Russia's Isolation from Europe

Was Russia, indeed, isolated from Europe for seven hundred years of its existence, until Peter the Great? Yes, it was, but not to the degree that the founder of this myth, Peter the Great himself, thought. Peter needed this myth for his breakthrough to Northern Europe. However, until the Tatar invasion, Russia had carried on intensive trade relations with the countries of Southern and Northern Europe. Novgorod belonged to the Hanseatic League. The Gotlanders had their own church in Novgorod. And even before that, the "Road from the Varangians to the Greeks" in the ninth through the eleventh centuries was the main trade route between the Baltic countries and the Mediterranean. From 1558 to 1581 the Russian state held Narva, to which, bypassing Revel (Tallinn) and other ports, not only the English and the Dutch, but the French, Scots, and Germans came to trade.[4]

In the seventeenth century the majority of the population of Narva still consisted of Russians, who not only carried on extensive trade but were also engaged in literature, as is clear from my publication, "The Lament of the River Narova in 1665," a lament in which the inhabitants of Narva complain in poetic form of their oppression by the Swedes.[5]

The Englishman Giles Fletcher, in his essay on Russia,[6] writes that when Narva was Russian, up to one hundred vessels, laden with Russian flax and hemp, passed through customs each year.

Serfdom

It is said and written that the institution of serfdom has formed the Russian national character, but the fact that the entire northern half of the Russian land never knew serfdom and that serfdom in the central section of Russia was established relatively late is never taken into account. Serfdom arose in the Baltic and pre-Carpathian countries before it did in Russia. Iurii's Day, which permitted peasants to leave their landowners, restrained the cruelty of serf dependence, until serfdom was abolished. Serfdom was abolished in Russia before it was abolished in Poland and Romania and before slavery was ended in the United States of America. The cruelty of serfdom in Poland was accompanied by ethnic strife. Polish serfs were, for the most part, Belarusians and Ukrainians. The slaves in the United States were black.

The foundation was laid for the full emancipation of the serfs in Russia under Alexander I, when limitations on serfdom were introduced. In 1803, the law on free tillers of the soil was announced, and before that, in 1797, Paul I promulgated a law that established three days a week as the maximum labor a landowner could require of a serf.

If we look at other facts, we cannot help but note the organization of a peasant bank for subsidizing peasant purchases of land in 1881–84. Under Alexander III a whole series of laws were passed to benefit workers: limitations on factory work by minors in 1882, before analogous laws were passed in other countries; limitations on night employment of adolescents and women in 1885; and laws regulating factory labor of workers as a whole in 1886 and 1897. Some people may object that other contradictory facts illustrated the negative actions of the government. Yes, especially during the revolutionary period of 1905 and the years following. Yet, however paradoxical it may seem, the ideological significance of positive phenomena is strengthened only when they have to be fought for. Therefore, the people struggled for the improvement of their existence and fought for their personal freedom.

The "Prison of Peoples"

One often reads and hears that tsarist Russia was a "prison of peoples." But at the same time, no one notes that other religions and faiths were preserved within Russia: there were Catholics and Lutherans, as well as Muslims, Buddhists, and Jews (in St. Petersburg, next to the Mariinskii Theater, from my childhood I remember a Jewish high school where Jewish theology was taught for the many Jews who had the right to live in the city).

As has often been noted, in Russia there was the usual law and the usual civil rights. In the Polish kingdom the Napoleonic Code continued to function, in the Poltava and Chernigov *gubernias* Lithuanian statutes were in force, in the Baltic, *gubernias* had the Magdeburg Law. The Caucasus, Central Asia, and Siberia had their own local laws. In 1885 in Finland, which had a constitution, Alexander III organized a four-chamber Sejm, which had the right to initiate legislation.

And once again, it is necessary to say: yes, there was also ethnic oppression, but this does not mean that we must close our eyes to the fact that ethnic enmity never attained its present scale, that the majority of the Russian nobility was of Tatar and Georgian origin.

Russians have always been attracted to other nations. This attraction has also easily turned into its opposite, as in a magnet. The attraction to other peoples, especially weak, small populations, aided Russia in preserving almost two hundred ethnic groups on its territory. One must agree that this is no small number. But this very same "magnetic effect" continually repulsed energetic peoples such as the Poles and Jews. Even Dostoevsky and Pushkin found themselves drawn into the force field of Russia's attraction-repulsion for other peoples. Dostoevsky emphasized the Russians' all-embracing humanity; yet, at the same time, and in contradiction to his central convictions, he frequently lapsed into ordinary anti-Semitism. Pushkin, declaring that all the peoples living in Russia would some day come to his monument ("each language in her, and the proud Slav's grandson, and the Finn, and the now wild Tungus, and the Kalmyk, friend of the steppes"), nevertheless wrote a poem called "To the Slanderers of Russia" in which he described "the uprising of Lithuania" (that is, in the terminology of the time, Poland) against Russia as an argument between Slavs, in which other ethnic groups should not interfere.

Tsar Alexander III, whom many see as Russian chauvinism incarnate, wrote to Konstantin Pobedonostsev in 1886: "There are those men who think that they are Russian, and nothing else. Do they think that I am a German or a Finn? It is easy for them with their *farcical patriotism* [my italics], when they are responsible for nothing. I will be the one to defend Russia."

Cultural Backwardness

There is a widely held opinion that the Russian people are extremely uncultured. What does this mean? True, the behavior of Russians at home and abroad "leaves something to be desired." It is not always the best representatives of the nation that go abroad. This is well known. It is also known that bureaucrats, and especially bribe takers, were considered the most reliable and "politically literate" people during the seventy-five years of Bolshevik power. How accurate the evaluations of the "organs" (the KGB) were is generally known. However, taking into account the entire thousand years of Russian culture, I would say that it is undoubtedly "higher than average." It suffices to mention a few names: in science, Mikhail Lomonosov, Nikolai Lobachevskii, Dmitrii Mendeleev, V.I. Vernadskii; in music, Pyotr Ilich Tchaikovsky, Modest Mussorgsky, Mikhail Glinka, Aleksandr Scriabin, Sergei Rachmaninoff, Sergei Prokofiev, Dmitri Shostakovich; in literature, Gavrila Derzhavin, Aleksandr Pushkin, Nikolai Karamzin, Nikolai Gogol, Fyodor Dostoevsky, Leo Tolstoy, Anton Chekhov, Sergei Bulgakov, Aleksandr Blok; in architecture, N.I. Voronikhin, V.I. Bazhenov, V.P. Stasov, I.E. Starov, A.I. Shtakenshneider. Must one name all spheres of culture and enumerate their representatives? They say that Russians have no philosophy. True, there has been little of the type produced by Germany, but there is a great deal of the Russian type: Petr Chaadaev, Nikolai Danilevskii, Nikolai Fedorov, Vladimir Solov'ev, Sergei Bulgakov, Semen Frank, Nikolai Berdiaev. And the Russian language, its classical period, the nineteenth century? Does not the language itself testify to the high intellectual level of Russian culture? Where did all of these scientists, musicians, writers, artists, and architects come from if not from Russia's culture in its highest manifestations?

In the nineteenth century, Russia's libraries were among the greatest in the world. Besides the imperial public library in St. Petersburg, which ranked third in the world in number of volumes held, there were many others: the Academy of Sciences libraries, the Rumiantsev library, Kiev University library, the libraries of the theological academies in St. Petersburg, Kazan, and Kiev, and the libraries of universities, institutes, military academies, secondary schools, and trade schools. There were wonderful private libraries as well and especially the libraries of country estates, thanks to which in the provinces, even sometimes in the villages, wonderful writers and scholars were educated.

In the 1920s and 1930s, books were taken out of Russia by the wagon and train load, thanks to the efforts of the Soviet "International Book" company agency and those of private rare book antique dealers. To this day, Russia continues to be a gold mine of rare books.

What, then, has happened to Russia? Why did so large and populous a country, with so great a culture, end up in such a tragic situation, with tens of millions of people executed and tortured, dead of famine, perished in a "victorious" war; a country of heroes, martyrs, and jailers. Why? What for?

Once again people are searching for Russia's special "mission." This time the most widespread idea is the old one turned upside down: Russia is fulfilling its mission to save the world from the destructiveness of artificial states and social formations, to demonstrate that socialism, which fueled the hopes of most "progressive" people, especially in the nineteenth century, is not viable, that it is a catastrophe. This is incredible! I refuse to believe that such a "mission" has an iota of merit. Russia has no special mission and never has had!

The fate of a nation is no different from the fate of an individual. If a person enters the world with free will, then he can choose his own fate, take the side of either good or evil; he answers for himself and makes his own judgment about his choice, condemning himself either to extraordinary suffering or to the happiness of acclaim; he ascribes his participation in the Good, not to himself, but to the Highest Judge (I am intentionally choosing my words carefully, for no one knows exactly how this judgment will be made manifest). If this is so for an individual, then just as surely every nation answers for its fate. And one nation must not blame another for its misfortune; neither should it blame cunning neighbors, or conquerors, or chance, since chance itself is far from being accidental, not because there is some sort of "fate," destiny, or mission but because accidents have their specific causes.

One of the many causes of many such "accidents" is the Russian national character. It is by no means monolithic. It combines not only varied traits but a number of different traits in "a single register": religiosity and extreme atheism, generosity and miserliness, pragmatism and utter helplessness when faced with external circumstances, hospitality and misanthropy, national self-humiliation and chauvinism, an inability to fight and sudden manifestations of an extraordinary capability for military staunchness.

"Senseless and merciless," said Pushkin, describing a Russian uprising, but during an uprising this description is above all applicable to Russians themselves, to the rebels who give up their lives for the sake of a meager and poorly articulated idea. "Expansive, Russians are very expansive —I would narrow them," declares Dostoevsky's Ivan Karamazov.

Those who speak of Russians' tendency to extreme measures of all sorts are completely correct. The reasons for this tendency would require a separate discussion. I will say only that they are quite specific and do not require a belief in national destiny and "mission." Centrist positions are always difficult for Russians, and sometimes are simply intolerable.

This preference for extremes of all kinds, combined with an extreme credulity, has led to the appearance in Russian history of dozens of self-appointed leaders—full-fledged or half-baked—and contributed to the victory of the Bolsheviks. The Bolsheviks were victorious partly because, in the view of the masses, they wanted "bigger" (*bolshie*) changes than the Mensheviks, who supposedly proposed fewer and lesser (*menshie*) changes. These and other such arguments, which are not reflected in the contemporary documents (newspapers, fliers, slogans), I nonetheless recall quite clearly, for they happened within my memory.

The misfortune of Russians lies in their credulity—above all in their credulity. This is not the same as frivolousness, not at all. Sometimes their credulity takes the form of trustfulness, and then it is linked with kindness, responsiveness, and Russia's famous hospitality (now disappearing). Sometimes, however, this credulity leads to the devising of simplistic plans of economic and state salvation (Nikita Khrushchev believed in hog farming, then in rabbit raising, then he worshiped corn, and this naiveté is very typical of simple Russian people).

Russians often laugh at their own credulity: we do everything "on the off chance" and because of what is "most likely" or on account of "what if"; we "hope" that "luck will be on our side." All these phrases and expressions typify Russian behavior, even in critical situations, and are untranslatable into any language. This credulity is not frivolousness in the face of practical questions; it cannot be interpreted that way. Rather, it expresses a belief in fate that takes the form of distrust of oneself, a belief in one's own predestination.

We either believe in foreigners, or we attempt to blame these same foreigners for all our misfortunes. There is no doubt that the careers of many of "our" foreigners were influenced by the very fact that they were not Russians, but Georgians, Chechens, Tatars, and others. But this same fact also played a role in their demise.

And by the way, those Russian philosophers who believed in the mission of the Russian people, of Russia, were typical Russians without realizing it. The Slavophiles and the Westernizers alike—Konstantin Leont'ev, Nikolai Danilevskii, Fyodor Dostoevsky, Vladimir Solov'ev, Nikolai Berdiaev, Georgii Fedotov—and to one degree or another the entire Russian intelligentsia, even now, represent the typical Russian thinker, who seeks the meaning of existence and ends up looking for a messianic destiny for Russia, in order instinctively to relieve the Russian people of taking responsibility for their own actions.

The drama of Russian credulity is deepened by the fact that the Russian mind is not engaged in everyday cares but strives to make sense of history and its own life, of everything happening in the world, in the deepest sense. The Russian peasant, sitting on the stoop outside his home, talks to his friends about politics and the fate of Russia.

Russians are prepared to risk what is most precious to them, and they are adventurous in the fulfilling of their proposals and ideas. They are ready to go hungry, to suffer, even to commit self-immolation, as did hundreds of Old Believers for the sake of their beliefs, their convictions, their ideas. And this devotion was not just in the last century; it is true now as well. Have not we not recently seen people who were waiting for the end of the world commit suicide? Did the voters not recently support promises that were patently unfeasible, as if operating on the theory, "what if it works out?"

While not agreeing with the myths about Russian history and Russian culture that were created for the most part under Peter the Great, who had to turn away from Russian traditions in order to move in the direction he wanted (a slap in the face of traditional Russian culture), I do not mean that we should calm down and consider ourselves to be living in a "normal situation." No, no, and again no! A thousand year old cultural tradition creates many obligations. We should, we are obliged to, we must continue to remain a great power, by virtue not only of our size and population but of our great culture. It is not by chance that when others want to belittle Russian culture, they juxtapose it to that of Europe as a whole, all the Western nations rolled into one. This consolidation is not deliberate, but it does show that Russia, in and of itself, *can* be compared to Europe.

If we can preserve our culture and all that enables it to develop—libraries, museums, archives, schools, universities, and periodicals (the "thick" literary journals typical of Russia); if we can preserve unspoiled our rich language, literature, musical education, scientific institutes, then we will indisputably occupy first place in Northern Europe and Asia.

And what can be said about the economic policies of Russia in the future? I believe that economists should speak about economics, and factory managers about production. I will say only this: the relocation of our national capital to the north of the country should be given serious consideration. In this respect the opinion of Academician Nikolai Ivanovich Vavilov takes on special significance. He pointed out that the North of Russia has certain advantages, if this fact is understood. The North suffers to a much lesser degree from crop failure and drought. It is easier to fight wet soil in small farms. It is easier for small farms to deal with the difficulties of the local landscape, the stoniness of arable land. Rye and oats withstand the particularities of the northern climate quite well.

That's it!

Translated by Jamey Gambrell

Notes

1. V.I. Sergeevich, *Veche i kniaz': Russkoe gosudarstvennoe ustroistvo i up-*

ravlenie vo vremena kniazei Riurikovichei: Istoricheskie ocherki (Moscow, 1867).

2. K. Lehmann, *Kniazhoe pravo drevnei Rusi*, trans. A. Presniakova (Moscow, 1993), p. 61 (originally published as *Der Königsfriede der Nord-germanen* [Leipzig, 1886]).

3. R.P. Dmitrieva, *Skazanie o kniaziakh Vladimirskikh* (Leningrad, 1955).

4. S.V. Bakhrushin, *Nauchnye trudy* (Moscow, 1954), 2:110.

5. D.S. Likhachev, "Plach o reke Narove 1665 g.," in *Trudy Otdela drevnerusskoi literatury* (1948), 6:333–38.

6. Giles Fletcher, *On the Russian State* (St. Petersburg, 1906).

WHERE ARE WE GOING?

5

Daniil Granin

New Dangers, New Hopes

For the last two years, the most commonly used phrase in Russia has been, "We're on the brink of the abyss!"

Before the elections to the new Russian parliament, called the Duma, each candidate began his campaign speech with a description of the troubles and horrors wrought by the previous rulers—inflation, crime, poverty, the mortality rate exceeding the birth rate, the plundering of national resources, the breakup of the Soviet Union, the failure of economic reform, the violence in American movies—everything was invoked, everything was dumped into one big pile.

The enumeration of our ills has long ceased to be a courageous act; on the contrary, it has become commonplace, and people are sick of it. For the political candidates, the listing of woes has served as a kind of preface, and an incomparably long one at that—but a preface to *what?* Surely a promise to fix everything and make it right. No one has said yet how they will do that, or on what their confidence is based. It seems as if most of their promises are merely a form of campaign propaganda—and nothing more.

There have been, of course, serious speeches by economists like Egor Gaidar and political scientists like Anatolii Sobchak and Sergei Shakhrai, who did have some proposals and programs. However, I will admit that I have become convinced in these last years that our government has only moved forward by using the trial-and-error method. I am not a specialist; I can judge the actions of leaders only as an ordinary resident of this country, a person upon whom ever new reforms are being experimented. I am a patient person, a good subject for an experiment.

In fact, it is not even an experiment but something else, more likely a desperate attempt to fight our way out of the trap of socialism, the planned, socialist system, the state capitalism in which our country is entangled. No one really knows how to get rid of this system. No matter how many congresses and symposia are held, no matter how many experts from various countries are invited here, they have not come up with a formula or agreed about anything among themselves. There is no experience, no example to follow—at least none are appropriate for us, a country where the people have lived more than seventy years in the socialist barracks.

I am reluctant to accuse the government, the ministers, and the governors. The failures we see now are from the past, after all; we are all wise after the fact. There are no specialists who can predict the future and find the right solution. And the trial-and-error method, the cautious, groping search, is probably inevitable. I was persuaded of that numerous times at meetings of the Presidential Council, of which I have been a member since its inception.

The situation was exacerbated by the fact that the actions taken by the government's policy team were blocked by the parliament. This is all well known, and I do not intend to analyze or evaluate the struggle at the top and the events of October 3–4, 1993. That is a matter for specialists, politicians, and historians.

The writer's specialty is to study human beings—what is being done to them, how they are changing in the course of events in Russia, and what they hope for. Their expectations are especially important because that infamous Russian endurance, about which the commentators love to write, also has its limits. If people are still enduring in spite of everything, that means they still have hope, although in the last year, hope has dwindled markedly. Prices are rising on everything and just keep skyrocketing. It is impossible to plan an individual budget or save money for a purchase because of inflation.

Nevertheless, some old hopes remain, and some new ones have appeared. It is about these new hopes that I wish to speak, about these hopes and the accompanying dangers, mainly moral dangers.

The Russian has never had a normal attitude toward private property. The peasant never succeeded in becoming a farmer. Until 1861, he was a serf. After the abolition of serfdom he was still tied to the community landowner. Petr Stolypin's reform of 1907 was never completed; he was assassinated. After the Revolution and the Civil War, not even ten years passed before collectivization began. Land was taken away from the peasants, and once again it became "not mine."

V.I. Lenin's New Economic Policy brought back private trade, stores, workshops, and factories, but not for long. Everything was taken away and prohibited, and the idea of private property was anathematized. The psychology of the private property owner was branded as a "vestige of capitalism." These "vestiges in people's consciousness" were uprooted by all possible means—communal apartments, dormitories, collective farms, state farms. Nothing private remained, and even a person's private life fell under suspicion. Any effort to start one's own enterprise was condemned as a "private-property, petty-bourgeois instinct." I remember how in the late 1970s, the Leningrad Communist Party boss Grigorii Romanov vigorously blocked the allocation of garden plots to urban residents. Factory workers tried to obtain some tiny parcels of land on the Karelian Peninsula, an uninhabited, empty area. They were finally allocated plots of unwanted swampland where there were no roads.

Meanwhile, collective farm workers built five-story concrete houses on the Karelian Peninsula and were resettled there "in order to eliminate the difference between the city and the village." They were stripped of the customary routine they had established in the village with their homes and animals. Instead, they ended up on the fourth floor of a building in the middle of the woods and fields, not sure whether they were peasants or urban dwellers. The kind of ideology that produced this plan is deeply rooted and persists to this day, and not only among people of the older generation.

When people talk about the threat of a rebellion of the "blind and ruthless," about the tendency of the Russian to be drawn into such a rebellion or revolution, it is not merely because of some national traditions but mainly because Russians have never had private property. A hatred of materialism was instilled in even the urban dweller. A room in a communal apartment was the extent of his possessions, and even that room belonged to the government. He had nothing to settle into, nothing from which to make a profit, nothing to give up, and nothing even to regret or lose. Everything around him was "not mine." The collectivist mentality was the psychology of the homeless.

Finally, the "vestiges of capitalism" were eradicated. Now it is not so easy to restore them. A morality based on the negation of private life has taken root instead. The primacy of public interests over private is considered to be socialism's crowning achievement. Moral problems were easily resolved; what was moral is whatever helps the cause, and whatever helps the cause is what serves the Party's interests.

Oh how those vestiges of capitalism would come in handy now! But instead, the government is offering land to collective farm workers and the people are saying they do not want it! The government is offering the city residents opportunities to manage, trade, and manufacture, and they are saying: "Why should we, when it will be taken away from us anyway? We don't believe in it! Would Soviet people turn into speculators, would we ever exploit other people? Not for anything! Would we ever work for a boss? Never!"

These deformed vestiges of socialism and communist ideology continue to weigh us down. How can we overcome them? We cannot use violence; after all, you cannot force a person to be a private property owner. You can make a key for a lock, but you cannot make a lock for a key.

Strangely, urban dwellers are more strongly drawn to the land than the collective farm workers. For years I have observed how city residents work and tend their garden plots. On their tiny little patches of land, with Chinese-like attentiveness, they produce record crops and feed their families at least with fruits and vegetables. They have no farm machinery or fertilizer; they do everything themselves, cultivating the earth by hand, which requires enormous labor and effort. It is not true that Russians are lazy, that they are drunkards and dreamers.

There are hundreds of thousands of such garden plots surrounding every city. There are little homemade huts and windmills on them, miracles of inventiveness. It is amazing what the Russian people are capable of when they are at last given a chance to be property owners. I remember how Grigorii Romanov, the Leningrad Party boss, and other Party ideologists argued that these plots of land distracted people from their regular jobs, that food shortages could not be solved in this way. But the real reason for their objections was that the owners of these garden plots had gained a sense of independence, a feeling that the Party dictatorship could not tolerate.

In fact, as I observed, all my acquaintances who worked in their gardens achieved a tremendous satisfaction from being an owner, from having their own property, even if rented, even if only a piece of the government's land. After the deadening effect of officialdom all around them, here the illusion reigned that they had something that was theirs, made with their own hands, a world of their own.

True morality apparently lies, not in a conscientious attitude toward public property, but in respect for your own and other people's labor, which means for private property. It is difficult to reinstate that respect. I myself still find it hard to connect all the hopes for a healing of public morality with the introduction of private property, with the transition from collectivism to individualism.

We should not be surprised that private farmers are harassed and blocked and have their crops burned. Rather, we should be amazed that there are people who are prepared to be private farmers under these conditions. Their numbers are growing, although the law on private ownership of land has not been passed in its entirety.

Before the Revolution, Russian capitalism did not find support in society, even from the intelligentsia. The businessman was never a positive figure in Russian literature. The nineteenth-century Russian writers Anton Chekhov, Leo Tolstoy, and Ivan Goncharov were hostile to the appearance in Russia of industrialists and entrepreneurs.

From time immemorial in Russia, making a profit was perceived as something wrong. Rich people were not respected. "A rich man is like a horned bull" was a folk saying. Most of our proverbs are hostile to rich people: "If you let your soul go to hell, you'll be rich," or "You'll sleep sounder without money."

Fledgling capitalism tried to break these stereotypes and win society's sympathy. Merchants and factory owners built schools, orphanages, and hospitals; they founded institutes, art galleries, and homes for the elderly. Nevertheless, this prerevolutionary attitude toward the entrepreneur still prevails in society. For the Soviet person, the entrepreneur is above all an exploiter, prepared to commit any crime for the sake of profit. Everything amoral is concentrated in the image of the capitalist. People who are successful traders, those who open banks and firms, are considered dishonest, morally reckless people. They provoke envy and sometimes even hatred. The existing mind-set of our citizen simply cannot undergo the reorientation necessary so as to give credit to business people's hard work, enterprise, inventiveness, and initiative.

Commercial talent has not been acknowledged in our country. Trading has been considered the occupation of swindlers. Contemporary Russian businessmen are compelled to overcome this attitude toward their activity. They have had to revive the traditions of philanthropy, known in Russia as the *metsenat*, the Maecenas, or patron. Wealthy businessmen have begun to sponsor theatrical shows, television films, literary journals, and universities. The public takes science and education seriously, so private support is viewed sympathetically. But people are still far from showing sympathy to the individuals who provide the funding.

They are irritated by the fancy cars, the balls, the presentations, the security guards, the newly appeared marks of luxury that are ostentatiously displayed with the thrill of the *nouveau riche*. Notably missing in the new community of the wealthy are commodities manufacturers. There are still no factory owners, entrepreneurs who could provide the market with new, quality domestic goods. There are still no small businesses, no owners of small workshops, creameries, dairy plants, repair shops—everything that today makes up the basic strength of such highly developed countries as Germany, Switzerland, and France, where the small producer is the chief producer of the nation.

Russia does not need private owners who are millionaires as much as it needs millions of private owners. This is precisely the reorientation of people's lives that provokes such brutal resistance from the neocommunists.

One serious hope is breaking through the garbage-strewn, rocky plot of our consciousness. A longtime acquaintance of mine, a screenwriter of middle age and middling talent, opened a small publishing house while continuing his writing. Business gradually got under way, and soon the publishing house turned into a firm selling southern wines, tea, and preserves. Trade is now brisk. The screenwriter showed he had what it takes; it turns out that his calling was commerce and not art. Thank God, the man has found himself.

Another acquaintance of mine, a researcher with a Ph.D. in science specializing in cybernetics, found an effective method to organize a factory's freight forwarding. Now he is a partner in a joint venture with a South American company. He told me that only now has he understood what real work is. Before he thought he was putting in a full effort. But now there is no comparison. He spoke of the great gratification he receives from his current job.

People are testing their abilities, measuring themselves, proving themselves. There are some bitter discoveries. More often there are real finds. The tribe of young bankers, brokers, investors, and dealers has burgeoned incredibly, and they are aggressively making themselves known. Experience has forced them to pick up foreign languages quickly and even more rapidly to become conversant in the intricacies of stock fluctuations. Others are carefully following the new operations of the joint-stock companies—what are they all about, where vouchers should be invested, what should be deposited. Gradually, they are figuring out all of these horrors of capitalism.

The citizens of the country are learning to understand that electricity costs money, that heat is not free, that quite a bit has to be paid for a haircut in a salon because it is hand labor. Apartments are expensive; that concept did not used to exist. Gasoline is also costly. Bread should not be wasted. No one has to be convinced that throwing away bread is a sin; the cost of bread itself forces people to conserve every crumb. People have mastered this kind of economics perfectly; nobody has failed the test here. We have entered upon an unfamiliar relationship with reality; everything, all goods have their price. The world has become harsh and expensive.

The idea of the rate of the ruble against the dollar has become a household notion. People have to do some calculations and economize. They have to look for some extra earnings, and they appreciate work where the pay is good. They have realized that they have to figure some things out by themselves.

The failures of economic reform have led to the discovery that people have to rely on themselves. The government is no longer capable of providing education, housing, and medical care free of charge. The proverbs of the day are, "If you want to get along, you have to be quick on your feet"; "You can only get free cheese in a mousetrap." A different perception of the authorities is growing. Ministers make mistakes, they are not flexible, there are too many bureaucrats, they eat up our money, and in general, the people are smarter than their government.

So people's minds have cleared somewhat. And that is the success that has come out of our failures. The enlightenment has been painful. Russia is not a superpower. Nuclear arms do not increase either the happiness or the welfare of the citizenry. Whether we like it or not, we have to reconcile ourselves to this fact and moderate our opinion of ourselves. For the first time, we have begun to evaluate our merits soberly. It turns out that there are not many of them, but there are some.

Russian business is getting its start in a country with an educated populace. Any social system has its pluses and minuses. To the credit of the Soviet system, it did much for the education of its people. And although Aleksandr Solzhenitsyn ridiculed our "education mania," it has proved useful today.

The business community has no shortage of specialists. To be sure, there is a brain-drain, but the value of our brains on the international exchange also means something.

A new third estate is taking shape, a visible social force actively supporting reform policy. This estate is primarily made up of the intelligentsia.

During the decades of stagnation, an enormous amount of unspent energy, intentions, and projects accumulated, and people developed a desire to become involved in something that really used their heads. They had grown sick and tired of the poor management that was so prevalent. It was painful to watch how the country was being drained of raw materials.

Now, at last, there is an opportunity to flourish. That is why the demand for reasonable taxation is heard so persistently. Let us breathe, let us do business!

These stormy processes in the country are changing the destiny of the Russian intelligentsia. In this new, pragmatic, rational world, less and less space remains for the previous spiritual communion, with all the charm of the heated interest in the new books, the theater premiers, the exhibits. We lived for art. The "thick" literary journals had hundreds of thousands of subscribers. The monthly journals *Novyi mir* and *Znamia* each had circulations of more than a million copies. Now their circulations are down to under fifty thousand, but not only because the price has gone up. People just do not have time to read. And they do not feel like reading.

The intelligentsia is finding a different base. People are going into business. The dissident movement has run out of steam. The intellectual opposition today has no program. Among the thirteen parties that took part in the December 1993 elections, there was virtually not a single one that could be considered the party of the intelligentsia. The intelligentsia has splintered. Its most active part is becoming the "business class" and is unlikely to leave this class. The old Russian intelligentsia is disappearing and may grow extinct. That is a loss, of course, but it is hopeless to stop this process, just as it is pointless to attempt to revive the Russian nobility.

All society is changing. Political and economic consciousness has appeared, and there is an emancipation from the psychology of dependency. The Soviet person had become accustomed to living as a parasite. Everything he had came from the government. The government taught him, told him where he would live, thought for him, decided for him, established what he should and should not know. It freed him from any sense of guilt or responsibility. It was supposed to take care of him until his very death.

For the time being, the process of people straightening themselves up, liberating themselves from the barracks to enter a free life, proceeds in secret, in minds and hearts. The kernel is germinating, but its shoots are still not visible on the surface. It is a rapid process, though. We have never lived such full lives. To be honest, life in the West now seems sleepy and slow moving.

Factory engineers are becoming managers of companies or directors of large firms. This is a time for transformation and unheard-of careers. The visible changes are breaking through all cracks. In the St. Petersburg district where I live almost all the ground-floors in the buildings have been remodeled and furnished. The furious trading from hand to hand has stopped. The buildings are now being repaired for use by private firms. You enter another neighborhood and do not recognize the new signs and new store windows.

The stores are filled with goods. The prices are high, very high, but on the other hand for the first time, the people of St. Petersburg can buy pineapples, bananas, and kiwis in the wintertime. They can buy fish and meat, fur and cars, refrigerators and television sets. To be sure, most of the goods are imported, but it is just a question of getting the money together. Making money is defining people's activities now.

The media are completely preoccupied with the subject of people's suffering. It is considered in poor taste to say something positive. There is plenty of bad news, of course, but if it were really all as bad as they say, we would not be surviving. No, life is becoming renewed with new—actually old—simple human values.

Recently I was in Leipzig in the former German Democratic Republic and saw that the scene was similar to ours. There are the same loss of the common idea of life, disappointment, high expenses, impoverished people, and many offended people. But with each passing month people value freedom even more and want less and less to return to the former GDR. As a rule, those who want to return are former members of the party autocracy, Stasi officers and aging specialists on Marxism-Leninism. There are very few young people among them.

It is all the same as in our country, except that there the process of transformation is being helped by the powerful economy of West Germany. And in our country there is still a great chance that things could return to the status quo ante.

The economic crisis here has increased the influence of the neo-communists. They are straining every nerve to get to power. They are not averse to an alliance with outright fascists. They have common slogans, promises to restore the Soviet empire and along with it the previous "cost-free life" and to kick out the foreigners and the democrats. They toss onto the political market attractive packages charged with fascist dynamite. The neocommunists are a previously unseen hybrid of Browns and Reds.

The difficulty is that Russia knows fascists only in the form of Adolf Hitler's soldiers with machine guns in hand. The modern-day brown communists march under red banners that depict not the hammer and sickle but a swastika. They carry portraits of Stalin and Hitler.

We must understand what fascism means for Russia: first of all, the militarization of life, an increase in the size of the armed forces, a rise in military expenditures, nationalism, alienation from the democratic nations, and, in the final analysis, a course toward war.

But a flow of other events runs to meet these dangers. In spite of everything, life is organizing itself. The people's sorrowful memory of wars and purges is still alive and restrains them from new bloody actions. People see that there is no clear and convincing alternative to what the president and the government are doing.

The silent, invisible battlefront is located in people's hearts. There, a war is being played out between old and new conceptions of the world. There, fears and hopes are born and perish.

Foreigners often describe our people as savage, wild, and sick. My country is good, those foreigners tell me, but the people ought to be changed. The country will never have another people, however. We are drinking bitter medicine now and poking fun at ourselves. It is a time of sobering up, as after a severe hangover. That process is always hard, but that is how healing begins.

How can the greatness of a country and a people be measured? Not through the size of its territory or the number of millions in its population. And not through missiles and nuclear bombs. We are beginning to understand that arms and force instill only fear, not respect The measure of the greatness of a people is its contribution to world culture and science, that which the people and the nation have given other peoples and all of civilization.

Russia has a great culture, a saving strength that supports a sense of dignity. There is the history of Russia, during the course of which it has managed to come out of wars and destruction strong and renewed. And there is the example of other peoples, all of whom in one way or another have embarked upon the universal human road of progress.

Translated by Catherine A. Fitzpatrick

6

Konstantin Azadovskii

Russia's Silver Age, Yesterday and Today
Questions in the Void

As we look back at the last seven or eight years, so tempestuous and brimming with amazing events, we often ask ourselves: When did we really, totally believe that new times were coming? Was it when Mikhail Gorbachev came to power? when the war in Afghanistan ended? when Academician Andrei Sakharov was allowed to return from his exile in Gorky to Moscow? One hears all sorts of opinions. But for me personally, so-called perestroika began with an article in a journal in the fall of 1986.

I well remember my astonishment when, opening the latest issue of the magazine *Ogonek* (at the time the most hard-hitting and "progressive" of the Russian journals), I suddenly saw an article on the hundredth anniversary of the birth of Nikolai Gumilev, the remarkable Russian poet whose name was banned in the Soviet Union. Gumilev is a symbolic figure in many ways. He was ordered shot in August 1921 (allegedly for participating in an anti-Bolshevik plot), and for six and one-half decades he personified the tragic fate of the Russian pre-revolutionary (before 1917) culture—suppressed, exiled, destroyed.

The era in which Nikolai Gumilev lived is now known as the Silver Age, an analogy to the Golden Age, the age of Alexander Pushkin, in

Russian culture. The Silver Age (which in fact lasted only a quarter of a century) was noted for an extraordinary outpouring of creativity in philosophy, literature, painting, ballet, and theater. It was a kind of Russian Renaissance, as many people call it even today. The artworks created in this period are widely recognized throughout the whole world. Every educated person (not only in Russia) knows the names of Sergei Diaghilev and Igor Stravinsky, Vasilii Kandinskii and Konstantin Malevich, Aleksandr Blok and Leonid Andreev, Osip Mandelstam and Marina Tsvetaeva. Nikolai Gumilev is at the same level as these figures and has long held a place of honor in the Parnassus of the Russian Silver Age.

Suffused with the militant spirit of class warfare, the Bolshevik dictatorship (calling itself "proletarian") that established itself in 1917 was obviously incompatible with the high civic and moral principles instilled in Russian society by the Silver Age. Despite its elitism and aesthetic refinement, the Silver Age was a period of surprising artistic freedom; the prerevolutionary generation breathed that freedom like air. Plunged, after 1917, into an abyss of physical and spiritual slavery, our country was, of course, not permitted to know anything about all that.

And so began the annihilation, the gradual and deliberate destruction of our country's culture. Along with all of thinking, active Russia, the Silver Age was pushed up against the wall, or brought to its knees, or thrown in labor camps, or forced into emigration. And not only people were destroyed and persecuted, but also the works of their hands, minds, and talents. Manuscripts and books, documents and letters, photographs and paintings, were obliterated. Untold numbers of enormously significant historical and cultural artifacts were confiscated during searches and thrust into nonexistence. To this day, these materials, with a few exceptions, have never been returned from the depths of the Lubianka or from the Big House.[1]

Thus the Soviet enforcement agencies vigilantly guarded the country from "bourgeois" and "decadent" influences, and many philosophers and poets, artists and musicians, sociologists and commentators, became "enemies" of Russia. The authorities tried to hush up their names and consign their works to oblivion. Nikolai Gumilev thereby became an enemy, too. Possession of his books, especially those published in the West, was not without its risks; such possession cast a shadow on the owner. Too zealous dissemination of his poems—if it became known— could threaten one even with criminal prosecution.

But was it only Gumilev who shared this fate? After all, for about thirty years, from the late 1920s to the Khrushchev "thaw," it was as if the Silver Age had never existed. It was a closed or semiclosed topic even for specialists, cultural historians, literary critics, art critics, and bibliographers. The study of Russian symbolism, even the work of Aleksandr Blok (the author of the "revolutionary" poem, "The Twelve") or the work of Valerii Briusov, who had joined the Communist Party, was not encouraged, to put it mildly. One could not even think of studying the writers and artists who had emigrated; and, of course, it would have been seen as outright subversion to refer to the works of Gumilev and of Nikolai Kliuev, who were executed, of Sergei Esenin and Marina Tsvetaeva, who hanged themselves, and of Osip Mandelstam, who perished in a labor camp. Matters were also complicated even with such seemingly canonized authors as Vladimir Mayakovsky and Maxim Gorky; former Count Aleksei Tolstoy, who became a deputy of the Supreme Soviet; Aleksandr Kuprin, who returned from emigration; or Ivan Bunin, who did not return but who won the Nobel Prize. Until very recently, there were some sensitive subjects even about these authors that were taboo—Kuprin's severe chronic disease, Tolstoy's "decadent" past, the actual circumstances of Gorky's or Mayakovsky's deaths. (In general, the topic of death was particularly alarming for the curators and adepts of "life-affirming" Soviet art.)

The situation changed in the second half of the 1950s. The "thaw" restored to us the works of Esenin, Bunin, and some of Tsvetaeva's writing, although restrictions remained in effect on these names, primarily on the foreign editions of these authors that had managed to reach us from abroad. Confiscation of Russian books published abroad (including Vladislav Khodasevich, Vladimir Nabokov, Lev Gumilev, Osip Mandelstam, and Anna Akhmatova) became a kind of routine; these books were automatically seized during any search—to say nothing of works of Russian philosophy (Nikolai Berdiaev, Lev Shestov, Sergei Askol'dov, Semen Frank, and others).

Nothing surprising in this! After all, despite the repressions, the Silver Age was and still is the spiritual realm where our intelligentsia has dwelt and for which it has yearned. A pure oasis in the desert of militant vulgarity, a source of forbidden or semiforbidden fruit, our Silver Age fulfilled a rather important social function during those years: it shaped one's outlook on the world, aesthetic taste, and morality. It was eagerly embraced by the postwar generation, which had acutely and painfully sensed the insurmountable gulf between official Soviet pseudoculture and the richest heritage of the Russian Renaissance. This was a generation for whom later the poetry in Boris Pasternak's novel *Doctor Zhivago* would become a tremendous event, a generation that would stay up late at night reading Mikhail Bulgakov's *The Master and Margarita* and would endlessly argue about Vladimir Nabokov's *Lolita,* passing it from hand to hand in its foreign edition only.

The role of poetry in the Soviet era was enormous and truly indispensable. But how difficult it seemed at times to obtain any of the volumes of Gumilev, Mandelstam, Khodasevich, and the other poets! Without the opportunity to publish openly in the Soviet press, they came to their readers silently, in secret. They announced themselves from the literary underground, which began to be called *samizdat* (literally "self-published" literature) in the 1960s. Those slender *samizdat* booklets, copied out by hand or retyped, nonetheless outweighed the works of Mayakovsky and Dem'ian Bednyi, A. Prokof'ev and Aleksei Surkov, which were printed at times in the millions of copies. We remember well those *samizdat* days that lasted certainly more than two or three decades. In 1926, a contemporary of Gumilev, the poet Maksimilian Voloshin, who retired from upheavals of the revolutionary years to his home in Koktebel',[2] wrote these verses:

> My lips have long been hushed . . .
> But do not let them part!
> It is a greater honor to be learned by heart;
> And copied out in secret, in a nook;
> To be within one's lifetime just a notepad, not a book.

Thus, after decades of silencing, oblivion, and destruction, an official Moscow journal publishes an article in commemoration of Gumilev's birth. And not just anyone's article, but one by V.V. Karpov himself, who was at that time one of the secretaries of the Union of Soviet Writers, the editor-in-chief of the Moscow journal *Novyi mir.* The article was comprehensive and, on the whole, kindly disposed. Gumilev had already entered into Russian literature, the author maintained, "He has lived, is living, and will go on living regardless of any temporary, opportunistic accretions." These were new intonations we were not accustomed to hearing, and they signaled the birth of a different historical era.

Exactly seven years have passed since then, and today many of the premises of that article seem cautious, even timid. In the subsequent years, Gumilev has become a classic. Starting in 1987, his works have been published and repeatedly reissued; memoirs about him have appeared, and hitherto unknown details about his life and his academic research have surfaced. Gumilev's verses have been put to music; they resound over radio and television programs. At long last, the poet has taken his rightful place in Russian letters.

Gumilev was fated to lead the cohort of "returnees." Along with those who had been repressed (the new peasant poets, the Oberiuts,[3] the philosophers Pavel Florenskii, Aleksandr Meier, and others) one after the other, members of the first wave of the emigration after the Revolution, the writers (Dmitrii Merezhkovskii, Zinaïda Gippius, Vladislav Khodasevich) and the thinkers (Nikolai Berdiaev, Lev Shestov, Nikolai Losskii) began to return. And many, many others. There began a time of republication (which continues up to the present); what had at one time been published in the West or in Russia before 1917 could be reprinted in the USSR without restrictions. Two streams of Russian culture that had been artificially parted in their day by the powerful impulses of history were rapidly merged into one.

But was it not too late? This vexing question emerged, in 1986–87, at the dawn of perestroika. For virtually none of the figures of the Silver Age sent to labor camp or hounded into emigration had survived until the mid-1980s!

There were still a few survivors, though. The poet Irina Odoevtseva, a student of Gumilev, returned to Russia not only through her books but in person. Having lived in France for sixty-five years, Odoevtseva revisited her native St. Petersburg in 1987 and spent the last three years of her life on the banks of the Neva.[4] Her return to Russia was a colorful public event at the time.

Or take, for example, Nina Berberova, a widely known Russian writer who died in 1993 in Philadelphia. She left Russia in 1922 (along with her husband, Vladislav Khodasevich) and followed the itinerary so characteristic of the Russian emigration—Berlin, Paris, the United States. She was also fortunate enough to see the great changes in Russia, to visit Moscow and St. Petersburg once again, and to see with her own eyes the people who read and treasured her books.

The process of return and reevaluation of values extended not only to the Silver Age. It also encompassed the West European *fin de siècle*, modernism, and the avant-garde, which is today emerging full-blown before our eyes. At long last the "bourgeois" authors, branded in their day as "decadent," "anti-Soviet," or simply "ideologically alien," have broken their silence and speak to the modern Russian reader. Friedrich Nietzsche and Oswald Spengler, Sigmund Freud and Carl Jung, and Rudolf Steiner, who were also semibanned, have returned as well. With them have also returned the Russian "idealist" philosophers, long expunged from Russian cultural history by the Bolsheviks—Konstantin Leont'ev (who died in 1891), known as the Russian Nietzsche, Vladimir Solov'ev (who died in 1900), the spiritual teacher of Blok and the other symbolists, and Vasilii Rozanov (who died in 1919), the philosopher. Along with these names have returned others who had seemed forever buried under the rubble of Marxist-Leninist dogma.

Today at the end of the century, just as at its very beginning, Russia's "eternal" questions are once again being discussed on the pages of our journals: the country's true path, its identity, the people, the intelligentsia, the Slavophiles and the Westernizers. The arguments broken off during the fateful years of the Revolution and the "triumphant procession of Soviet power" have been resumed. Who is to blame? Why did Russia allow itself to be drawn into the abyss? Can Russia be "renewed"? Our grievous experience (revolution, wars, labor camps, emigration) has hardly brought us closer to the answers to these questions. Just as before, Russian society is split into separate tendencies, groups, circles, and parties; at times the ideological and political disputes among them assume fierce, brutal forms.

But still, it happened! What none of us could have dreamed about even ten years ago has happened. The system has collapsed. The lying, the mythology, the substitution of the false for the real have disappeared. The legends so firmly rooted in our consciousness have collapsed under the pressure of the facts. The history of Russia has turned out to be different from the one we recited in school and university. The Revolution, the Civil War, collectivization, the Great Patriotic War (World War II)—all have turned out upon examination to be a distortion or often a forgery. Soviet culture, too, proved to be a pseudoculture; it collapsed along with the empire. The films about the shock-workers of socialist labor, the novels about our valiant Chekists,[5] the "folk" songs about the happy life on the collective farm, the majestic statues of leaders or athletic girls adorning the "recreation parks" and "palaces of culture"—all have vanished. Authentic culture—the Silver Age—has come to take the place of Soviet pseudoculture. Now joined with the outlawed art of the past (the novels of Aleksandr Solzhenitsyn, the poetry of Joseph Brodsky, the songs of Aleksandr Galich) and the homegrown avant-garde emerging from the underground, the Silver Age determines to a significant extent the face of contemporary Russian culture.

How joyfully we welcomed, in the first years of perestroika, the return of Gumilev, Merezhkovskii, and Berdiaev! It seemed as if the connection between time past and time present was being restored, and we were coming back to our own roots, from which we had been violently cut off. It seemed as if we were reacquiring lost values, a fulcrum or place from which to take a bearing, from which everything could now start afresh. Time passed, however, and the ecstatic joy of the first emotions was replaced by doleful, skeptical second thoughts.

Starting in about 1988–89, commentators began to complain that an excessive fascination with the past, and particularly the Silver Age, was leaving its mark on the contemporary literary process, and not a beneficial one. "By adopting the stepsons of the past epoch," wrote Alla Latynina, a prominent literary critic, "perhaps we are turning the sons of today into stepsons." That thesis seemed to be borne out. In reality, what had the perestroika era, rightfully called "revolutionary," given us? Where were its bards and artists? Where was the plethora of new names, the diversity of styles? If you did not count the ephemeral, accidental butterflies who were born and died in one day, there were none. That seemed strange, especially if we recall the tumultuous events of 1917–22, which produced so many outstanding works infused with the powerful enthusiasm of a new vision of the world. Why were no new bright stars burning on the horizon of contemporary culture?

Not surprisingly, however, it was not only modern art, which had forged a path for itself to the future, that ended up as a "stepson," but the long-established classical heritage, or at any rate some of the classics. In fact, these were primarily the authors accorded heightened attention during the Soviet era, about whom people had written dissertations, books, and articles, whose lives and works were studied scrupulously (whereas the Silver Age had been an undesirable topic).

But recently, everyone has seemed to change places, and a definite shift has occurred—and, unfortunately, a warping. Every era has its chosen ones and favorites. Today it is Gumilev and Akhmatova, Merezhkovskii and Nabokov, Berdiaev and Rozanov. Today Russia pays them its due, and there is a certain logic, a certain justice in that. But is it fair that there is virtually no public interest in Ivan Turgenev or Aleksandr Herzen, the Decembrists, the democratic writers?

Is it fair for historians of Russian culture and social thought to display such an obvious indifference to the great victims of the nineteenth century who suffered in prison, who were exiled to Siberia, who fled from Russia?

Is it fair, for example, to have in our country a distrustful, ironic attitude toward Nikolai Chernyshevskii, an outstanding Russian essayist, revolutionary, and scientist, who for decades languished in prison and exile? It is not fair. But there is a kind of appropriateness in that injustice. In his accomplished novel *The Gift*, Nabokov "exposed" Chernyshevskii, depicting his yearning for a social reconstruction of Russia as a pernicious, "amoral" tendency. For Nabokov, Chernyshevskii was one of those who laid the groundwork for the Russian Revolution. With his book, Nabokov reinforced among our intelligentsia negative perceptions of the "revolutionary democrat," who summoned Rus "to the ax." All of us, including Nabokov, knew quite well the nature of that revolutionary ax—terror. But is Chernyshevskii himself to blame for it? Is it not time to investigate who Chernyshevskii really was, the author of the famous novel *What Is to Be Done?*, a work so resolutely rejected by new generations?

Time has ordered things as it wishes, and the victim Gumilev triumphs today over the victim Chernyshevskii. The toppling of idols has naturally affected not only the Russian classics but the pillars of Soviet literature—Gorky, Mayakovsky, and Mikhail Sholokhov. A prejudiced attitude toward these authors reigns, and even the publication of previously unknown texts (of Gorky, for example) is primarily designed to expose them. The desire to condemn clearly prevails over the wish to understand. When will we at last perceive our great writers and their destinies and works in all their contradictory and tragic entirety?

We are settling scores with our history. We are hastening to rid ourselves of the burdensome legacy of the era of the Great Falsification. We are dividing our past into executioners and victims, prison guards

and inmates. While exonerating some, we demand the immediate con-
demnation of others. That can be understood. But are we impartial?
Are we not in our haste committing new blunders?

This is only one problem on our current cultural scene. There is
another, perhaps no less serious. The high culture of the Russian Renaissance, until recently the provenance of only a few "chosen," has
suddenly flooded the book market, becoming commercialized and, inevitably, vulgarized.

Actually, what happened has occurred many times before in the
history of culture and not only Russian culture, of course. When high
culture "descends" to the masses, it becomes the property of those who
have not yet matured sufficiently to appreciate it properly. A struggle
of sorts begins. Authentic art, opposing the nature of the masses, still
conquers and subdues the crowd, which, for its part, unwittingly
strives to cheapen the elite work of art, to accommodate it to mass
taste and understanding. This process is natural, necessary, and well
studied—and completely harmless if it proceeds gradually and
smoothly.

But in Russia, the process was rushed. The removal of the barriers of
censorship unleashed a powerful avalanche of names and works that
were banned and almost inaccessible until recently. Of course we all
welcomed this sudden breakthrough to freedom, reveling in it. We did
not notice right away that the eulogizing of the same names over and
over, like the quantity of printed production piling up around them,
was beginning to reflect badly on their quality.

The problem, of course, is not that Mandelstam's poetry or Nabokov's novels ceased to belong to a narrow circle of the intelligentsia and
acquired hundreds of thousands of readers and admirers among the
most diverse social classes. The problem was that the number of readers
(that is, essentially the number of copies sold) proved for many publishers to be an end in itself, and they were prepared to engage in profana-
tion in order to achieve it. What is depressing is not the mass
production, but the cheapness, not the high price, but the low level of
the book. Now and then we will see that a Silver Age book has a cover
like a spicy detective novel or a mediocre piece of erotica. Yes, of course
today's starving Russian public greedily consumes subject matter not
even printed yesterday. The works of Ivan Barkov (and everything else
ascribed to him) are printed and reprinted. But it is sad and somewhat

awkward to see the works of Tsvetaeva, Mikhail Kuzmin, and Fedor Sologub jumbled together in an anthology entitled *Russian Eros.*

What can we do? Is it possible to preserve under modern conditions that "mountain air," that "pure music" permeating the masterworks of the Silver Age? This is not an easy question. The abrupt collapse of the former structures in Russia left culture to its own devices. The ensuing freedom placed culture in harsh circumstances. The state has neither the means nor the capacity to support it; the new merchant philanthropists, for which Russia was renowned in the past, have yet to be born. Culture, including our cultural past, has frankly and sometimes unabashedly become a commodity. The fate of a book is in the hands of a publisher. But the modern Russian publisher usually does not want to burden himself with extra expenses—good paper, illustrations, a jacket, a highly qualified commentator or author of a preface. Why should he? People will buy it anyway—if not for the author's name, then at any rate for a garish title such as *Russian Eros.*

What is needed? First of all, of course, a clear understanding of what Russian culture was on the threshold of 1917 and what was done to it in the next decades; respect for our Silver Age, a sense of its stature and worldwide significance.

Second, culture needs support—the support of all authentically cultural undertakings for everything that is trying today to survive, to germinate and sprout.

Here are several characteristic examples. It is no secret that the manuscripts of many monographs, collections, and publications, completed back in the era when science and culture were supported by the government, are now gathering dust on the shelves of publishing houses. Of course the publishers are in no hurry to publish what in their view will be a commercial failure. Thus several volumes of a unique series, Literary Heritage, enormously valuable for the history of Russian culture (it has appeared since the beginning of the 1930s) languish in Moscow, "frozen." Collected back in the late 1970s and early 1980s, the volumes have yet to see the light of day. Among them, for example, is a volume containing the unknown letters of Valerii Briusov and his fellow symbolists. Another volume, absolutely essential for any researchers of Russian symbolism, is devoted to Aleksandr Blok; it is the last of five volumes and includes all the name indexes. The absence of this volume is an enormous nuisance because it deprives readers of the ability to use the first four volumes published in 1980–87. As for the institutes of the Academy of Sciences, where Literary Heritage was based for a time, they are in no position to change its pathetic and humiliating fate.

The plight of museums and reserve collections charged with conserving and propagating the culture of the Silver Age is also not enviable. Long-established academic centers with rich collections and experienced staff members are now forced to raise the entrance fee to their museums and look for handouts, even to issue a guidebook or an advertising prospectus. And there can be no thought of holding the conferences that at one time attracted wide public attention, or of publishing materials, articles, or theses.

In the same position are the Aleksandr Blok Museum in St. Petersburg, for example, which has long attracted people who study (or simply love) the Russian symbolists; and the relatively new Anna Akhmatova Museum (Akhmatova was Gumilev's first wife), where everything relating to these poets and Russian acmeism[6] is carefully collected and studied. The Maksimilian Voloshin Home Museum in Koktebel' must also be mentioned here. All of these museums are poor and preoccupied with making ends meet. Is not the heritage of our great poets worthy of a better, brighter fate?

We are now suffering a difficult, fateful time. We are infected with nostalgia for prerevolutionary Russia. We want to immerse ourselves in the age of 1910 as deeply as possible and to bring back—at least in part—the atmosphere and spirit of that era, to transport it to our troubled days. It is precisely there, in the past, that we stubbornly seek the answers to the burning questions of the day. We are restoring the pillars of that life—the nobility, the cossacks, Orthodoxy, autocracy. Is it for nought? Are we not living with illusions just as before? Are we not idealizing "the Russia we lost,"[7] failing to see that we have lost it forever? *That* Russia can no longer be reborn; it is long gone and exists only in memory.

But culture does not belong only to the past. The Silver Age lives on. It nourishes and perhaps by degrees is putting us to the test. For how long? Will we preserve this heritage? Will we maintain it at a worthy level? Will that culture not lose its value for us? Are the spiritual demands of modern life compatible with the metaphysical quests of the Silver Age? Who will say a grateful word to that age for what it meant to us in the difficult years? There is a long list of troublesome questions directly facing many of us. But only the future can provide the answer.

Translated by Catherine A. Fitzpatrick

Notes

1. Lubianka is the street in Moscow where KGB headquarters was located and where its successor agency can still be found today. The Big House is the name of the KGB Directorate (and its successors) in Leningrad (now St. Petersburg).

2. Koktebel' is a village in the Crimea on the shores of the Black Sea.

3. "Oberiut" was based on the acronym for Ob''edinenie real'nogo isskustva, the Association for Real Art. The Oberiut group of Leningrad included Daniil Kharms, Aleksandr Vvedenskii, and other poets.

4. The title of Irina Odoevtseva's memoir is *On the Banks of the Neva.*

5. "Chekist" is from ChK, the Russian initials for Extraordinary Commission, the name of the first secret police created under the Bolsheviks (later KGB).—C.A.F.

6. Acmeism is a school of Russian poetry of the Silver Age represented primarily by Akhmatova, Gumilev, and Mandelstam.

7. *The Russia We Lost* is the title of a famous film directed by Stanislav Govorukhin (1991).

7

Ales Adamovich

"But Where Is the Tsar?"

Amid the raucous flock of Soviet jokes from the perestroika era, one stood out: The Russian people wake up seventy years after the Revolution, look around in astonishment, and ask, "But where is the tsar?" And where were a lot of other things—where had *they* gone? With great difficulty, the people struggled to remember that everything was a result of what they had wrought themselves; they had brought it down on their own heads.

During my speech at the First USSR Congress of People's Deputies in 1989, I told this silly anecdote. And I received an angry dressing down from a very patriotic Russian writers' newspaper (the word "Russophobia" was then in fashion).

I shall recall in more detail the thoughts I had in 1989 about the prolonged sleep into which the Bolshevik terror had plunged the country. When my friends and I were transcribing the terrible recollections of Belorussian peasants who had survived the tragedies of hundreds of villages where people were burned alive by SS punishment squads (our book was called *Out of the Fire*), I was particularly amazed that under terrible conditions, a person can sometimes fall asleep from the horror. This is especially true of women and children. All around are screams and shouts of people being murdered, neighbors being burned alive, but a woman would fall down in her garden and go to sleep. She would wake up—if she was not found or shot—to find her village gone and nobody and nothing around.

This ability to fall asleep is the mind's defense mechanism against an overwhelming situation. Is this not what happened to millions of people in a country where, with overwhelming brutality, for many decades, the Leninist-Stalinist experiment of building a "new society" was carried out?

When Stalin died, the mass repression seemed gradually to recede into the past, but the machinery of persecution, its weapons, signs, and symbols (the Communist Party, the KGB, and so on) remained in place. It was always before your eyes. And while deep sleep may have subsided, a half-sleep remained at the level of consciousness, of the subconscious, even during the time of perestroika. The life experience of tens of millions of people was too much of a nightmare. The dissidents and the generation of writers who flourished in the 1960s worked to unfreeze people's psyches and consciousness; Aleksandr Solzhenitsyn's books seemed to have been read by many people; and, in the eyes of the entire country, Andrei Sakharov stood as a stubborn reproach in the path of an all-powerful system. The "solution" had reached the saturation point, and the crystals of a completely new psychological reality were just about to appear. But one more final push was needed, some unique little crystal.

I believe this catalyst was the two-week nationwide live television broadcast of the First Congress of People's Deputies. It was one thing to have Sakharov and what was done to him in the faraway closed city of Gorky, under the hue and cry of the Party's propaganda machine. But it was something else to have Sakharov live on the television screen at home, speaking persistently about the abusive government and the unjust war in Afghanistan. For two weeks, an enormous country seemed to stop working and was glued to its television sets or radios. An amusing newspaper photograph of those memorable days showed a man taking out a garbage can in one hand to a dumpster in a back alley and, with the other hand, pressing a transistor radio to his ear.

Something similar happened in 1975 on the Soviet cruiser *Storozhevoi*, when the ranking political officer aboard broadcast an antigovernment message over the airwaves from international waters. (In the United States, a novel—later made into a film—was written about this incident, called *The Hunt for Red October*.) Much later several documentary films were shown in Russia, and there was even a "public trial," which found Captain Valerii Sablin, who had been executed by a firing squad for treason, to be not guilty, despite the opinion of many military people that his broadcast had violated military duty.

I would like to emphasize the parallel between what happened in 1975 on that ship and what happened in Russia in 1989 during the First Congress. At the "trial," Captain Sablin's former shipmates were asked why they had supported him and dared to become involved in such a risky gesture that was probably doomed to failure. (Believing the whole country would support them, they had intended to sail to Leningrad and deliver an ultimatum to the Central Committee and the Politburo, demanding television air time.) The sailors followed Captain Sablin because for the first time they saw and heard, not just a boss, but a *political leader* (that is, a representative of the Communist Party itself) *openly* expressing their secret thoughts and feelings.

Now imagine that the thoughts and feelings of millions of people could suddenly be heard, not just anywhere, but directly from the Kremlin, from the tribunal of supposedly the highest alternative to the omnipotent Communist Party, a kind of new power and authority, the Congress of People's Deputies! It was only much later, after many events and disappointments, that the words "democrat" and "people's deputy" virtually became swear words for a great number of people. But in 1989, at that time, a deputy could not go out on the street without being grabbed at by dozens of hands and caressed by dozens of happy eyes. He would be dragged to some elevated place, a park bench or a pedestal, and urged to speak. Tell it like it is! Tell us what you said there, at the Congress! Perestroika was still having its honeymoon in those days; it was a foretaste of changes to come, fledgling democracy! But now that time of our stormy awakening already seems like a dream.

If you look at the country now, you will have the opposite impression from those heady days when we looked to the future. Now there is too much nostalgia for the past. Sure, there was the Brezhnev era of "stagnation," but prices were not high, people were not shot at, the streets were safe. (For decades the government and its "organs" of state security were far more terrible than any murderer or criminal; but in time, people are liable to forget this fact.)

In the 1980s and early 1990s, there did not appear to be many advocates of the so-called socialist choice. Meanwhile Mikhail Gorbachev, who kept invoking this alleged "choice," seemed to be committing political suicide. Now in the 1990s, these adherents have once again made themselves heard, claiming to prefer "developed socialism" to our "wild capitalism." Mainly elderly persons, they make up a significant portion of the population. Many people are inclined to think that it is not the charm of socialism that is diverting their minds to the past, but rather their exhaustion from life. Slavery debilitates people and thereby reinforces itself in their consciousness. The generation of "builders of communism" is simply worn out. In the past, these people had suffered so much hunger, vulnerability, alarm, and fear of what was to come that when they discovered that the path to the market would mean years and years of new sacrifices and suffering, many people were overcome with a sense of hopelessness and were suspicious of those who had once again lured them to a "bright future" (only it was capitalism this time). It seemed as if they had been deceived once again. And now the communist liars and murderers could hide in the shadow of public indignation and soon reemerge into the political arena, now in the role of saviors of the "socially defenseless."

In the last years of his life, I would think such a man as Stalin would have been bored and irritated that any kind of serious—even potential —opponents of him and his regime had vanished. His was the ennui and contempt a rapist feels after he has broken and defiled a woman.

When you see the old ladies at the "Red" rallies, worn out by life, carrying portraits of the angry, mustachioed executioner, you are seized by a sense of powerlessness in the face of human deafness, blindness, and deep sleep.[1]

Marching ahead of these unfortunate women with the portraits of their rapist and tormenter (but that is all in the past) are the Gennadii Ziuganovs, the Anatolii Lukianovs, and the Aleksandr Prokhanovs, who are the new little leaders of stupidity, envy, and lawlessness born out of bloodshed.

The wonderful Russian writer Viktor Astaf'ev remarked that a neocommunist leader "had the face of Chichikov," the hero of Nikolai Gogol's novel *Dead Souls*. It was the noble, deceitful physiognomy of the opportunist. No wonder Gogol is recalled; Russian history was not born yesterday. And no wonder the author of the Russian *Iliad*, the epic of Russian reality, *Dead Souls*, hit upon the theme, the pathos of the "flying troika," the horses and carriage racing ahead—but whither? This was the image of Russia itself. And really, what Russian Achilles does not love fast travel? The carriage hurtles forward and is just about to smash itself to death, along with all the people standing on the curb, gawking. The coachman is Selifan, who had wondered for a long time whether the wheel would stay on or fall off but never answered the question, and in the carriage is the opportunist Chichikov, who is choosing the route. Crash, bang! And the wheel cracks and falls off, but, more important, they were rushing in the wrong direction. It was the usual mistake for the nth time, and they had to go back to the fork in the road. Over and over again in embarrassment, Soviet Russia had to go back behind "other peoples," who, like Gogol's spectators, had just "stepped out of the way" of its onward victorious march. We are sorry, it was just a mistake—the cult of Stalin, collectivization, this problem or that. And in the wake of the "first country of socialism" trudged the vassals, the "countries of people's democracy"—this embarrassment was repeated over and over, a parody of Gogol's flying troika.

And now there are new Selifans, new communist Chichikovs, tempting Russia to a new leap into the bright distance.

This movement is appearing not only in Russia but in Ukraine and in my native Belarus and other countries emerging from the vast reaches of the former USSR. Curiously, in the years of communist domination, Russia was, in the eyes of the nomenklatura, the essential foundation not only of the Soviet Union but of the whole "socialist camp" (this was said outright). But today, this same Russia is the biggest headache for the states that have broken away but are still united by the mentality of the procommunist nomenklatura. If the radical democrats in the countries of the "near abroad" (as Russians now call the other former Soviet republics) are outraged by imperialist recidivism in Russia (real or imagined), then the communists of Belarus, Ukraine, Central Asia, and so on are frightened by Russian democracy. Thus in one way or another all of them are overt or covert opponents of Boris Yeltsin.

Before the collapse of the first coup of August 1991, the Belorussian Communist Party apparatchiks did not want to hear a thing about the market, or democracy, or an independent Belarus, with its own symbols and national flag and so on. But when Yeltsin and the democrats prevailed in Moscow, in order to hide from them, to distance themselves from them, the Belorussian communists embarked on an act of apparent political suicide. They consented to the ban on the Communist Party (although they could have easily opposed it in the Belorussian Supreme Soviet) and supported the proposal of the People's Front to declare independence and Belarusian statehood. Since all the levers of economic and, of course, political power remained in the hands of the

nomenklatura dinosaurs, after a few years they could once again legalize the Communist Party and, after the second coup in October 1993,
turn the procommunist structures of Belarus into a kind of "Paraguay"
for the Moscow putschists. Coup plotters would flee into hiding in
Belarus to save themselves, just as in 1945 the Nazis ran to the "rat
holes" in Latin America. (It is a coincidence, but such a vivid statement:
the editors of both the Russian and Belorussian procommunist newspapers have the same last name. Is it a hellish phantasmagoria? Chikin,
the editor of *Sovetskaia Rossiia*, which was shut down by Yeltsin, greets
the fugitives at the entrance to the "rat hole," and at the exit they are
met by another Chikin, editor of the filthy, vulgar Belorussian newspaper, *Chas i my*)!

In the days of perestroika, when conservative Politburo member
Egor Ligachev loved to visit Minsk (just as later Ruslan Khasbulatov, the
speaker of the rebel Russian parliament, and Konstantinov, Baburin,
Prokhanov, and other reactionary leaders loved to come to Belarus),
the Belorussian communists were very much offended that they were
the reason Belarus was called the "Vendée of perestroika," after the
backward French province that opposed the French Revolution. (Later,
they were proud of the nickname.) Now they have a reason to be both
proud and insulted at the name "Paraguay"—of course, on behalf of the
Belorussian people and the country of Belarus. They have learned at
least that lesson well: always identify themselves and their interests with
those of the whole nation.

When these nomenklatura people discuss a new association of former republics in something like the Soviet Union (although they speak
mainly of the need to restore economic ties), the main impetus for
their enthusiasm and energy is the desire to return the Communist
Party to its former ruling position. Now that Belarus is just one of many
small countries, they do not have the same confidence as before. They
were accustomed to living in an enormous "camp" that took up one-
sixth of the whole planet.

Thus, when speaking about "Russia's awakening," we must keep in
mind that this process is not isolated from events in other former Soviet
republics. There is a complicated interaction, a process of both acceler-
ation and braking. It is no accident that groups of gunmen from many
of the countries of the "near abroad" were sent to defend the procommunist "Khasbulatov" Supreme Soviet. Not long before the second

coup attempt, emissaries from the Moscow communo-fascists were seen in Kiev, Minsk, the Caucasus, and Moldova.

Still, what goes on in Russia per se is especially significant. What and who prevails in Russia may well have a definitive influence on the whole process of democratization of one-sixth of the planet. The success or failure of a process so important for the entire world community depends largely on what happens in the depths of the peoples of enormous Russia, in the consciousness of the Russian.

So just what is happening in Russia? What latent phenomena seem particularly visible now to us? Our attention is usually drawn to paradoxical facts and manifestations. The suspicion arises immediately, and with good reason, that precisely at these points some very important, momentous events and processes intersect.

For example, an unpleasant and offensive fact for any cultured Russian is that domestic fascism has found refuge in St. Petersburg, which has traditionally considered itself as the most civilized of all the Russian cities, the focus of culture, libraries, museums, a city with not only a highly educated intelligentsia but a very intellectual working class. And suddenly there is this incongruity, this shame: right in St. Petersburg, there are profascist publications, the constant, defiant gatherings, the pro-Nazi prosecutors and judges, the reactionary television show *600 Seconds*, and so on. And the milieu of Leningrad/St. Petersburg does not reject them. Or perhaps this very "milieu" has changed, unnoticed by all of us?

When Daniil Granin and I recorded the stories of the people who survived the siege of Leningrad, the terrible starvation and mass deaths during World War II (which we later published as *A Book of the Blockade*), we were amazed not only by the horrible instances of cannibalism because of starvation, but also by the opposite: how, under the conditions of a nine-hundred-day blockade, this great city was able to survive not only physically, but for the most part mentally as well. We kept thinking that for any other city under these circumstances, the panic, breakdown, and cannibalism would have been far worse. And there would have been much less of that exceptional human dignity with which the Leningraders died. We could only explain the fact that these people withstood everything both physically and spiritually under those circumstances, going beyond the limit, because of the exceptional nature of the intelligentsia in this northern Palmyra. What the Bolsheviks (and the Nazis, by the way) thought of as human weakness ("those little frail intellectuals!") turned out to be an irreplaceable "vitamin" of stoicism and endurance under prolonged torture. It was the spirituality, the intellectual quality of the Leningraders that was a substitute or a "filler" for the last piece of bread, when there was no bread or when they shared their bread with their fellow Leningraders.

But even during the war Leningrad was not like the former St. Petersburg/Petrograd. The Bolshevik leaders had worked hard to weaken its spiritual potential, with the executions after the Kronstadt mutiny and the purges of the 1930s. Then there was the war, and hunger destroyed another third of the city's natives. After the war came the show trial of the "Leningrad Affair" and more persecution of the great city, continuing the physical depletion of Leningraders, undermining their spiritual and moral potential. The city's awareness of itself changed, its "soul" was transformed and shrank in the process. St. Petersburg, the city that had always felt itself to be "the window on Europe," with pride of place among the other cities of Russia, which for many years had rivaled ancient Moscow in its role and significance, had turned into Leningrad and gradually began to feel like a provincial city, huddled in fear, "effacing itself" (to use the term invented by the St. Petersburg writer Fyodor Dostoevsky), following in everything the principle of not sticking your neck out, never being smarter than the village priest.

Now the name of St. Petersburg has been returned to Leningrad, but its previous sensibility and memory have not been immediately restored, the feeling that it really was the city of Aleksandr Pushkin, Fyodor Dostoevsky, Dmitrii Mendeleev, Aleksandr Blok, the Petrine Academy, the unique museums, libraries, the unique intelligentsia and working class, making it a city of the intelligentsia.

Instead of all this, there is only the memory of it, and the birth of the fascist movement Pamiat' and other such organizations.

These are the paradoxes in Russia after seventy years of the "sleep of reason," of Bolshevik experiments. But these manifestations do not reveal the whole picture. "St. Petersburg is never to be empty," as the poet has said. There are quite different forces and tendencies growing and becoming stronger and even prevailing in the great city. They gained the upper hand during the first coup of 1991, they made themselves known in St. Petersburg during the second attempt at a communofascist coup in October 1993, and confidence is growing stronger that the future belongs to these forces in the cities of Russia.

Events in the Russian village are evolving just as ambiguously as in the city and are at times paradoxical. Even twenty or thirty years ago, the Russian village (like the villages of Belarus, Ukraine, and the other republics) preserved within it, if not hope, then at least the eternal peasant dream of having one's own land, not the state's collective farm but free labor for oneself, for one's family. During the war years, when we partisans came to the villages, people would talk about this and ask questions. "You're out there fighting the Germans, you're getting killed, we're getting burned, the marauders are killing people, but when it's all over, God willing, and we chase out the Germans, what then? The collective farms again?"

And we ourselves believed, but yet did not quite believe, that after such sacrifices, such suffering, the peasant people would not once again be kept in serfdom. We tried to persuade our rural benefactors and helpers, and ourselves—surely after the war, after such a war, everything will change! But it did not. Only in the 1990s did the opportunity arrive to make radical changes in the village. But perhaps it was too late? The powerful collective farm lobby, consisting of the procommunist chairmen of such farms now at all levels of government, would not have such influence and force if it were opposed by a clear and direct expression of the peasantry's desire to regain the right to private property and the fruits of its labor that had been stripped from it.

Private farmers have emerged, and it seems private farming is growing, but there is not the anticipated powerful movement from below. The nearly century-long policy and practice of "depeasantifying" the country, during which not only the class of working peasant farmers was destroyed but the psychology of the farmer, have yielded their regrettable results—lack of resolve, fear of initiative, reluctance to take risks, mistrust not only of the bosses and their "undertakings," even democratic ones, but worse, lack of faith even in oneself. This is what the Russian peasantry has become after years of being disenfranchised in the collective farm system, the *agrogulag*.

It will not be simple or easy to overcome this degradation, as recent events have proven. But it is also clear that the process of renewal of the peasantry in Russia is inevitable, since it is so vitally necessary. Without the peasantry, the earth, like a field stripped of its humus, does not bear fruit or feed people. Only bookish Marxists and dogmatic Leninists can imagine (and act accordingly) that, "stripped" of the sense and instinct of the private property owner, the village (like the field "stripped of humus") would yield "high productivity." And the result is what we are trying with such difficulty to rectify today: an enormous country with boundless farmlands, yet one that is unable to feed itself.

If we add to that the difficulties and complexities of reforming Russian industry, which has been heavily militarized, and the halting (and not very skillful) conversion of the military-industrial complex, which threatens unemployment and food shortages for millions of workers, then the unbelievable difficulties that Russian democracy has encountered and will continue to deal with become obvious.

A brief discussion is in order about our writers, primarily because in the Russian tradition, a writer is capable of having a noticeable and sometimes enormous influence on the state of people's minds, on public awareness. (In the West, such authority for a writer is a great rarity.) Thus it mattered a great deal which side a writer was on, during both the first and the second coup (just as it did during the First Congress of People's Deputies), although many supposedly well known writers are only apparatchiks whose fame was manufactured at one time by Party propagandists. Their works were the so-called secretary literature produced by the official secretaries of the Writers' Union (all those Markovs, Proskurins, Prokhanovs, and even the more talented ones, like Bondarev). They were the product of Stalin's literary policy, later administered by Mikhail Suslov (for many years the Party's ideology commissar). This was the era when pseudoart and pseudoliterature substituted for real art. (Just as Lysenko's pseudobiology replaced biology, there was a kind of special "Soviet" physics and mathematics.)

At first those members of the Writers' Union who devoted themselves to pseudoliterature preserved some quality, or at least some feature, of real literature. It was a kind of writers' collective farm, where all rights were reserved for the chairman, the foreman, the Party organization, and the "people with briefcases." Obviously these people opposed any reforms that would deprive them of such a comfortable position in literature, with power, large press runs, trips abroad, and inexhaustible financing from the Literary Fund. And they were the ones to defend the coup plotters, Generals Valentin Varennikov and Vladimir Kriuchkov, in August 1991 and who, in October 1993, backed Aleksandr Rutskoi and Ruslan Khasbulatov.

A small yet indestructible and unquenchable hotbed of future upheavals in Russia is still buried in the depths of the writers' community, especially because some of these writers are under the special care not only of our own guardians of the purity of "democratic principles" but of Westerners as well. As soon as one hears the "voice of the law" or even reproaches against the provocateurs and inciters of civil war, the wail immediately goes up, the moaning about "witch hunts," about "a return to 1937." For example, among those attacked in these terms were those who charged the newspaper *Den'* with responsibility for abetting the explosive hatred and violence with which it had filled its readers.

Well, all right, our seemingly democratic press and our television stations, flirting with independence, want to demonstrate they are always in opposition to everything. But when respectable human rights organizations in the United States, France, Finland, and other democratic countries speak in the role of preservers of profascist and procommunist bacilli, those hotbeds of future coups that Russia will not be able to overcome, one wishes to ask: at home, in your country, do you allow newspapers (like *Den'*, *Sovetskaia Rossiia*, *Pravda*, and so on) to call the democratic government "occupiers" and the president "an agent of influence of a foreign government"? Do you let newspapers call for the forming of "combat groups" and urge readers to prepare for "Day X," when "we will lead the democrats around the streets of Moscow" (like German prisoners of war) and, if we have to, we will hang them (and what is more, "upside down")?

But what of the press? You are standing at a streetcar stop (two days before the October 1993 coup) and a tall citizen with a mustache, who appears to be normal, recognizes you: "You," and he calls you by name, "and the criminal government are to blame for everything. But it's all right, soon you'll be hanging from the trees!" And you *would* be hanging, and they *would* hang you, and they are prepared to do all that tomorrow. Is that an opposition that should know no restrictions? Or at least the restrictions established in countries with a far more stable internal situation, unlike ours?

Russia today is changing its faith, virtually its religion, trading Marxism for Russian Orthodoxy and other traditional beliefs once again. In the past this was a violent process, the forcible inculcation of belief in the leaders, their dogmas, and their infallibility. Of course the revival of the Christian, Muslim, and other religions is taking place under conditions of freedom of conscience to which we are unaccustomed. Clearly a great deal of drama is accompanying this process, and it is not simple. But it is interesting that the country of "triumphant atheism" within a short time became (or is becoming) an international center of widespread and sometimes fervent religiosity. So much for your Marxism, your communism, your Marx, your Lenin, give us back our Christ, our Mohammed, our Buddha!

But to whom is this being said? Who is stopping people from taking back their religion? Curiously, it is not just our atheists and Leninists. There are many abroad for whom our parting with the "socialist choice," with the Leninist experiment, brought no joy but, on the contrary, distress. I am not speaking about those whom the Communist Party supported abroad by robbing its own country. There are many very decent, independent leftist intellectuals—I have heard them myself and have debated them in the universities of the former West Germany, Finland, even in the United States—who are inclined to believe that we were too hasty in parting with socialism. It is just that we Russians, we Soviets, "ruined" a good idea, but if we could just try to correct, or change, or adjust the practice and the policy, why, look what we would achieve. Well, whoever thinks this way, fight for the cause yourself, that will be plenty! Trying to talk us into continuing the building of communism, socialism with a "human face," is the same as trying to convince the residents of Chernobyl that "clean" and "safe" nuclear power is possible.

In Japan, the *Izvestiia* correspondent Sergei Agafonov and I were bowled over by a Japanese philosopher and wise man who made the following paradoxical statements: Evil in the world is a constant. Whenever a quantity of evil is eliminated, it is replenished, and even more is added. You Russians and Soviets, said the Japanese man earnestly, have already adapted to life under socialism. Now you are rejecting it, and the evil is migrating to other countries. And now other people are becoming accustomed to it and adapting. Thus you would be more humane if you could go on carrying that historic burden.

Well, at least this fellow had some humanitarian considerations. In Germany I heard purely pragmatic arguments: While the nightmare of "real socialism" existed in real life, Western entrepreneurs, sensing the threat to their interests, met the demands of unions and workers halfway, agreeing to broader social programs. But now they would be stingily cutting back—and all because the socialist camp collapsed. The moral is that you should go on living in the "camp" so that we who live in freedom will be able to deal with our own problems more easily.

Even Pope John Paul II considered it necessary and timely to inform his flock around the world that the communist ideology had a "kernel of truth." Capitalism, so to speak, is changing, and has changed largely thanks to socialist thought, which gave rise to such "social buffers" as trade unions, government oversight, and so on.

If that is true to some extent, then it is only with one reservation, but a very important and necessary reservation: the implementation of the communist idea and purposes on the scale of a state, as the many years of practice of a large number of countries have shown, is impossible in principle. Such a state inevitably mutates into totalitarianism, universal constraint, economic stagnation, and slave labor. That does not preclude the existence and even the flourishing of some individual voluntary "communes" like the Israeli kibbutzim or some that I had the opportunity to visit in the United States. But to cite individual and isolated examples of successful communities or "ideas" in books and to ignore the horrible experience of hundreds of millions of people is possible only under the conditions of Western plenty. Jean-Paul Sartre once seriously praised the attraction of the Maoist "cultural revolution," a wonderful example of an intellectual "playing at communism" from a safe distance, where people are spoiled by the good life. Whoever wants "communism" and whoever still pities their people, well, it is a free country, go and see the late Kim Il Sung's paradise in North Korea— thank God such preserves are still maintained.

Among the many designs for a memorial to the victims of totalitarianism was an antimausoleum on Red Square. Like a reflection in the water, opposite the Leninist cubist structure of the mausoleum, another would be built, but turned upside down in the earth. It could contain documentary and other evidence bearing witness to the regime's crimes during all the years of its existence. And one can imagine the two adjacent queues—to the mausoleum and to the antimausoleum, people could pick whichever one they liked best.

During one of the "Red holidays" back in the Gorbachev era, something like this happened: There was a celebration rally, a holiday in honor of "Great October," on Red Square, and a funeral memorial march at the Solovki Stone[2] on Lubianka Square. People in the column heading toward Lenin's mausoleum broke off and went to the monument to the victims of Leninism and Stalinism, stood for a while, then rejoined the others. Some people remained; others left the stone to go back to the "official" column. That is how the "Brownian movement" occurs in our society, diverse oscillations of the most incongruous purposes and aims.

Where is such a contradictory Rus—Russia—headed? Where is it moving? What awaits it in the future? These questions torment us, and the entire world as well. That is how it should be: what happens in Russia influences everything, it affects and will continue to affect the interests of many peoples and countries, just as it did after 1917. The reverse movement, the historical turn of the tide, the return of an enormous mass of humanity to the channel of common development, is a process that is planetary in scale. The legacy of the Soviet military empire inherited by democratic Russia, however, is harsh, and it is too great a risk to leave Russia alone with its problems.[3]

Notes

1. Here is a letter I received after the "October events," the reaction of one such woman to my radio speech (I have preserved her style and spelling). The letter was sent to a Minsk address, since the woman understood that "Adamovich" was a Belorussian name. But she found it more convenient to settle scores with a "Jew"—a technique widespread in the "patriotic" press, which had formed her values, views, and style.

Dear A.M. Adonovich,

Having heard your "heroic" speech over Russian Radio on October 10, 1993, I want to express my opinion or actually to ask you: do you have the right in general to speak and not only speak but to live in Russia? I'll answer you—no! Do you have the right to condemn such outstanding people like Rutskoi, Khasbulatov, Boburin [Baburin], Makashov, and the other leaders and heroes of the people, heroes of ours, what were the victors of Soviet power in 1917. All democrats are traitors! They sold themselves to capitalism, they sold themselves to enemies of socialism, twice over. You Jews, God himself damned you, what else do you want? They gave you, A.M. Adonovich, air time, that doesn't mean that after your preaching the people leapt up! No, they hate you all the more, and you can take your little article to Israel, and don't forget to take with you Boner [Elena Bonner, widow of Sakharov], she always tried to defend traitors over the air. But whoever hears you is laughing at you. Sooner or later the soc. [socialist] order will be restored and that'll be the end of you Jews! That [October] was the Bloody Sunday of "1905"; now there will be "1917." People will understand that the soc. order is the order of Russia. Now they didn't have enough strength but they will be restored by the coming generation and this generation of 30–40-year olds will be old people if they survive, well, then they'll feel what it's like for the old folks now. This doesn't concern you 'cause in Israel there will never be socialism. How I hate your ugly Jewish mug! And there are a lot of traitors like that in Russia! We need a second Stalin in order to destroy you all here. Don't be so happy about what happened to the heroes of the soc. battle, everything's still to come. There are a lot of us, the process has started, half the country's already for the soc. order! Just a little more, just a little bit! The last battle it's the hardest.

2. On October 31, 1990, on Political Prisoners' Day, on Lubianka Square across from the KGB headquarters building, surviving victims of Stalin and activists of the civic organization Memorial, which is devoted to exposing and remedying the abuses of totalitarianism, unveiled a monument made from a stone hauled from the Solovki Monastery in northern Russia, once used as a labor camp.—C.A.F.

3. I have a collection of articles on my desk from a Tomsk newspaper for chemists called *Dialog*, which has broken the alarming story to the public of Tomsk–7, a closed city. For many years, specialists appealed to Central Committee and Politburo members and to scientific academicians in Moscow. Now they are appealing with the same degree of success (or rather, without any hint that they are being heard or will get a hearing) to the Chernomyrdin government. The reaction is: it's their problem, their headache. I am not a specialist, but I will cite just one quotation from the newspaper *Dialog* from scientists and practicing chemists:

A. *Boltachev:* "Thus, a crime has been committed. A crime against humanity and everything living. No less than 850 kilograms of plutonium and two metric tons of highly enriched uranium from one (!) factory were dumped into an open reservoir. (Other factories were not napping at the time.) Go and check it. And if it is not proved, I am ready to answer to the law. But the fact is that I myself have analyzed these solutions. Without going into detail about this criminal technology (A.V. Striapshin, a former worker of OTK Factory–25, has described it in detail in his articles), I will say only that even then I understood that something criminal was going on."

A. *Striapshin:* "The nuclear materials of the SKhK [the Russian acronym for a "chemical plant" that makes the plutonium "product"] that were dumped into the reservoir and burial sites were deliberately reported as less radioactive than they actually were and this fact was concealed by the directors of the plant with the knowledge of the Ministry, the KGB, and the city and regional committees of the Communist Party. . . .

Here are two figures: 740 grams [the weight of the bomb dropped on Hiroshima] and 63 kilograms [the official figure for the Chernobyl fallout]. But the chemical plant quietly, without fuss, dumped into Mother Earth several tons (in my secret letter to the ministry specific figures are cited), whereas the maximum standard for technological waste can be no more than 10–15 kilograms. The accumulated above-standard waste from the chemical plant (factoring in the standard waste of nuclear products)

for Plant SKhK–25 alone is a fantastic quantity that could cause an ecological disaster, incomparably more dangerous than Chernobyl."

A. Boltachev: "What would happen to Tomsk province, to the entire globe,
if this 'national treasure' were accidently to evaporate into the air (for
example, if a tornado occurs, or a plane or missile falls into this lake)?"

One plant alone—and so many remain from the Soviet military-industrial
complex—caused such a threat to humankind and everything living on the
planet. How can this superexplosive lake be cleaned? What fantastic sums
would be needed? Some scientists believe that spontaneous combustion
could occur again, as it did in 1957 in Cheliabinsk province. And then
what? Countless tons of active plutonium in this and other Siberian lakes
and reservoirs!

Translated by Catherine A. Fitzpatrick

8

Leonid Batkin

The Minefield of Russian Constitutionalism

Before and After October 1993

After tanks stormed the massive headquarters of the Russian Supreme Soviet, and after those involved in the insurrection of October 3–4, 1993, were dispersed and several of their leaders arrested, Boris Yeltsin hastened to announce in his address to the nation that "there are no victors." As early as October 4, Yeltsin was already referring to the situation as "a tragedy in which there are no victors." Considering the blackened walls of the White House and the 150 or so dead found within, the comment did not sound at all unreasonable, and it was quickly adopted as a catchphrase by the mass media. But Yeltsin's phrase had nothing whatsoever to do with the political reality.

There were those who suffered defeat; this means that there were also victors. And victorious they certainly were: the policy makers who rushed in with indecent haste to shape the future government of Russia according to their own convenience (as they understood it) have in no small measure been successful. As I write this (in November 1993), the politicians and the newspapers are discussing the latest draft of the Constitution (which the powers-that-be and their supporters regard as "finally, for the first time, democratic") and are gearing up for the parliamentary election and referendum on December 12 (touted as "finally, for the first time, free").

The "Yeltsin" Constitution (which, insofar as it was developed behind closed doors by a small group of bureaucrats, could be termed a "Filatov" constitution)[1] should enter the *Guinness Book of Records* for its brazen simplicity and the speed with which it was drafted. For precisely this reason, however, it will hardly be the final one: it is unlikely even to last out the remaining years of what for Russia has been an agonizingly interminable century. The December elections, of course, will also by no means be free in any substantive (that is, socially meaningful and civically responsible) sense. And this is true not only from the perspective of an outsider.

On the contrary, many of Russia's political activists—including the most "democratic," and especially those from the ruling Moscow intelligentsia—could hardly conceal their triumph, their righteous exultation, and, it goes without saying, their career calculations. In the early hours of October 4 I received an anonymous telephone call from someone expressing drunken sympathy that "you are not with us celebrating." All of these people (most of whom, in former times, did quite well for themselves and even belonged openly to the Communist Party) —former people's deputies, insipid or downright fraudulent "writers" of one kind or another, "champions of justice" (as they hurriedly proclaimed themselves to be two years ago), intriguers from the leadership of Moscow's Democratic Russia movement or, I am sorry to say, from the current membership of the Moscow Tribune club (created by myself with help from Andrei Sakharov, especially)—the whole crowd of them have insinuated their way, pushing and shoving, into the ranks of the new Duma.

However! Although independent, worthwhile individuals are few and far between among the Yeltsin crowd, and although the post-October consolidation of presidential power does not give me the slightest cause for optimism, I cannot agree with those (including, for example, my friend Andrei Siniavskii) who have found nothing better to do than to proclaim, with surpassing naïveté, that although the burned-out Supreme Soviet may have been hollow and corrupt, it was still, nevertheless, a parliament (a *parliament?!*). And that, consequently, Yeltsin's decree of September 21 violated the Constitution. And that on the night of October 4 democracy was crushed. Well, well . . .

Imagine if the Soviet generals who vacillated for so many hours had not finally given the necessary orders! Like many others, I spent that entire night nervously waiting and hoping for tanks to appear on the streets of Moscow (and, God willing, to turn in the right direction). How frighteningly sad that we should have to *want* such a thing.

After the storming of the Ostankino television station and the pogrom in the municipal building, military intervention was once again the only thing possible to hope for. Our fate as a nation hung in the balance. If the attack plans of the Makashovs and Barkashovs and their ilk had prevailed, then Russia really would have fallen (perhaps not for the long term but with grave bloodshed) under the dictatorship of the very worst of the neo-Soviets and Russian fascists. It is quite beyond me how intelligent people can fail to recognize such an elementary and obvious fact.

After October: Heading into a Historical Unknown

On the other hand, the reversal in attitude referred to above, which to me is entirely natural, has somehow eluded large numbers of the intelligentsia. I am talking about two positions combining to make one purely democratic, consistent, and balanced view: first, the sober ability to look with understanding and sympathy upon the *immediate* significance of the upset of September 21 (although, as events soon proved, it was unforgivably risky and ill planned in practical military terms), followed by the most determined support for those who opposed the occupiers of the White House on October 3 and 4 (which does not, of course, mean approval of all of the specific acts and behavior of the high-ranking Yeltsinites or, for that matter, of the subsequent disorder and police brutality); second, the very clear opposition to the president's regime immediately after his victory. At the time I formulated my attitude in the following terms: I breathe a great sigh of relief and rejoice sincerely in the defeat of "those" but not, in any way, in the victory of "these." In this victory there is much to be sad about, in both a political and a human sense.

The confusion on the part of some liberals, and equally the profound apathy and disgust that most of the population feels toward what has been going on, is not unfounded. The circumstances and aftereffects of the president's Decree 1400 abound with discouraging contradictions and do not merit summarizing (*although*—or even *because*—we have passed the point of greatest danger). And we therefore find ourselves for the first time at something like a historical crossroads. The current situation is not the final chapter, but a beginning.

In any event, the collapse of the Communist Party political system—which occurred in three successive stages—perestroika, August 1991, and October 1993—is only now complete (and has left, by the way, an enormous manpower, administrative, economic, and psychological legacy). Only now can we look at what has happened without the distressing need to glance behind us for the threat of the crudest kind of reaction. Only now are we liberated at last from the ideology of the "lesser evil"—a circumstance that may not, it is true, lead us "out of the frying pan and into the fire," as the Russian proverb warns, but it may certainly land us in a good-sized pile of manure, and in short order.

Now that the worst elements among the Russian leadership have been driven out of the political spotlight, there is some prospect that a more concerted radical democratic opposition can arise, made up of critics "from below" of the entire horde of presidential followers. (How much needs to be done to organize such an opposition is still unclear, but that is a separate issue.) This is another reason why I supported the decree of September 21. After all, when the lesser evil gains the upper hand over the greater, it naturally becomes the only evil, and therefore assumes the status of the greater evil.

No one will deny that the three stages in the breakdown of the neototalitarian Khrushchev-Brezhnev order have had enormous positive significance or that each stage has been more progressive than the one before. The current post-October stage, however, involves not only the dismantling of Soviet power but the setting of conditions for a whole new era in Russia's existence. An era of transition, yes, but the change will be much deeper, longer lasting, and more fundamental in nature than the term "transition" suggests.

Between January 1987 and December 1993 the direction of reform, for all its dramatic and unforeseen twists of fate, was actually fairly primitive: it was anti-Soviet and nothing more. To climb out of the hole we were in, we at each point had to grab the nearest foothold, whatever that might be. Accordingly, the choices were simplistic and, invariably, crudely personalized. We were reduced to choosing between Egor Ligachev and Mikhail Gorbachev, so to speak, and later between Ruslan Khasbulatov and Boris Yeltsin.

Now, however, the range of our options is mushrooming. We have passed the stage of debating about whether there should be any reforms at all and moved on to a set of more significant issues—more radical versus less radical reform, specific details of the reforms, common interests and goals, legislative and judicial mechanisms, the rate and social costs of change, and so forth. We are now truly in virgin territory and heading into a genuine historical unknown.

I have selected the problem of "constitutionalism" for this article because it has been the most prominent issue in recent events and has been the subject of the greatest dispute.

Democratic Hopes Deferred

From the legacy of the Soviet past and through the efforts of the group of gradualist reformers within the ruling elite that, fortunately, prevailed (although they are far from democratic by nature in behavior), it would appear that an authoritarian, bureaucratic regime has been hatched. Like its predecessor, this regime will be morally unattractive in the eyes of most people. It will have a highly dubious claim to political legitimacy and, because of its specific domestic provenance and social nature, it will hardly be capable of effectively bringing about a competitive modern market economy in Russia.

Russian authoritarianism never expected the current level of sophistication in society. It will never succeed in creating its own party. An authoritarian government will inevitably be weak and unstable on the whole. (Perhaps that is fortunate?)

I reiterate: *this* October of 1993 (unlike the October of 1917) was not a disaster; on the contrary, it saved us from the most terrible turn of events. Nevertheless, the democratic hopes aroused by the strange August 1991 coup (almost a "velvet" democratic revolution, one that was not only without revolutionaries but without democrats as well) rapidly disintegrated during the following two years. Since the government's victory over the nationalist-communists last October, these hopes must be deferred even longer.

To find appropriate criteria to evaluate such a paradoxical and confusing situation, it is useful to place the events of September 21, when the parliament was dissolved, in both near- and long-term historical perspective.[2] That will facilitate the transition to my discussion of the

October 1993 regime (its Constitution, its parliamentarianism) and my thoughts about the "Russian path" in the coming years.

The Subversive Tactic—"Respect Your Own Laws"

Even before September 1993 some sincere and well-intentioned people supposed that it was better to have the strained pretense of "constitutionality" before us publicly every day than to reject even its outward appearance. I believe they were deeply mistaken. They misread the situation at that time and compared it to the struggle for human rights of the 1970s, although that was entirely different. Beginning in 1968, the human rights activists who put forth the labored, but nonetheless sincere watchword "Respect Your Own Laws"—as if they believed the Soviet Constitution was a reality—were trying to destroy Orwellian "doublethink" from inside the system. Each year, on December 5, the Day of the Soviet Constitution, they gathered on Pushkin Square to protest, with startling simplicity, the Soviet government's violations of its own Constitution. Each year, the pensive statue of Pushkin bowed his head toward them and observed a moment of silence along with them.

Of course, this gathering was also a stratagem of war. The KGB understood this, and the dissidents knew that they knew, and the KGB knew that the dissidents knew that they knew. But why did this stratagem turn out to be fairly successful, while retaining its acuity, and why did it serve as a source of inner strength? Because the Soviet government did not observe its own laws; they had not been passed for that purpose. But they were passed for some reason, after all. Who was the padishah here, and who was Scheherezade? One way or another, without these tales, the thousand and one nights that we lived through would have been inconceivable. The human rights activists sacrificed themselves for the sake of the literal meaning of "permitted speeches." They took this literal meaning as reality, and in doing so made the case that Soviet reality was absurd and had to be changed.

In response, the authorities realized it was necessary to amend the Constitution by adding Article 6, which established the "leading role of the Communist Party" in Soviet society and thus made the interpretation of all laws subject to party interests. The authorities also added Article 190.1 to the Penal Code, making it a punishable offense to

circulate "deliberately false fabrications slandering the social order"—
that is, they also behaved as if they themselves took the laws seriously.
The mendacity of the system was so deeply rooted and total that it
needed a systematization of lies. The illusoriness was something far
deeper than simply propaganda. It *was* reality; its lie was the truth.
Molière's Tartuffe was not merely a deceiver. More subtly and earlier
than others, George Orwell understood the deep-rooted nature of the
Soviet absurd.

Such was the hypocritical nature of the authorities and the tragic
duality of its open opponents, who dared to hope to live to see the day
when the regime would become more open, more soft—but never
dreamed they would see its collapse.

From Constitutional Rituals to Parliamentary Battles

Under Gorbachev, to this illusoriness was added a wider range of tolerance for the elements of public political debate, which rapidly flew out
of control and assumed an avalanchelike effect. The new political ritual,
even if it was quasi-parliamentary, even if it had inherited the decora-
tive, false features of the previous ritual, had nonetheless shed its stiff-
ness, its studied effects. While the whole country was watching on
television, it placed demands on the skills of the administrators and
politicians. Elements of improvisation began, and there were the inevitable surprises. Millions of people watched the parliamentary debates
and awaited them with great anticipation. Along the way the public
began to assimilate some unfamiliar "legal" rules of the game. Highlighted by glasnost, worked out in public, and then immediately trampled upon (but also in public!), methods of something like politics (was
it really a parliamentary battle?) really began to emerge as a specific
form of activity (and not, as before, an all-intrusive context for the
evaluation, significance, and control of any human phenomena).

But the situation after the First Congress of People's Deputies in
1989 remained ambiguous. Hopeful signs of change as well as elements
of the former mimicry were superimposed on one another. Everything
of which Soviet constitutionalism was capable was extracted from it. But
for that very reason the congress sounded its death rattle, became a
slapstick comedy accompanied by constant violations of the rules of
order, falsifications of roll calls, and so on. All of this continued in the

post-August Russian "parliament" and finally led to its degeneration. By provoking society's outrage and ridicule, that body became the source of even greater legal nihilism and political collapse. Although the Russian parliament had played a useful and expressly subversive role in bringing about the end of the party regime of the USSR, as an artifact of the alleged "constitutional sphere" of the Soviets it was unquestionably a dead weight on democracy.

"Constitutionalism" Hits a Dead End

In 1992–93, "constitutionalism" became a refuge for reactionaries, communists as well as nationalists, who wished to restore the status quo, serving as an ominous sign that the Yeltsin early-reformist stage was absorbing the previous Gorbachev prereform stage as it was frozen in 1990–91. Egor Gaidar's reforms were like a stick upsetting the anthill of the state economy and played a useful role as a prod. By the summer of 1992, however, the reforms had run out of steam and come to a halt. When Gaidar then made a sharp retreat from monetarism, it became clear that he was not able to fulfill even his own limited goals.

Gaidar and Yeltsin hid this fact, though, and continued to pretend that reform was moving ahead. In August 1992, five members of a group called Independent Civic Initiative, including myself, sent the president a confidential memorandum that expressed our deep alarm about the halt of reforms. We know that Yeltsin read our paper, but he never replied. Only in December 1992 did Gaidar speak some of the truth at a speech in parliament before he stepped down. To this day it is hard for me to forgive Gaidar, although he is an excellent person, for his conduct during the months between July and December. His lack of political honesty and courage, a result of his previous career, gave him away.

At that time I subscribed to the opinion that we had no parliamentarianism, no Constitution, and therefore no Constitutional Court. I wrote in the journal *Novoe vremia* (New Times) that I had no desire to take part in skirmishes over a vacuum—the "constitutional space" as it was known in official parlance. "Some persons have supposedly come out of this space, and others have not 'come out' of it. You should go into the space first," I wrote.

It became obvious that moving toward a rejection of the Soviet Constitution and government by means of that same Constitution and that same government was impossible. And the increasingly rough and chaotic clash of the two groupings among the neo-Soviet rulers became inevitable. "We have to get out of the vicious circle somehow, precisely through politics. Somehow we have to get out of the dead end of the current 'Constitutionalism.' Because it is this 'field' that threatens to produce the most filth and bloodshed." This phrase about bloodshed concluded my article, which came out more than six months before the October 1993 events.

And I also wrote in the same article: "In my opinion, this matter will be decided through political force. How? Just as the question of the USSR Congress of People's Deputies and that of the USSR president was decided."

I was recognizing the expediency of using force against the moribund inherited government institutions of the Soviet Russian Republic, but not, God forbid, against human beings. It would be done through a peaceful coercion and purely political action; it would not be a legal resolution of the problem, because that would have been impossible. "Law is above politics only when and where politics creates law, that is, politics precedes law. Although we are acting for the sake of the ideals of *the law*, it is time to restore to Russia the grandeur and dignity of a no less civilized word—*politics*."

Any appeal for the direct manifestation of political will, however, and for the dissolution of the false parliament would have been entirely justified, I added,

> only if it reflects the force of a society that has matured sufficiently to take such action and is not the work of the apparatus of coercion. . . . Such a display of will requires not only a favorable public attitude and not only decisions made "on high," but an influential, powerful democratic movement independent of the government. Otherwise the danger is too great that this expression of political will can turn into arbitrary measures and chaos.

We should have realized that even a relatively favorable outcome to the struggle at the top, which is what happened in October, could not have by itself become a victory for democracy, nor would it "open the direct route to a civil society based on the rule of law."

While I fear the coming to power of the nationalist-communists, I cannot predict without alarm what will happen if the "democrats" should win.

The Yeltsin Constitution

Although I cannot get into an exhaustive analysis here of the text of the new Constitution, I will draw some conclusions and possibly fill in the picture better.

First of all, the very method by which the new Constitution was drafted and presented to the country for approval was startling.

The Constitutional Conference that took place in mid-1993 included a rather peculiar collection of participants, chosen by various methods, and it lacked procedures for approving summary decisions. It appeared to be a very subservient body, kept in the president's vest pocket and taken out when needed for use against Khasbulatov's Supreme Soviet. After October 4 it was jettisoned altogether as irrelevant. Only the first two chapters of the draft produced by this summer conference were retained: several general statutes and the section on "human and civil rights and liberties." The draft was fairly easily formulated at the time, and it passed without too much difficulty because most of the conference members appointed by Yeltsin were preoccupied (with good reason) by entirely different matters: the structure and nature of the federation; the system of federal and local government; the structure and function of parliament; and the status of the president. All were crucial elements for which constitutions are required in the first place, and they affect the degree to which declared civil rights will become a reality. But these matters of governance remained uncoordinated and in a total muddle.

Now, of course we can express satisfaction that the broad constitutional definitions and the civic principles enunciated for the most part look fine. There is much here that is new and substantive for citizens of Russia, although it is like a suit of clothes they must grow into. Some day, all of the declarations will be implemented and will be imbued with practical meaning. For selfish reasons I am sad that I will never see any of this myself.

But as we know, didn't Stalin's Constitution have some fairly good clauses about human rights? As one of the exhausted and disbelieving aborigines of the USSR, I am interested now in one thing: Who will really rule us, and in what way and how will this damned government be structured in reality? What reforms of property relations and government can be expected in the foreseeable future, along with the modernization of the economy and the emergence of a civil society?

But everything to do with the new government system was cobbled together in a few days by a bunch of bureaucrats appointed by the president, the so-called Working Group, whose composition was never made public. Actually, one of its sessions was shown for a moment on the television news. And who should I see sitting at the table—was I mistaken?—but Mr. E. Sevastianov—who else! (I did not recognize any of the others.) Sevastianov is a young, terribly democratic chief of Moscow State Security, the KGB's successor as political police organization, which has retreated into the shadows for the time being (but has still remained the same as before). He surfaced as one of the cooks serving up the new constitutional dish.

The Working Group kept stirring this dish and salting it and muttering chants over it right up until the eleventh hour. Then, waving away the objections of the already obsolete Constitutional Conference, it pushed the document through some sort of "constitutional arbitrage" appointed by the president on the spot and presented it to the public. One hundred million Russian voters had the opportunity to study the Constitution's 137 articles and 429 paragraphs and clauses for an entire month, meanwhile having the wool pulled over their eyes by television coverage that was completely run by the government. Actually, it was important, as Yeltsin observed, to grasp only the fundamental points.

All right, I'll try to do just that.

Let me note only that all the references to precedents that were bandied about (mostly the analogies to Charles de Gaulle's France) are not serious. When the presidential-parliamentary Fifth Republic was created, it was a question of a package, obvious to everyone, of article-by-article amendments concerning the main governmental powers and procedures. The draft Constitution of France was commissioned by the parliament and it was approved by the State Council, a body that was not appointed by de Gaulle.

More important, the de Gaulle Constitution was approved in a country where people were accustomed to private property, independent courts, political parties, and constitutionalism in general. It was merely a question of the continuing process of repairing an ancient "bourgeois democracy" in a republic that had fully emerged at least one hundred years earlier. It was *not* a country where a totalitarian regime had just collapsed, where economic and political gulfs had just yawned open, where there was terrible confusion in everyone's minds and actions, where there was virtually no privately owned manufacturing, nor democracy, nor normal courts, not to mention authentic political parties and real federalism. As Voland, Mikhail Bulgakov's Prince of Darkness, said in *The Master and Margarita*, no matter what you grab hold of, there's nothing there.

And now we have a "Russian de Gaulle," as another close friend of mine, Kronid Lubarskii, has said heatedly about the president. Forgive me, he's not de Gaulle, after all, but Yeltsin, who is trying to rearrange Russia in one swoop to his personal taste while proceeding entirely from the current correlation of forces, under the heavy influence of his recent clashes with Khasbulatov's Supreme Soviet. Yeltsin conducted a constitutional referendum by rules that he himself prescribed (half the votes of half the list of registered voters was sufficient for approval, that is, only 25 percent of the electorate). Moreover, he scheduled this referendum on the same day as the elections to the Federal Assembly, a body that was to be established under this Constitution, which technically had not yet been passed. The elections were held under a proportional system that was transparently phony, in our conditions, because half of the seats were guaranteed to politicians from quasi-party "blocs" created especially for the occasion. A sufficient level of voter participation was defined as 25 percent of the list of registered voters. Moreover, only one round of balloting was prescribed, so that a majority of votes in a district that had a large number of contenders could theoretically be obtained with a minuscule proportion of votes, say, 5 or 7 percent.

Worse, on the very same day, we had to elect city dumas, or councils. It was also unclear how their structure, function, and number were to be defined, and by whom.

As Sergei Shakhrai said in a television interview at the end of October, "Our choice was limited." In other words, either we had to adopt the Constitution quickly, or there would have been only presidential power, without parliamentarianism, for a long time to come.

A third alternative, which many people tried to get Yeltsin to focus on and about which Shakhrai was silent, was to pass a Provisional Constitutional Act, valid for perhaps two years, during which time a Constituent Constitutional assembly could be elected and elections held to approve a permanent Constitution that the assembly would draft.

But no! What you got on December 12 was not merely a permanent

Constitution but one that is almost impermeable to future legal amendments, a Constitution set in concrete!

Look at Article 136 of the Constitution, with a reference to Article
108: to amend Sections 3–8, "no less than three-fourths of the votes
from the total number of members of the Council of the Federation
and no less than two-thirds of the votes of the total number of members
of the State Duma" are required. In our current political circumstances,
there is no chance that such a qualified majority in opposition to Yeltsin
will be formed.

The circumstances of drafting and the period of time allowed for
presenting this Constitution to Russia were all obviously motivated by
the desire of opportunists to seize the moment. It was a dangerous sort
of arrogation of power, and I think revealed a lack of foresight as well as
contempt for Russian society.

But in its own way, the text of the Constitution itself is a remarkable
document.

The Powers of the Presidency—A Fourth
Branch of Government?

The president of the Russian Federation is the "guarantor" of the Constitution and of individual rights and liberties. What does that mean?
Nothing is said about the Federal Assembly, the Constitutional Court,
or any other branch of power because that would be a politically dangerous (as well as legally meaningless) formula. The president "ensures
the coordinated functioning and interaction of governmental bodies"
(Art. 80.2). It is not the branches of power independent of each other
that are to ensure their own functioning and interaction, but Himself.
Thus, the president is removed from the category of these bodies and
placed above them all. *His* "functioning and interaction" are not en-
sured by anyone. He is answerable to no one. He is the head of the
government, and not in the customary judicial formal sense. Although
under Article 10 there are only three forms of government power—legislative, executive, and judicial, the president is obviously *not included in
the concept of executive power*. In Article 11, among those who "embody"
government power, the president is named *before the parliament*. The
president can issue not only administrative directives but the ukases, or
decrees, to which he and Gorbachev were accustomed. How decrees

differ from laws is not explained; they are both called "*normative* acts" (Art. 125.2a, Art. 15.3). That is, they are legal acts, not on a case-by-case basis but permanently in effect. (I recall that in ancient Rus there were imperial ukases that were not just decisions concerning specific cases but were normative; later there were the ukases of the Presidium of the USSR Supreme Soviet, or standing parliament.) To be sure, the ukases should not contradict the Constitution and other laws; but neither should legislation adopted by the parliamentarians.

The Russian president is clearly elevated above the three branches of government. He is like a fourth branch, or to be more accurate, the first and chief branch and in some sense, even the only branch. Otherwise, how can we account for the fact that only about the president and him alone is it said in the Constitution that he "determines the fundamental directions of the domestic and foreign policies of the government"? Does that mean the Federal Assembly does not determine any policy? In fact, that is the way it is.

From these facts ensue numerous intriguing details. The Russian president will combine *all the advantages* of both the American and French presidents and will have some powers they do not have, but he will have *none of the limitations* imposed on these presidents. Thus, his power is comparable to none, except perhaps the president of Peru. Even analogies with the Communist Party's general secretary are weak, because after Josef Stalin, the power of this official was limited by the oligarchy of the Politburo and the Central Committee and circumscribed by virtual rules of order. In fairness, though, I will say his power was based not only on a chaotic and rapacious vertical hierarchy of bureaucrats but on the omnipotent, regimented party apparatus and thus was more inviolable than that of today's president. The Russian republic thus created is most like a constitutional monarchy but it is not a dynasty, which is why Yeltsin has come up with the thought, which he has expressed with charming candor, that "a successor must be prepared" and citizens must become accustomed to him.

Our president will have the right to chair sessions of government and, in essence, lead it, like the president of the United States, but he will also be able to dissolve parliament, like the French president, although for more simple reasons. On the other hand, he will not have the equivalent of the U.S. Congress, which cannot be dissolved for any reason and which is equal to the president. He will also avoid the

French president's obligation to assign the formation of a new government to the leader of the party securing a parliamentary majority after national elections.

Whereas, for example, ambassadors appointed by President Bill Clinton must be confirmed by Congress, President Yeltsin will appoint them only after an ill-defined "consultation" with parliamentary committees. As for the appointment of cabinet ministers, unlike Presidents Bill Clinton or François Mitterrand, our president does not even have to consult with parliament. Ministers are not selected by the prime minister, who essentially is appointed by the president; they are appointed both de facto and de jure by that same president.

The Russian president may also suspend the laws of the Russian constituent states within the federation until the Constitutional Court accepts a case for review of the constitutionality of those laws; in this respect he assumes the role of conducting a preliminary judicial hearing.

The parliament will not have to trouble itself with overruling a state of emergency or martial law declared by the President. The president has merely *to inform* parliament about the imposition of these measures.

Nonetheless, there is a clause for impeachment, although an unprecedented miracle must occur—the Federation Council does not have the right to invoke it and the Duma may invoke impeachment only by a two-thirds vote. The Duma cannot make a final decision to impeach the president, since rulings by two different courts are required, whose members are to be proposed by the president and who are not appointed for life, in addition to a specially created commission. Grounds for impeachment cannot be an ordinary crime committed by the president but only "state treason or another serious crime."

I suppose that for impeachment ever to happen in Russia, the full moon would have to fall on a rainy Thursday.

Finally, just so that the "guarantor" would not be offended even by the above provisions, the entire impeachment procedure must be completed within three months. If you do not meet the deadline, tough luck. With a ninety-day statute of limitations, even "state treason" can be forgiven.

Critics of the Constitution are startled by the fact that the president may dissolve the Duma after three consecutive refusals to approve his appointment of a prime minister. And what of the fact that after three—no, after only *two* tries the Duma may be disbanded! All that is required is that it get the idea *by itself* to pass a vote of no-confidence in the government. After the no-confidence vote, though, nothing, not a darn thing, happens. The president doesn't even have to sneeze.

But if the Duma deputies, fearing nothing and scorning death like samurais, give a second vote of no-confidence within three months—well, what then, surely *something* happens? Not quite. In that case the president is required to focus on the situation and either send his prime minister into retirement or, the opposite, send the Duma to the devil's grandmother and call for elections ahead of schedule! Thus the Duma may express its disfavor of the government only by committing hara-kiri, triumphantly falling on its sword.

It will be interesting to see how many times in the course of the whole historical period that the new Constitution will be in effect that the Duma will want to use this mechanism to make its own modest contribution to the "determination of the fundamental directions of domestic and foreign policies."

Constitutional Illusions, Political Traps

I have left out another topic, just as important—federalism. I will note only that the list of administrative units of the former Russian Soviet Federative Socialist Republic (RSFSR) within the USSR, like the list of the fourteen subjects of "joint jurisdiction," exhausting all conceivable and inconceivable spheres of governance, is not, in my view, sufficient so as to say with assurance that there really exists some kind of federation in Russia. The list leaves no place for any *definite spheres* (nowhere mentioned in the text) of jurisdiction of *only* "subjects of the Russian Federation" (compare Art. 73) It is as if they are saying, everything else, which will be "given," that is yours, gentlemen subjects, and it shines on in "the entire fullness of government power." Meanwhile, unitarian, *central* power is *called* "federal"; at least under Communist Party rule, they did not use this word as a cover.

Finally, there is a definition of the composition of the upper chamber of the local legislative and executive powers, that is, essentially, the *appointment* of Russian "senators." All this should be seen in the context in which governors themselves are appointed to regions once again by the president; that is, there is a lack of separation between local and federal power. Article 77.2 states that in this unlimited joint jurisdiction, "the federal bodies of executive power and the bodies of executive power of the subjects of the Russian federation form a single system of executive power in the Russian federation." All of this gives reason to doubt that our "federation" has ever left the RSFSR.

The federation has only to be constructed some day by holding several regional referenda, creating it anew, and investing it with meaning. This method would amalgamate the regions (oblasts) on the basis of the referenda, in the manner of the German *Länder* or the Indian states, with a very high degree of internal governmental sovereignty.

This Constitution, however, which is anti-Soviet in form but very much Soviet at the level of its political comprehension, and which is tightly protected by Section 9 of the preamble, apparently foresees no further movement of history.

I believe this Constitution is a senseless trap, a potential source of new conflicts and upheavals. Some people ask: "What if such an authoritarian Constitution should be used in time not by Yeltsin, but some other, less nice person?"

Indeed.

In fact, even Yeltsin was elected in one of the republics of the USSR when the term "president" had a different meaning. The transitional clauses of the new Constitution, however, provide for Yeltsin's remaining president until 1996.

I am the first to admit that Yeltsin has not thus far gravitated toward dictatorship. In fact, he has a great many virtues. But, as Prime Minister Viktor Chernomyrdin put it, "He and I have a similar background." Therefore our president is capable of exploding like an angry boss during one of his "walkabouts" to "meet with the people" and firing a local meat plant director on the spot because of high prices and the shortage of sausage. With an even grander gesture, he may announce that he is returning Andrei Rublev's famous *Trinity* icon to the Russian Orthodox Church, thus confiscating it from the Tretyakov Gallery. It never even occurs to the president that laws and courts exist for such matters.

So I think to myself: why lead a person with such a mentality, who is unwittingly and inevitably a product of a career in the party nomenklatura, into temptation? He has already committed an unbelievable number of very grave mistakes (including promoting Ruslan Khasbulatov, Aleksandr Rutskoi, and Viktor Barannikov, the former head

Ministry of the Interior). Why, indeed, lead such a man, who is, on the whole, a nice fellow, lively, despite his background, into the severe temptation of a new Constitution? Why not avoid the devil and all his works?

But things have already gone too far. What's next?

"Let it begin, the Russian delirium," the Russian writer Aleksandr Blok once wrote.

Thus we now have an illegitimate president and as a consequence of a real innovative spirit we have a Constitution imposed upon us by that president. We now have a kind of mirror-image of Soviet "constitutionalism." It is a more authentic kind of constitution than the previous one. Nevertheless, because of the political expediency that shaped it, its elite provenance, and the fraudulence of its "approval" by the people— in short, because of our lack of a civil society—it is still an illusory constitutionalism. It is more like a politicians' show than serious politics.

We have traveled a journey of thousands of miles from the tsar's autocracy of the turn of the century, from Stalin, from Leonid Brezhnev —and even from perestroika—but how far we still are from reaching the end of the twentieth century!

My friends object: What's all this romanticism? What do you want? Straight to democracy after the tanks shelled the filthy White House? And people who write for the newspapers, who conveniently accommodate themselves to the new government, for those louses, different from the Russian intelligentsia, the main thing is *always* to strut around and assert themselves in opposition—in opposition to *any* government, whatever its nature and whatever the circumstances, without analyzing that government's actions.

That is not true, of course. Many people, following Sakharov's example, declared their conditional support of Gorbachev. Only when Gorbachev finally retreated from his reform program did Sakharov say, before his death, that it was necessary to move to the opposition. In the same fashion people spoke of conditional support of Yeltsin, and when those conditions were not fulfilled, they had to withdraw their support. I myself only arrived at such a decision, publicly stated it in the summer of 1992, and had to stand in opposition to Yeltsin. (Nevertheless, on the morning of August 19, 1991, and in the evening of August 20, as well as September 21 and October 4, 1993, without the slightest hesitation one had to be on Yeltsin's side—and I really was on his side then.)

It does not pay to consider the domestic members of the Russian intelligentsia (there are not that many of them) to be "eternal oppositionists," thick, obstinate people, or even complete idiots. All they have done is logically formulate what for millions of people remains largely at the level of an attitude or swear words.

Russia and the West—A Widening Gap?

In 1988, in *There Is No Other Way,* the anthology prepared by many of the leading figures of the liberal intelligentsia at the time, I called myself a "gloomy optimist." Now I would say that I have become a resigned pessimist.

I have the impression that after August 1991, we somehow missed a turnoff, where a liberal-democratic alternative could have been some kind of reality.

Russia could not help but move slowly, with pain and difficulty. But what is important is the direction in which it is moving. I may know that I have to walk two hundred more miles on foot, but at least I have to know that I am headed in the right direction.

Perhaps something that depended on the quality of political energy and organization is now irretrievably lost. Some overall outlines of the economy and the system of government have already been traced. We still keep thinking: just a little bit more, and then somewhere, just around the corner, something different will start happening, something more serious and real.

I ask myself: What if it never does start? What if we now embark on a period that could drag on for ten or twenty years, never bringing stability, when authoritarianism will become a regime that is fundamentally new compared to the previous, totalitarian-party regime but that is a kind of next evolutionary stage of that regime? Can we employ here the concept of the "Latin American version" of development?

Are there similarities—a delayed type of development of the market and capitalism, in a very impoverished and archaic society with primitive roads and infrastructure? Is the difference that our Russian backwardness is not of the colonial or feudal type but of the posttotalitarian type, with a powerful military–industrial–raw materials complex? We see the leading role of state capitalism (there you have the "special Russian path"), the same kind of *compradore* bourgeoisie made up of financiers

and commodities brokers engaged in grafting capital onto the bureaucratic, indestructible system of government corruption. And finally
there is the shadow economy, which overlaps with the criminal under-
world. All these elements turn out to be integrated somehow, a large
percentage of the population makes a profit, although opportunities
for medium-sized and small business are limited.

It is not clear how "Latin Americanism" will get along with Russia's
military-industrial complex; the interests of one part of the ruling class
may clash with the interests of another. The difference is that Latin
America fell into its rut during classical capitalism and is now starting to
climb out of it. We will be in a somewhat similar situation at the end of
the twentieth century. I am afraid that as a result, the gap between
Russia and the West will be even greater than it was under Brezhnev.

Even so, private shops and computers will pop up everywhere in our
country, and the rate of inflation will be stopped at an acceptable level.
I do not expect an economic disaster. Our people have developed an
amazing ability to adapt and survive. It is now much easier than it used
to be for sane people with initiative to make deals. Profits are possible.
And people have begun to do business.

But the problem is that fifteen years from today, the West will be
something we cannot even imagine now. If Russia turns out to be un-
competitive in the major areas of industry, its lagging behind will become chronic and it will grow stagnant.

As a result of such slow movement—but movement of some kind at
least—by the year 2010 our standard of living will be on the level of, say,
Europe in the 1960s and 1970s. With such a slow form of evolution in
such a gigantic and unevenly populated country, however, there will be
all sorts of imbalances: between the top and bottom segments of society,
between the developed and the backward regions—not to mention the
ethnic problems and the tense and critical belt of the Commonwealth
of Independent States surrounding Russia.

All these problems could lead to temporary aggravation of the growing imbalances in various areas. Here my pessimism grows more acute.
Political instability can hardly be expected to diminish under these
circumstances.

Just a year or two or three ago, many of us were expecting there to be
hunger and civil war in the country and practically the end of the world.
Now it seems the doomsday has been canceled. That is wonderful, but it

does compel us to wonder what we will have instead of the day of judgment. It is hard to believe that there will be steady progress and a decent life in the near future.

No, there will be something else.

Translated by Catherine A. Fitzpatrick

Notes

1. For a contrasting analysis of the December 1993 Constitution, see the essay by Alexander Yakovlev in this volume. —H.I.

2. See Leonid Batkin's article in *Novaia zhizn'* (New Life), no. 17 (April 1993), for an earlier statement of his views, upon which he has drawn for this essay. —H.I.

9

Galina Starovoitova

Modern Russia and the Ghost of Weimar Germany

During the period of transition from the old world order to the new one, which has not yet established itself, and with the advent of newly independent states on the Eurasian continent, it is quite natural for the inhabitants of the multinational Russian state, and especially for the nearly 150 million ethnic Russians, to ask themselves the eternal questions of being.

As more changes affect the world map, Russians are faced with finding their place not only in terms of geographical coordinates but also in history, among European and Asian civilizations and cultures. Traditional myths, illusions, and stereotypes are being replaced by new ones; Russian society is subject to rapid stratification, with each stratum addressing the problems of political sympathies and antipathies in its own way and asking questions about the criteria of the ethnic identity, openness, or isolation of a future Russia.

Some people are nostalgic about the past—about the times when the Soviet superpower ruled supreme and instilled fear in the whole world—while others are striving to join the family of civilized Western democracies, and still others are confused, disappointed, and apathetic.

Although systematic sociopsychological studies of post-Soviet society are just unfolding (science itself is in a severe crisis), surveys of the behavioral patterns of large groups of people during elections, referenda, and formation of political parties, as well as an analysis of a wide range of the print media, and, finally, reflections on history allow us to draw some conclusions about the changes in the world outlook and mood of the Russians as the world itself changes.

Russia Between Asia and Europe

Throughout the ages, in the course of the historical development of culture and social thought in Russia, two orientations, two cultural models derived from European and Asiatic civilizations, have always fought each other. Ancient manuscripts tell us that Grand Prince Vladimir, who baptized Russia, faced the same choice. Having received envoys who described the different forms of worship among Muslims, Jews, and Christians, he decided that Christianity (in its Byzantine interpretation) would be Russia's choice. Thus Vladimir determined Russia's millennium-long link to European values, to the Western understanding of good and evil. Prince Yaroslav the Wise, who had his children marry members of European royal families rather than Iranian or Chinese princes and princesses; some heretics among the clergy; Tsar Alexei Mikhailovich, to say nothing of his son, Peter the Great; and writers such as Denis I. Fonvizin, Nikolai Novikov, Petr Chaadaev, Vissarion Belinskii, and Aleksandr Herzen can all be characterized as advocates of the Western path of development.

In our century the most ardent adherent of the liberal ideology of the West was Andrei Sakharov, who in the 1960s put forward the concept of convergence. Even among those who preached messianic views of Russia's unique path of development (for example, Moscow as the Third Rome) and among the Slavophiles, there were outstanding thinkers, both religious and secular, such as Aleksei Khomiakov, Petr Kireevskii, Ivan and Konstantin Aksakov, Vasilii Rozanov, and, perhaps, Fyodor Dostoevsky. In our time it is Aleksandr Solzhenitsyn who is most closely associated with the issue of Russia's "uniqueness."

Both the supporters of Russia's "unique way" and the Orientalists have long criticized those who advocated a Western course of development. In reply to such criticism, Petr Chaadaev wrote in 1836:

It is true that we live in the east of Europe, but nevertheless we have never belonged in the East. And now a new school of thought— oblivious of what the West has done for us, showing no respect for the great man [Peter the Great] who made us into a civilized nation has come to the fore, denying both Europe and that great personality. Carried away by such a frenzy, this kind of newly fledged patriotism is hurrying to declare us all the beloved children of the East. What's the need for us, they preach, to be educated by Western nations? Didn't we already have all the necessary prerequisites of a social system that is incomparably better than the European one?[1]

Thus the isolationists of 150 years ago used the same arguments against the reformers that are being used in Russia today. "I have never learned to love my country with my eyes closed, my head bent down and my mouth shut," Chaadaev declared to "the newly fledged patriots." He added: "The time of blind love is gone. Now our primary debt is the debt of truth to our Motherland."[2]

Aleksandr Pushkin, who could not love his country blindly either, took issue with Chaadaev:

There is no doubt that the Schism [within the church] has separated us from the rest of Europe and that we have not taken part in any of the great developments which have been shaking it, but we have had our special mission. It was Russia with its endless expanses that absorbed the Mongol conquest and thus Christian civilization was saved. To achieve this goal we had to exist in a unique manner: we remained Christians, but at the same time we became alienated from the Christian world. This is how, as a result of our martyrdom, Catholic Europe could make energetic progress without any hindrance.[3]

Professor Ralf Dahrendorf of Oxford, a contemporary historian, contends that the cultural boundaries of Europe coincide in the East with the former borders of the Ottoman and Byzantine empires and also with the divide between the Roman Catholic countries and the Orthodox ones.[4] Notwithstanding the political and economic reforms in Eastern Europe, Dahrendorf sees no immediate prospect for these "genuinely European" borders shifting eastward. He seems to attach too much significance to the cultural heritage derived from Greek Christianity, which accorded precedence to the interests of the state over those of the individual.

Pushkin's observation cited above suggests a parallel with the idea nurtured by the eighteenth-century French Enlightenment thinkers, specifically Montesquieu, who attached much importance to the geographic factor in history. Indeed, after Ivan the Terrible in the sixteenth century the Russian state progressed mostly through territorial expansion, which proved detrimental to the development of the newly acquired lands and the creation of a civil society. Nikolai Berdiaev wrote in 1915:

> The efforts of the people whom we tend to view, and not without reason, as focusing on their inner, spiritual life are subordinated to the colossus of statehood. The interests of creating, supporting, and protecting an enormous state occupy a unique and dominant place in Russian history.[5]

Berdiaev also referred to the special "power of space over the Russian soul." It is that same power over our souls that today seems to make so painful the loss of lands that Russians customarily viewed as the outskirts of their own country. Many Russians find it hard to reconcile themselves to the theory that geography is the main outcome of history. However, despite the dualism of the Russian mentality, which is based in deep-seated historical and geopolitical roots, the majority of Russians (we shall speak about the minority later) have in recent years shown an affinity with the values of Western democracies. The striving to express their will in free elections and their views in the independent press; respect for the free will and self-determination of other nations; the desire to exert influence on government policies, to exercise civil control over the power structures of the state, and to be full masters of their property; to say nothing of the right to travel freely inside the country and abroad—all these features inherent in an open society have emerged in Russia after seventy-five years of totalitarian rule (in fact, the lifespan of three generations!) with amazing speed.

In my opinion, the unarmed people who came out against tanks and submachine guns during the August 1991 coup to defend their newborn democracy are the best evidence that Russia is part of Europe. And the same people who voted in the April 1993 referendum for carrying on the painful but inevitable economic reforms made it clear once again that the Russians are Europeans, perhaps even the most patient of all Europeans. The well-known poem by Fedor

Ivanovich Tiutchev is quite popular among the opponents of this viewpoint:

> *Russia is understood not by the mind,*
> *Nor by a common rule.*
> *She has a special stature of her own:*
> *In Russia one can only believe.*

But the practice of developing a market economy and the first steps taken toward a civil society in Russia are giving the lie to this poetic assertion. Rational ways *can* be applied to this country, too. The Russians are just like any other nation, although no country is without its specific traditions. The institutions of Western democracy and market models are working in Japan, a "unique" and exotic country, so why can't they be reintroduced to Russia?

The essence of the liberal model of governance consists in minimizing the state's interference in the economy, culture, and private life of citizens, leaving as much room as possible for every nation to display its ethnic and psychological originality. It suffices to watch the activity of the new entrepreneurs in any Russian city or to read the independent press to understand that our people are not inclined to embrace some kind of Oriental tyranny. Although they are suffering the inevitable hardships of the transition period, they nevertheless greatly appreciate the new opportunities that have opened before them.

From the Empire to the Commonwealth?

It would have been impossible to liberate people from totalitarianism without granting independence to the former USSR republics, which had been fighting for that independence with varying degrees of persistence. Six republics of the USSR did not take part in the March 17, 1991, referendum on the future of the Union, and they did not intend to sign the new Union Treaty worked out by Mikhail Gorbachev and other leaders in Novo-Ogarevo, outside Moscow. The results of the vote in favor of the Union were, in fact, rigged. The votes cast by citizens of the "disobedient" Soviet republics, such as the Baltic republics, Moldavia, Georgia, and Armenia, were excluded from the 100 percent base used for subsequent calculations, although the question asked in the all-Union referendum had been substantively reworded for those republics and the votes cast in Ukraine and Kazakhstan were added to the affirmative replies. As a matter of fact, the sovereignty of these two republics was made conditional on their remaining within the USSR.

As a result of that trickery (in which the leaders of the former Supreme Soviet of the USSR played a part), the government could claim that more than 70 percent of the voters who went to the polls cast their ballots in favor of preserving the Union. Meanwhile, in major cities and in republican capitals, the proportion of affirmative answers varied from 31 percent in Ekaterinburg to 50 percent in Moscow and St. Petersburg, and the percentage was even lower in Lvov (western Ukraine), for example. But the actual percentage of the entire population of the former USSR (approximately 300 million) who said yes to the USSR remains a mystery.

That vote-rigging strategy explains the contradiction (which puzzled the West) between the returns of the USSR-wide referendum and the results of referenda on the independence of the former Soviet republics held later in 1991. Two events played a decisive role in the collapse of the Soviet empire: the failed August coup, when, as one Russian politician put it, "The imperial center committed suicide" by thwarting the Novo-Ogarevo talks on the new Union Treaty; and the December 1 referendum on Ukraine's independence. The size of the Ukrainian vote for independence came as a shock to most Russians as well as to the Union leaders. (A week before the referendum, Mikhail Gorbachev had declared sharply that it was absolutely impossible for Ukraine to secede; his pronouncement undoubtedly boosted the number of votes for independence as a counterweight to "imperial pressure from the center.")

The idea that the Russians were "the elder brother" in the family of the Soviet nations, which had been preached over the years, undoubtedly bore bitter fruit. Since the time of Stalin, the policy of Russification and assimilation of the USSR nationalities, as well as attempts to create an interethnic community called the Soviet people, who would speak a nationwide language, had taught the average Russian to look down upon the cultural specifics of other nations, to consider them as vestiges of an archaic past to be overcome on the way toward the integration of all nations. The assimilation of the Slavic nations—the Ukrainians, Belorussians, and Poles—as those standing closer than others to the Russians, was pursued with particular assertiveness. The ethnic characteristics of these nations were ignored; their languages were deprecated as distorted variants of Russian.

Ukraine's stand has raised the question of Russia's own self-determination. Acting largely out of habit, the ethnic groups living in the conflict-ridden regions of the former USSR as well as the ethnic minorities elsewhere that are exposed to discrimination—including Russians who have found themselves outside Russia, Tajiks, Ossetians, Abkhazians, Armenians, and the Trans-Dniestrian and Gagauz residents of Moldova—continue to appeal to Russia. They hope that Russia will have to formulate its policies in the former Soviet republics with an eye to retaining the support of its "geopolitical friends," with due regard for the traditional cultural, religious, and economic ties with Russia and with a commitment to the continued use of Russian as the lingua franca and the ruble as the standard currency unit.

However, both ordinary Russians and the politicians have become increasingly confused. The formulation of a new foreign policy concept proceeds haltingly.

Over the last four centuries, Russia has existed not by itself but only as the central domain of a multinational empire and thus has had no chance to concentrate on its internal development—a point that Aleksandr Solzhenitsyn recently made. The Russian Federation, moreover, appears to be no less multinational than was the Soviet Union. According to the latest census, it is inhabited by 126 nationalities comprising distinct racial and linguistic groups and devotees of many different confessions, including Muslims, Jews, and Buddhists. Interethnic tensions have been acute in the North Caucasus and in southern Siberia, a fact that prompted the authors of the new Russian Constitution to focus on the principles of federation deriving from the equality of the subjects of the federation, irrespective of the ethnic makeup of their population.

At the USSR Congress of People's Deputies in 1989, the Siberian writer Valentin Rasputin, an advocate of nationalistic views, responding to charges of "Russian imperialism" advanced by the envoys of the Baltic and Transcaucasian republics, threatened that Russia could choose to secede from the Union—a statement that was recognized as a way of cutting off further attacks by "the younger brothers." Shortly thereafter, the First Russian Congress of People's Deputies unanimously adopted on June 12, 1990, the Declaration on the Sovereignty of the Russian Federation (then no more than a geographic part of the USSR). The democrats and the communist nomenklatura voted together, although they must have had different views of how a sovereign Russia, weary of carrying its imperial burden, would benefit.

After the August 1991 coup, democratic Russia voluntarily gave up its role of the "elder brother" and recognized the independence of the new states. But Russia's position was ambivalent on the question of the inviolability of the existing borders between the republics of the former USSR. These borders often criss-cross ethnic territories—for example, those of the Ossetians, Lezghins, Buryats, and Armenians. The borders have never been drawn in accordance with international standards, often exist only on maps, and cannot be identified on the ground. Twenty-five million ethnic Russians suddenly found themselves émigrés against their will, and under a flawed principle of collective responsibility they have frequently been made scapegoats for the past wrongs inflicted by the empire on indigenous peoples. Russian nationalists and procommunist chauvinists have capitalized on this discrimination to promote their call for the restoration of Russia as a superpower. Vladimir Zhirinovskii made a special appeal to members of the Russian Diaspora during the December 1993 election campaign.

The exodus of Russians from Tajikistan, Azerbaijan, and Chechnia and the adoption of discriminatory citizenship laws in Latvia and Estonia cannot but worry public opinion. However, measures to protect the rights of ethnic Russians living outside Russia (like those of other ethnic minorities who, out of habit, expect Moscow to protect them against the local authorities) have encountered difficulties because of recognized principles of international law, notably those of noninterference in the internal affairs of sovereign states and inviolability of existing borders proclaimed in the Final Act of the Conference on Security and Cooperation in Europe (CSCE) in 1975.

Despite the new political realities and recent changes in the political map of Europe (the reunification of Germany, disintegration of Yugoslavia, breakup of the USSR, separation of Czechoslovakia, and partitioning of Cyprus) the inviolability-of-borders principle is still invoked by many (CSCE) states with regard to "unpleasant" cases of peoples expressing their will—in Kosovo, Krajina, Macedonia, South Ossetia, and Nagorno-Karabakh—in order to avoid confronting difficult problems. Moscow's leaders, however, find it more difficult to dismiss the appeals of the peoples of the former USSR because, like much of the population inside Russia, they feel that Russia's responsibility for the destinies of the peoples of the former empire cannot vanish overnight. When imperial powers withdraw from trouble spots in their colonies without helping to resolve the conflicts there, the international community inherits conflicts that simmer for decades (consider, for example, Pakistan and India, South Africa, and Palestine).

At the same time, Russian society generally (and part of the country's top leadership) is unwilling to recognize that the disintegration of the USSR was the result of a logical historical process. Instead, they cite the results of the rigged referendum of March 17, 1991. These political forces prevent the formation of a consistent, democratic policy on the nationalities issue and with respect to countries of the "near abroad." Part of the military leadership defied the civilian authorities and took part in armed clashes outside Russia in Trans-Dniestria, Abkhazia, and Tajikistan. Moreover, North Ossetians who were ethnically Russian fought together with South Ossetians against Georgians; Chechens and other North Caucasians backed the Abkhazians; Ukrainian mercenaries often fought on the side of Georgia and Azerbaijan, while Russians of different political persuasions have fought on opposite sides in the conflict between Armenia and Azerbaijan. All these actions complicate the problem of Russia's federal structure by aggravating the cultural and religious contradictions between its peoples.

Federalism in Russia is a complex problem of long standing. In the 1820s the Decembrists supported a federal structure, although their proposals did not take national criteria into account. The first post-revolutionary Constitution of 1918 introduced what amounted to a territorial-national principle within a federal structure, granting a measure of independence both to territorial (regional soviets) and ethnic-territorial entities. Thereafter, under the constitutions of 1924, 1936, and 1977, a federal-autonomous structure prevailed in the USSR and in the Russian Federation.

Three basic structures of multinational states are known in international history:

- the unitary state, in which ethnic minorities have no real self-government and are politically and economically subordinated to the preeminent nation while preserving their cultural and linguistic features (for example, China, India, and the USSR);

- an asymmetric federation, in which some regions receive special rights and a significant degree of independence within a federal framework (for example, Puerto Rico and the Virgin Islands in the United States);
- a federation of equal entities irrespective of the ethnic groups in their population (for example, the new state structure of Spain).

After the conclusion of the 1992 Federative Treaty, Russia embarked on the second road because some republics (Sakha, Bashkortostan) joined the federation on special terms, whereas others (Chechnia and Tatarstan) refused to sign the treaty and were engaged in negotiations with the center. However, these special demands of the national republics inside Russia sparked sharp opposition from the major regional leaders of Russia proper whose districts included major industrial and cultural assets, notably St. Petersburg and its environs and Ekaterinburg. The fact that several Russian regions proclaimed themselves to be republics prompted the Constitutional Conference, which was then drafting the new Constitution, to include a clause on the equality of all the constituent members of the Russian Federation and to delete the provision conferring the status of sovereign states on the national republics inside Russia.

The wounded pride of ethnic Russians, who make up 83 percent of Russia's population, also played a part in the decision to opt for an asymmetrical federation. At the same time, the military and civilian officials who were engaged in managing the ethnic conflicts flaring along the periphery of Russia were inclined to back whichever side (as in Trans-Dniestria and Abkhazia) favored the restoration of the USSR. The actions of these officials undermined trust in what the new Russia professed to be its foreign policy and delayed the emergence of effective administrative structures in the Commonwealth of Independent States (CIS). Nostalgia for superpower status and for political stability has strengthened the position of the antireformist elements in Russian society, especially in the army and navy, as manifested in the results of the parliamentary elections in December 1993.

Ideological Vacuum in "Weimar Russia"

The collapse of the communist system revealed the inherent weakness of internationalism as part of Soviet ideology. In practice the empire divided peoples into first-rate and second-rate citizens and fostered covert or overt xenophobia. The citizens of the closed Soviet society were told that they were living in the world's freest country, surrounded by hostile rivals. The world, in this archaic appeal to primitive and medieval consciousness, was divided into friends and foes. These deeply ingrained xenophobic stereotypes were inevitably reflected in the relations among the peoples of the USSR and on occasion became part of proclaimed government policy, as, for instance, official anti-Semitism during the crusade against "cosmopolitanism" in the late 1940s and early 1950s.

As the former idols toppled, communist ideology began to give way to nationalism, a process facilitated by the diffuseness of moral standards among large sections of Soviet society, which had been taught to put a class-oriented morality above universal human values. Relativity in the definition of moral imperatives permits the use of any means to achieve a goal. The high-ranking conspirators in the abortive August 1991 putsch were ready to use violence and spill blood in order to preserve the Soviet Union. Russian chauvinists who join forces with hard-line Communists in the National Salvation Front are prepared to resort to similar means.

Opinion surveys have revealed that support for the National Salvation Front varies from 8 percent to 20 percent in different regions—a minority of the population to be sure, but a minority that is ready to act resolutely and defy the law (witness the street clashes in Moscow on May 1 and in early October 1993). The aggressive antireformist wing commanded a disproportionately large number of seats in the former Supreme Soviet of Russia. The Russian Unity faction, for instance, brought together procommunist army generals, collective farm managers who feared privatization of land by peasants, members of the former Party nomenklatura, and the new Russian nationalists.

It will be recalled that the former Supreme Soviet was elected in the spring of 1990, before Russia's independence and before the repeal of Article 6 of the Constitution, which had officially vested the monopoly of power in the Communist Party; thus this body did not represent Russia's more pluralistic society. How representative the parliament elected in December 1993 will be is difficult to tell, since it was elected by about 53 percent of the electorate.

Although opponents of reform constituted less than half of the population (about 30–40 percent, judging from the results of the April 1993 referendum and opinion polls), they had a majority (more than 70 percent) in the former Supreme Soviet and today hold about one-half of the seats in the State Duma, the lower house of parliament.

One can note certain parallels between the Russian opposition movement today and the coalition between right-wing and left-wing extremists in Germany that eventually brought the Nazis to power. Like Russia today, the Weimar Republic was stricken by economic crisis and burdened with a sense of national humiliation. Defeated in World War I and deprived of its colonies, Germany found itself divided along new borders.

Like Russians today, Germans were experiencing a crisis of ethnic identity as a result of alterations in their political geography and reappraisals of their recent history. Nazism and communism alike exploited traditional ethnic values and historic events (whether the Nibelungen saga or the victories of Alexander Nevsky and Ivan the Terrible over Russia's Western neighbors). As a result, in our day Russians as well as Germans have come to associate the ideals and symbols of patriotic unity with totalitarian regimes. Russia's new democratic authorities can ill afford to remind their citizens of such ideals, whereas the Russian chauvinist opposition calls for a restoration of a regime that can whip up patriotic fervor and once again help the nation survive a time of great difficulty.

The most recent break with the Soviet past is undoubtedly much more drastic than that which occurred under Nikita Khrushchev's reforms or even under Mikhail Gorbachev's perestroika. Rapid social change has had a demoralizing effect on Russian society (in varying degrees, this observation also applies to the East European nations, as suggested by growing crime rates and the revival of profascist organizations). Expectations of an economic upsurge in Russia—in particular, the expectation that the wealth and privileges of the Communist Party would be equally divided among all citizens, a typical reaction for *homo sovieticus*—have failed to materialize. The old social values and standards have turned out to be false, but people were brought up on them and have no substitutes at hand.

Meanwhile, the new values are strange and not very clear. What does democracy mean to the ordinary person? Does majority rule really prevail when a minority has the right to fight for power and engage in endless mutual recriminations in the independent press? Clearly, that is not enough to provide a meaningful or inspiring vision of a new world order worth defending. The institutions of a democratic civil society, backed by the power of the state, are only beginning to emerge in Russia. In moral terms, the bloody events of October 1993 undoubtedly dealt a blow to the democratic administration in Russia, which had to resort to undemocratic actions.

Furthermore, people see that in many places, especially in the vast provinces of Russia, power remains in the hands of the members of the old political elite, who are not inclined to repent of their past actions. Contrary to some Western predictions, the fact that the indigenous Russian people suffered more from the totalitarian regime than the populace of other CIS countries has made it no easier for Russians to discard the communist legacy. Fortunately, the danger of a Russian version of the Nuremberg trials—judicial proceedings against the Communist Party of the Soviet Union (CPSU)—was averted by the decision of the Communist judges of the Constitutional Court in November 1992.

The pain and controversy that have accompanied the implementation of laws on lustration of former government officials in Eastern Europe and East Germany is one obstacle to the submission of similar legislation to the Duma, although many Russians support such a bill as a safeguard against a "comeback of the nomenklatura." The Democratic Russia movement approved a draft law on lustration at its congress in 1992, provoking a public debate on the subject and leading to the adoption by the former Supreme Soviet of legislation protecting records on secret informants of the security services from public disclosure.

In the period when liberal Russians secretly admired the dissidents who were ready to risk everything for the sake of freedom, many persons were confident that the West, with its advanced traditions of democracy, was the embodiment of the ideal of justice and would rush to support the defenders of freedom. Many in Russia, Armenia, and Ukraine believed that in the world on the other side of the Iron Curtain there existed some supreme councils of moral arbitration that would return a fair verdict on the fate of Armenians in Nagorno-Karabakh, Abkhazians in Georgia, and Tatars in Crimea, and would even pass judgment on the fates of individual political prisoners. The main problem, their human rights advocates believed, was to brave all risks and tell the truth about individual and collective violations of human rights to the United Nations, the European Parliament, and the CSCE. When the Iron Curtain came down, many private individuals in the West did demonstrate a readiness to help build a new society in Eastern Europe and Russia. Large and powerful states, however, preferred to wait and see how events would develop.

The fact that the West has assumed a guarded attitude instead of delivering prompt verdicts on human rights issues has disappointed Russian "Westernizers." The citizens of newly liberated countries are often more sensitive to human rights violations than people in the countries where the principles of defending human rights were first formulated.

Western leaders and experts often advise Russians to follow the example of General Augusto Pinochet in Chile and Deng Xiaoping in China—make the transition to a market economy but retain the coercive political system before allowing civil liberties. Apart from being morally unacceptable to Russians, that strategy could not have been implemented because no transition to a market economy in Russia would have been possible without first dismantling the authoritarian power structures. Advice of this kind, however, created among Russian liberals a certain mistrust of the Western democracies and provided ammunition for politicians in the mold of Vladimir Zhirinovskii.

Like Hitler in Weimar Germany, Zhirinovskii was not taken seriously in the early years of his political career. But he skillfully turned the confusion in people's minds to his own purposes and came up with a demagogic platform that promised something more than cheap vodka—to make people's lives meaningful again through the revival of the great empire.

In the spiritual vacuum following the collapse of communism, Christian and other denominations in Russia could have played an important role in restoring the system of values. But all the religions, having initially attracted many converts, seem to have exhausted their potential for increasing their flock. Their exhaustion has several causes. First, educated people who have for seven decades been brought up in the spirit of rationalist atheism find it hard to fall back on metaphysical spiritual experience. Second, many church hierarchies (including the Jewish and Muslim clergy) were exposed as former KGB agents, and people lost trust in the church. Third, the Russian Orthodox Church, while preserving the sumptuous liturgy it inherited from Byzantium, has been deficient in preaching skills and has failed to offer the faithful an answer to their fundamental questions. In the early months of 1993 the Russian Orthodox Church lodged a claim to an exclusive position in the state, seeking to ban the activities of missionaries and preachers from abroad, probably fearing competition in the struggle for souls. Some members of the church hierarchy openly support chauvinistic or isolationist ideas and align themselves with Russian nationalists, and this inclination also tends to diminish the potential social base of Orthodoxy in Russia.

The period after the August 1991 coup brought much disappointment, both because the pace of reform was slow and because real fruits of the painful "shock therapy" were lacking. As can be seen in Eastern Europe (notably Poland) and in Lithuania, Georgia, Azerbaijan, and Tajikistan, many voters, weary of the turmoil of recent years, are ready to vote for prosocialist parties. The same phenomenon has occurred in Russia. But the success of the nationalist Liberal-Democratic Party (LDP) —which has nothing in common with either liberalism or democracy— came as a surprise for most people in Russia.

Observers underestimated several important factors, including the hardship that economic reform brought to large sections of the population; the reaction to the humiliation of having 25 million Russians outside Russia and watching the rapid "parade of sovereignties" of the national republics within Russia; and, most recently, disenchantment with the democratic authorities who failed to prevent a bloody conflict during the October 1993 rebellion in Moscow. During those days, when the use of force turned out to be effective, Russians' belief in the feasibility of achieving a synthesis between morality and politics was shaken.

These factors evidently contributed to the failure of the democrats to win the victory they had expected in the December 1993 Russian parliamentary elections. These factors may also explain why opponents of the Western economic model voted in such large numbers for one of the most extremist parties in the political spectrum.

Nationalistic and neofascist parties, while not uncommon, usually conduct their activities underground. At present Russia may be the only country that permits such a party—the LDP—to become a legal parliamentary faction and, consequently, to have access to the parliamentary rostrum, television, press, and public opinion. The seed of fascism in Russia has fallen on fertile soil. New growth is to be expected soon. It is well known that the size of a tree is not proportionate to the size of the seed from which it developed.

One cannot say with confidence that the awkward preelection struggle between the embryonic political parties and the hastily organized elections presented a mirror image of the new Russia; more likely we saw a bitter grimace on its distorted face. The comparison of today's Russia to the Germany of the interwar period is nevertheless instructive: when Chancellor Paul von Hindenburg transferred his authority to Hitler, the world did not know what the future held. The present situation is different in the sense that fascism, *Kristallnacht*, and the gas chambers have already occurred. One hopes that the world community remembers this lesson and that it possesses an instinct of self-preservation sufficient to set limits on the principle of noninterference in the internal affairs of other countries by defining special conditions imposed by the nuclear reality of Russia.

In Germany in 1933 and in Russia in 1993, the majority of those who voted for ultrarightists did not realize that they had voted for future fascists. However, many Germans afterward claimed that they did not realize what they were doing when they operated gas chambers and carried out orders. They could not understand why they were placed on trial after the war.

Russian fascists, in their own minds, are also prompted by a noble idea: the revival of their once great and now oppressed country. The parliamentary elections held in Ukraine in March 1994 will probably register the support of an appreciable part of the population for the far right. In Russia, however, of the votes recently cast in territorial districts and for party lists, Russian nationalists received only about 12 percent of the votes and the Communists 11 percent.

Nonetheless, the drama that took place during the December elections destroyed the liberal illusions held by many democratic parties; they are ready to join forces upon receiving the first warning signals and create a reformist coalition in the Duma, where at the moment the contending forces are roughly equal.

In the meantime, it will be very important to determine which political groupings or leaders the 47 percent of the disenchanted population that did not appear at the polls on December 12 will support. Whom are they inclined to follow? Where are they turning their eyes—toward the West or toward the East? We remain with no answer to the classical question posed by Nikolai Gogol to the Russia of the nineteenth century: "Whither then, are you speeding, O my Russia? Whither?"[6]

Translated by the Federal News Service

Notes

1. Petr Chaadaev, *The Apology of a Madman*, in *Russkaia ideia* (Moscow, 1992), pp. 42–43.
2. Ibid.
3. Aleksandr Pushkin, "A Letter to P.Ia. Chaadaev," in *Russkaia ideia*, p. 60.
4. *Boardbook of Lufthansa*, October 1992, p. 41.
5. N.A. Berdiaev, *The Soul of Russia*, in *Russkaia ideia*, p. 299.
6. Nikolai Gogol, *Dead Souls*, quoted in Richard Hare, *Pioneers of Russian Social Thought* (New York: Oxford University Press, 1951), p. 85.

10

Denis Dragunskii

The Sign of Our Times
Democracy, Authoritarianism, or . . .

In late 1991, as I surveyed the specific alternatives that were available for carrying out market reforms in the economy and democratic reforms in political life, I reached a conclusion that for me as a democrat was anything but pleasant:

> At the start of the reforms [I wrote], a clear minority of our fellow countrymen will live in a reformed world, in an oasis of the market economy. Perhaps only one-tenth of the population will work in modern enterprises and live in houses that generally meet Western standards, earn a decent wage, buy food of good quality, have a car, and enjoy medical care, education for their children, and social security. The inhabitants of this privileged circle will even enjoy a much broader range of legal rights. The reforms will have secured a legal as well as a political and social bridgehead.

Elsewhere in that essay I wrote: "In the reform era the army must provide real protection for the frontiers of the first oases of the market economy. Bluntly put, the army must protect the rich from the poor."[1]

These statements drew a rebuke from both the communists (in *Pravda*) and the democrats (in *Izvestiia*). Unfortunately, events in Russia thus far have been developing along the lines of that bleak scenario.

However you may assess the Moscow bloodshed on October 3–4,

1993—whether as an armed uprising by the anti-Yeltsin group or as a carefully planned government provocation carried out on a grand scale against the opposition (which I personally find difficult to believe)—the meaning of what happened is clear. The authorities used the mailed fist to suppress resistance to radical economic reforms.

Resistance? Whose resistance? It would be naive to think that, except for the power-hungry former deputies to the Supreme Soviet, the rest of the Russian people embrace tough budgetary policies and favor a strong presidency and a unitary state. Although television is full of comforting opinion polls, many ordinary people firmly associate market reforms and the policy of democratization with declining living standards, the disintegration of the country, and ethnic conflicts. For them, reforms in Russia mean hunger, national humiliation, and war. The situation is somewhat eased by the new abundance of consumer goods in the market, but one must remember that many people cannot afford to enjoy this abundance. At least half of the population lives below the poverty line, and that proportion is rising ominously.

It serves no useful purpose to call those who came to defend the Supreme Soviet building "lumpens," "the mob," or "the herd," as some progressive journalists did during the days of the October bloodshed. Aside from being undemocratic and inhumane, this attitude shows political blindness. It is above all the millions of "lumpens" who make up the voting majority. If the political authorities and the ideological machine that caters to their needs continue to push the "lumpens" to the sidelines, the reaction of desperation will not be long in coming.

By the way, Stalin's regime exhibited a similar contempt for the peasants in the early 1930s. Maxim Gorky referred to them as savage, ignorant half-humans and half-animals who had to be made over or destroyed for the sake of the future industrial paradise. In all fairness, it must be said that Stalin's repressions against enormous numbers of people in the course of collectivization and industrialization had the goal of modernizing backward Russia. But the modernization was never completed, it never went beyond the phase of building the "giants of socialist industry," and it did not bring economic prosperity to the land. Most of the people were turned into "slaves of socialism" and barred from economics and politics.

The situation today is not the same, as market reforms are relentlessly pursued. People are bidden to be "slaves of the market" temporarily, while they retain their full economic and political rights and therefore have the opportunity to break through to the "bright realm of the market economy," thus extending that realm. The crux of the matter, then, is political guarantees. But the political results of the victory of the reformists in October boil down to this: one military-bureaucratic-industrial group (with its main power base in the federal center) dislodged another group (also military-bureaucratic-industrial, but having its principal power base in the regions, the so-called subjects of the federation). A new phase in the war for the Soviet heritage began, a war for property and power left without a master since the breakup of the USSR and the collapse of the Communist Party of the Soviet Union (CPSU).

The former proprietors (the directors of state enterprises, who use and dispose of "the property of the whole people" according to "custom and usage") are trying to legitimize their possessions. Together with the new property owners (the *nouveaux riches* of Russian business), they are making a bid for political power. The power structures—members of the old party and government nomenklatura (who still retain their positions) and those swept into power on the wave of democratic reforms —seek to control or possess property. Criminal organizations, ranging from underground business enterprises to illegal paramilitary units, play an active part in these struggles. After October 1993, the redivision of property and power began.

Analyzing this process is a task for the future, but one can already see that amid the "struggle among the giants," the safeguards for a socially responsible diffusion of wealth and free enterprise for ordinary citizens who are outside the above-mentioned groups are minimal—unless one considers the street vendor to be the chief protagonist in the market economy. The question, then, is this: can the crushing of the October revolt be seen as a victory for democracy? First, one has to define democracy. If democracy means democratic procedures and declarations of democratic goals, then the answer must be in the affirmative. But the reformers themselves have chosen to introduce democracy by highly undemocratic methods. Thus, in the context of present-day Russia, democracy, rather than providing the *norm* (that is, the rules of political conduct), is a *value* (that is, a matter of conviction and sympathies) shared only by certain social groups. The democratic values of some groups are imposed as universal norms on other groups that actually share a different set of values which they, too, consider to be democratic.

To cite but one example, under the new electoral law, elections are valid if 25 percent of the registered voters turn out at the polls. No such threshold exists in the advanced democracies. If all others were to decide, of their own free will, to boycott the elections, the vote would nonetheless be considered valid if even one voter cast his vote.

The Russian political mentality, however, has always prized "unanimity" and set great store by the opinion of the "overwhelming majority." That is why the foregoing provision of the electoral law (as well as the majority system rules) is seen as an official trick and has given rise to grounds for political speculation. Already there has been an outcry in the newspapers: "We are going to be ruled by people who represent the interests of 12.5 percent of the population. Is that democracy?"

Moreover, democratic procedures and democracy as a modus vivendi are entirely different things. Democratic procedures may accompany, cloak, or directly bring to power the most brutal of regimes. I am convinced that democracy is not just a form of government but a life-style based on inner commitment to goodness, tolerance, dialogue, nonviolence, and, of course, to conscientious work. This life-style has been formed over the centuries in the civilization of Europe and North America on the basis of an enlightened religious consciousness, and it has inherited the basic moral norms of ancient Greece. That is why it cannot be legislated into being by any government decree which is "valid as of the time of signature."

A character in one of Mikhail Saltykov-Shchedrin's tales warned that "enlightenment should be introduced with the least possible amount of bloodshed." In Russia, in those days of October 1993, blood was spilled in another attempt to "introduce democracy." On balance, then, the simple answer would seem to be that Russia has embarked on the road of authoritarianism.

It is true that because of its authoritarian elements, the new Constitution proposed by Boris Yeltsin offers an easy target. For instance, the president has the effective right to dissolve the Duma if the latter fails to back his candidates for top political posts, and to form a new government. This provision renders meaningless the very idea of conducting elections according to party lists and, consequently, the multiparty system in a parliamentary democracy.

The idea that in Russia only authoritarian rule can provide safeguards for democratic reform is one that many of our political scientists find attractive. Without examining the substance of that thesis, let me say that on all the evidence the "enlightened authoritarianism" approach has no roots in present-day Russian reality. An authoritarian regime, however variously that concept may be interpreted, nonetheless implies that a ruling elite controls society and the state. Curiously, people need reminding that authoritarianism needs to have a state—a unit of territory, a distinctive population, and the kind of political power that cannot be questioned by the populace or by officials at any level of the political hierarchy.

In today's Russia such prerequisites do not exist. The authorities, at least at this time, have little control over the situation in the country. The provisions of the new Constitution designed to stop ethnic, political, and regional disintegration are unlikely to work over the longer term. The government administration has no internal unity and represents an unstable balance between central and regional elites battling each other for control over territory, resources, and the population and for the right to impose taxes, customs tariffs, and export quotas. Russians themselves have no sense of national (all-Russian) identity and therefore no adequate notion of what constitutes their national interests, although both components are essential if an authoritarian leader is to gain nationwide support.

The violence that sporadically erupts in Russia is caused not by the authoritarian tendencies of the government but by its weakness. The authorities resort to incoherent repressive measures because operational law enforcement machinery, and even the state's traditional authority, is absent. Russia's freedom today stems not from democracy but from the lack of effective central rule (*bezvlastie*).

If we are not a democracy and not an authoritarian regime, then what are we? First let us think back a few years.

From *Politeia* to *Perestroika*

We have witnessed what is arguably the most significant event of history within memory. We have seen the logical conclusion of social utopianism, which started with Plato and his regimented state and was crowned with the achievement of "advanced socialism" under Yuri Andropov and Konstantin Chernenko.

The word *perestroika* (restructuring) fits well into the terminology of communist propaganda, somewhere between *piatiletka* (the five-year plan) and reconstruction. But I think it should be spelled in Latin letters, and not in Cyrillic, because it implies much more than a restructuring of politics and economics. It was the drama's final act, the burning at the stake of faith in a great utopia, the crisis of communism both as a geopolitical reality and the personal experience of hundreds of millions of people.

That event transcends history and therefore cannot be reduced to the sum of political, legal, or economic acts of restructuring. Similarly, Plato's *politeia* is a term denoting not just a governmental system (the literal Greek translation), but world reason as embodied in the perfect state.

But two qualifications are in order. First, the geopolitical collapse of communism has affected only the Europe-oriented community to which Russia (the former USSR) belongs, albeit with certain important reservations. China remains a bastion of communism. If you look at world history from the Chinese point of view, the games the "large-nosed white people" play occupy only a modest place in its pages. Second, the crisis of communism does not signal its death. Indeed, there is every reason to fear that as a result of the profound changes in the European labor market provoked by perestroika, communism (and more generally the political left) will resurrect itself as the ideology of the dispossessed.

Even so, perestroika helped a great many persons in the USSR and in much of the rest of the world shed their illusions about communism.

Second, perestroika managed to prevent (or to significantly put off?) a world war that was all but inevitable while a communist nuclear super-power existed on the planet. And finally, perestroika brought about the collapse of the last empire and its belt of satellites as the peoples of the USSR and Eastern Europe gained freedom and independence.

These transformations, though beneficial and redemptive in a historical perspective, have had most grievous consequences in the short term. The collapse of an entire life-style, impoverishment and social stratification, the emergence of focal points of instability, the brutalities of civil war, the refugee problem, and mass emigration—all these are compounded by a profound spiritual crisis being experienced by hundreds of millions of people. What makes the present trials and those to come almost unendurable is the collapse of basic values—to put it briefly, the collapse of faith in the good and in justice.

This collapse is also a logical consequence of the crisis of communism. The communist idea is by no means original. Quite the contrary, it reflects the main elements of the European social structure: *equality* (the redistributive function of the state) and *fraternity* (the humanitarian aspect). But under "real socialism" in the USSR these ideas were overblown to become a travesty of themselves and were put in the service of socially despicable individuals.

This is not to condemn such individuals, although nothing could be easier than to curse the people who repudiated God and arrogated to themselves the right to dispose of other people's wealth and lives. The Russian version of socialism fitted neatly into the matrix of an intimate, filial bond between the individual and the state. Socialism ended up as a reversion to an antiquated paternalism that, for understandable psychological reasons, is deeply embedded in human nature and is rooted more strongly there than democracy and freedom.

In Russia, in particular, paternalism was the dominant mode of political behavior. Fyodor Dostoevsky, in his message of greetings to Alexander II, resolved in quintessentially Russian style the conflict between freedom and power: "The Russian man's freedom is the freedom of children gathered around their father." Before the Bolshevik Revolution, the church was part of the establishment, and the people had an ignorant and slavish faith in a God identified with church, tsar, and fatherland. The Reformation, which Europe experienced in the sixteenth century, did not become possible in Russia until the early twentieth century. But it came too late to stop socialism. Under socialism the Orthodox Church tried to take an independent anticommunist stand and thus became an obstacle to the individual Russian's filial attachment to the state. The Russian people responded by destroying churches and murdering priests (at least the majority of them did nothing to prevent these actions).

But here is the paradox! The very qualities that we correctly described as socially inferior—passivity, apathy, and civic obedience—helped the Russian people to survive under socialism. One cannot condemn people for living under a regime that gave sustenance only to the meek, the obedient, and those who considered passivity to be a virtue. To this day, despite all the proreform propaganda, words such as "aggressive," "smart," "businesslike," and "entrepreneurial" carry a negative connotation.

Under "real socialism," the main function of the state as represented by its officials became the redistribution, plunder, and redivision of wealth. Fraternity in the name of equality took the form of secret denunciations and executions. Nevertheless, the two ideas survived as a myth that justified what was happening in terms of certain higher principles that, verbally at least, coincided with traditional European or Christian values. That myth has now vanished. Only *liberty* has remained, that liberty which until now has lived quietly in the shadow of equality and fraternity, mindful that it was nothing but a "conscious necessity."

"What is this freedom which so agitates men's minds in our time, which prompts so many crazy acts, so many crazy speeches, and brings such hardship to the people?" asked Konstantin Pobedonostsev, that tireless and relentless critic of democracy under Alexander III as well as Nicholas II. Freedom in the democratic sense, he went on to explain, means freedom to participate in running the state, but "only an infinitesimal part of this right belongs to every individual. How will the individual use it?"

The Russian citizen who has lived through perestroika has chosen to keep freedom for himself and use it for his personal ends.

Privatism: Watchword of the Era

What is happening in Russia is usually described as a "postcommunist" ("postimperial," "posttotalitarian," or "post-Soviet") process. Giving an object an accurate name goes a long way toward understanding it. I find that definitions with the prefix "post-" are unsatisfactory because they say nothing about the substance of the new process and its distinguishing features.

The Swiss politician and writer Numa Droz (1844–1899) is credited with introducing the term "étatism," or statism, signifying the triumph of centralized governance over freedom and individuality. The fullest embodiment of étatism is socialism, under which the state systematically acquires control over everything. Be that as it may, étatism has until recently provided the only civilized model for the development of human communities.

Étatism provided the basis for the spiritual identity felt by the nations of Northwestern Europe, a sense of belonging to the civilization of the democratic North, a point of reference of very high standing. Its horizontal structure is provided by Judeo-Christian morality (the commandments of Moses and the evangelical "golden rule" [Matt. 7:12]), and its vertical structure by the redistributive function of the state. These coordinates of the European social structure engender a political morality that is based on faith in the justice of the authorities and the kindness of one's neighbor. In recent decades, that structure has come under heavy strain from all quarters, because developing technologies no longer correspond to social institutions and changing social institutions diverge from traditional political morality. Moreover, the genocide perpetrated by Hitler and Stalin raised doubts about the effectiveness of the gospel of brotherhood, while the political, economic, and moral dead end of socialism demonstrated the inherent dangers of the doctrine of equality.

Perestroika and the ensuing chaotic shifts of power and property on a vast geopolitical space finally put into question statist values and paved the way for a new model of civilization—privatism.

Privatism, defined in general terms, is a mode of political behavior based almost exclusively on the will of the individual. A privatist community is structured along much more complex lines than is a statist one. If étatism endures because of the strength of the supporting beams, privatism endures because of the bond that cements the individual bricks.

Privatism came into being when it became possible for the individual to survive without the daily tutelage of a state that had willfully restricted his freedom. In a society with long-standing democratic traditions, privatism is achieved through striking a balance between freedoms and restraints, ultimately reaching a balance of interests. In its mildest form privatism is known as liberalism, which has been criticized on the grounds that liberal democracy "leads nowhere." Thus it can provoke a political reaction that can assume the form of a resurgent statist ideology, a reinvigorated government apparatus of repression, violent nationalism, and the like. In its crudest form, instead of a balancing of interests, privatism gives rise to power games. Russia's recent political experience, indeed, suggests that "power" is no metaphysical concept but has a brutally direct meaning.

From a common sense point of view, privatism is the child of European postindustrial society, which has these features:

- It has mastered high technology, notably in the information sphere. The computer, radio technology, and even the telephone have done more for individual freedoms than all the declarations on human rights. Communism, it was often said, would be destroyed by the personal computer, or by computer networks. In the late 1950s computers were unknown in the USSR, but the short-wave radios that did become widely available at that time began to destroy communism.
- It has attained the point of its ultimate development, the limit beyond which social structure becomes meaningless. Paradoxically, a socially oriented state creates the illusion that it is no longer needed, or, more precisely, that the kind of loyalty embodied in a patriotic and filial relationship to the state on the part of its citizens is no longer needed. The state becomes depersonalized— a process that flows directly from the development of social safeguards and the rights of the individual. A person (citizen) owes nothing to anyone, except perhaps to himself as a representative of the very electorate that has established all these safeguards.
- Families have comparatively few children, and the labor market is not overcrowded. Note that families with comparatively few children do not generate paternalistic and collectivist values. Privatism is best fostered in the contemporary family.
- Political and economic rights are extended more broadly in the nation, while capital, goods, services, and people move freely across state borders.

But there is a danger here. People cannot move from one job to another with absolute freedom, driven only by economic expediency, because this movement may strain the national labor market and in turn lead to the rise of protectionist forms of nationalism.[2] If absolute freedom of movement is realized, it will create a new political reality that will promptly be dubbed "poststate" reality, although it would really mean privatism in the context of how large communities operate.

By the way, this danger is fast becoming a grim reality in the former USSR. Migration processes have already upset the traditional ethnic and social balance in a number of regions, leading to outbursts of racism and a soaring crime rate. The state institutions, including the police and internal security agencies, have proved incapable of controlling the situation.

Why Russia Again?

For seventy-six years Russia became a test range for the building of "socialism as the highest form of étatism," although neither its government institutions nor the level of its economic development augured well for the success of the experiment. Now privatism is having a field day in Russia, of all places, while in the advanced industrial democracies it is still only a trend.

Northwestern European civilization is based on two principles inherited from antiquity: conscientious work and fair competition.[3] This genetic code has built into it the mild, liberal development of Northwestern European privatism as summed up in the dictum: "Work and compete and God will help you."

The assertion that Russia belongs to Northwestern European civilization requires a caveat. On the one hand, Russia belongs to the West historically and culturally (in some respects Western culture has been molded by Russia: Fyodor Dostoevsky is the only world classic writer who is read and not just spoken about; Anton Chekhov is a favorite playwright in the West, and so on). On the other hand, the primitive and militarized Russian monarchy, the lack of civil and human rights, and the ignorance of a religious people stunted the growth in Russia of a genetic type of European civilization.

What is the code built into Russian civilization? It is: "Do nothing and God will save you." Mind you, not help, but *save*. Civilization, for Russians, revolves around the idea of salvation. When salvation is the order of the day, democracy and freedom are no longer viable options. Freedom thrives as prosperity grows, but the salvation of society derives only from totalitarianism.

It is no accident that socialism, based as it was on faith in somebody else's power as the safeguard for one's own miraculously granted prosperity, took root in Russia. The "spirit of socialism and the Russian Orthodox ethic" is a theme worthy of special study.

It was in Russia that étatism, carried to absurd lengths, shaped Russian political culture during the Soviet period. That is why the public reaction to the collapse of the state has proved so violent. It was in Russia that we have witnessed the dramatic convergence of privatism as a general trend of West European civilization with "privatization," a political measure to expel the government from the property it had held. Institutions that traditionally embodied the state as the source of all good have passed into the hands of private owners.

A central element in the Soviet mythology of the state was that everything was free (housing, medical care, education, vacations, and so forth). I remember that in 1973 Brezhnev made an eminently sensible statement: "We are accustomed to saying that many things are free in this country, but, comrades, they have actually been paid for by the labor of the Soviet people." Most people with whom I discussed Brezhnev's statement simply did not understand, or chose not to, that they were paying indirect taxes that were higher than anywhere in the world and that from this wealth they were being handed out tiny crumbs for social needs. People sincerely believed that they were getting everything from the great, mighty, and just state. To inquire how the state came by all this wealth was preposterous, heretical. The state had taken the place of God; it *was* God.

According to Dostoevsky, if God does not exist, then everything is permitted. If the state does not exist, Russia plunges into general permissiveness, since the communists had already dispensed with God.

I am convinced that it is privatization that has administered the greatest moral shock to Russians, a greater shock than the breakup of the USSR, the collapse of the CPSU, and the toppling of the old spiritual idols. That shock is all the greater because the populace is largely unaware of it. People buy, sell, and even invest their privatization vouchers, but in the process, socialist ideology is not replaced by an ideology of democracy and the free market, but by something very different.

Here we should ask why the ideology of a deferred future—building communism for the sake of future generations—worked in Russia for so long. Actually, the future was not deferred; people were satisfying their needs day by day, minute by minute. The notion, however, met a spiritual need. Now our souls are surfeited, or, more precisely, they are envenomed by the communist hogwash. The time has come for us to satisfy our more earthly and materialistic needs.

The buzzword in Russia today is "here and now" (*hic et nunc* in Latin, so "hicetnuncism" could be a fitting name for the new ideology). This emphasis is highlighted by the way business is conducted in Russia. It is dominated by speculative capital. I do not think it is fair to blame everything on the "unsound" tax policy of the government. It may well be that this policy was tailored to the interests of the speculators and middlemen. The so-called selling off of Russia—that is, a free-for-all trading of its nonrenewable resources or its national heritage—is not a myth put about by nationalist communists but a sad reality. Most of the profits are taken out of the country. Last year more top-of-the-line Mercedes automobiles were sold in Moscow than in any other capital. According to a security guard in one bank, its "owners reward themselves for every day they survive." To be a big businessman in Moscow in 1994 is as dangerous as being a ranking official was in Moscow in 1937. One was liable to be shot by firing squad, the other by his business rival.

At the other end of the social spectrum, down-and-outs sell their flats (an option that privatization has afforded them), spend their money on drink, and swell the ranks of the homeless in train stations.

Atomization

Russian privatism has the following political features:

- Civil (national) identity has been almost entirely lost, to be replaced by ethnic identity realized in the form of ethnocracy—the emergence of nationalist regimes across the former USSR and in Russia's autonomous regions. Moreover, ethnic interests now supersede civil interests. Congresses (parliaments) of the individual nations populating Russia have become influential political institutions. In the eyes of the ethnically mobilized masses, the decisions of these bodies are fully legitimate.
- The vertically integrated federal government structure, the division between central and local authorities, has been destroyed. Regional elites have claimed sovereignty and now control large chunks of property in "their own" regions. There is no reason to believe that these elites will voluntarily accept the significant limitations on their rights envisaged under the new Constitution.
- The central state apparatus behaves as a "private legal person" or, more exactly, as a multiplicity of persons who are sovereign and possess both property and power. At the same time, the state apparatus is fragmented. For example, the executive branch has a Council of Ministers and an administrative office of the president, but the powers of these institutions and their administrators are not clearly defined. There are three federal press and information

departments. New executive structures are mushrooming (according to observers, there are now many more federal bureaucrats on the payroll than during the Brezhnev era). Thus, the central (federal) state apparatus is only one of the participants in the "war for the Soviet heritage" and has to compete with the regional elites and other agents of the political and economic markets.

- Transregional economic entities—concerns and holdings that emerged from former industrial ministries and components of the military-industrial complex—play a special role. Controlling a large portion of the former "property of the whole people," they are in fact subordinated to neither federal nor local authorities.

- In addition to the defense ministry, the interior ministry and the security ministry both have their own large contingents of troops. One can only speculate about the degree of loyalty that each of these institutions has to the federal authorities—in any case, the October events raised many questions. However, they understand their own corporate or institutional interests very clearly.

- Illegal (or semilegal) armed formations have begun to play a special role. Russian cossacks and "national guards" operate in the individual republics of Russia. Many business and financial organizations have their own security services; each one might number several hundred well-armed professionals. Political parties, especially the nationalist ones, and, naturally, organized criminal gangs have their own combat units. Autonomous formations (for example, units of veterans of the conflict in Trans-Dniestria) fight in ethnic conflicts as mercenaries. It would be no exaggeration to say that Russia today is covered with a web of illegal armed formations. Alarmingly, both branches of government have independent security services—one of the factors that triggered the October clashes.

- Criminal structures are being legalized, and legal institutions are being criminalized. Corruption has become one of the major problems in society.

- Finally, one finds a tendency to divide the country into "zones of law." The mayor of Moscow has introduced a visa system for those who wish to visit the city. If bankruptcy procedures are accelerated and lead to mass unemployment, this visa control system could be applied not only to citizens of the former USSR who are not ethnically Russian but also to Russian citizens living in these regions. For their part, some regions in the south of Russia are taking measures to restrict immigration, thus introducing a kind of "regional citizenship."

Disrespect for the law as a standard of behavior on the part of those in positions of authority has elicited a corresponding reaction across the social spectrum. Morality has deteriorated. Established social norms and prohibitions are eroding rapidly.

The atomization of individuals and of state institutions has been accompanied by the atomization of political life. Party alliances and political movements are usually temporary and fragile. Lacking confidence in the partner's reliability, political groups cannot unite around a common platform.

The time that has passed since the putsch of August 1991 shows that the Democratic Russia movement, intoxicated by victory, failed to capitalize on its results. Petty infighting within the democratic movement has resulted in a comeback of party and state nomenklatura, who have changed their colors.

Communists, too, have failed to learn the lesson of their August defeat. For some time thereafter the Communist Party retained the aura of a "ruling party," even if only as a toppled colossus. The Communists had only to change their name (to, say, "the Party of Free Labor") and introduce visible elements of social democracy in their program. Had they done so, most of their members, including government officials, would probably have remained in a renewed and renamed Communist Party. Such a party could have become the most influential political force in the country.

Communists, however, have been plagued by the very same problems as their democratic opponents: endless splits, reshufflings, and mutual accusations of backsliding from principles. As a result, the Communist Party is doomed (at least in the near future) to remain an "opposition of those below." In the meantime, the former party and state nomenklatura has broken away from the control of *any* political force (that is, from the control of a party accountable to the will of the electorate) and has been transformed into a network of central and regional ruling clans whose actions are dictated primarily by banal economic interests. This is why their struggle for the "Soviet heritage" is so ruthless and uncompromising.

After the presidential decree of September 21, 1993, dissolving parliament, the opposition held all the trump cards. Had the antireformist forces displayed a little patience and common sense, political power, like an overripe fruit, would have dropped into their hands. Members of the Supreme Soviet should have donned the solemn masks of martyrs in the name of parliamentary democracy, left the White House at once, and begun forming a broad election coalition. Had they done so, the opposition would have won the election. Parliamentarians and their supporters, however, preferred atomization; they preferred to take the risk and act independently from each other and without coordination. The victorious reformers, too, failed to form a single election bloc that would have mobilized a solid majority of voters.

The absence of any mobilizing slogan for the nation is also a mark of privatism. As soon as a mobilizing slogan does appear, it would signal the counterattack of those advocating a return to statism. Moreover, all the institutions that are now flourishing under privatism—from regional elites to criminal armed units—will bitterly oppose any regime's effort to unite society. It is difficult to say which tendency will prevail. In all likelihood, Russia will continue to seek a path between statist nonfreedom and privatist permissiveness for a very long time to come.

Afterword: Implications for Western Policy

Developments in Russia cannot be assessed within the framework of traditional concepts of either democracy or authoritarianism. The country has seen the rise of privatism, that is, of social organizations that are beyond the control of state institutions. This trend could well lead to the emergence of a new model of human society. Thus far, however, events in Russia have been taking a dangerous turn, threatening its own citizens as well as the international community.

As a result of the surge toward privatism, the average citizen has been left to himself. In effect, he is a puppet in a vicious game for power—a bystander in the war for the Soviet heritage. If social stratification becomes more acute, it could play into the hands of those working for a communist restoration.

The erosion of state institutions, political authority, and family morality has turned Russia into a transshipment point for the export of arms, drugs, and contraband. Domestic instability, illegal armed units, and an uncontrollable domestic weapons market, all aggravated by growing nationalism, can stimulate new major conflicts within Russia along its borders.

Under these circumstances I believe that in framing its policies the international community should:

- Give Russia every opportunity to concentrate on its own domestic problems. Do not force upon it the role of a regional superpower, either as Eurasia's gendarme or as the guardian of order within the former USSR. This approach will give Russia an incentive to avoid participating in endless and exhausting border wars and could help to liberate it from the fatal idea of Russia's "special destiny."
- Introduce a greater degree of differentiation in carrying out measures of economic cooperation with Russia. Forge economic ties not with the entire state, but with its separate economic and political regions and entities. This approach will encourage the development of privatism.

With all of its defects, Russian privatism may be the logical next step on the road toward overcoming the totalitarian legacy and finding the way to civil society and to real rather than formal democracy. Naturally, this road is very long. But Russia has already taken the short road.

Translated by the Federal News Service

Notes

1, Denis Dragunskii, *Vek XX i mir*, 1992, no. 1; see also *Novyi mir*, 1993, no. 1.

2. S. Sato, "Iaponiia o sebe i mire," *Konets XX veka*, 1993, no. 11.

3. For more on this topic, see D.V. Dragunskii and V.L. Tsymburskii, "The Genotype of European Civilization," *Polis*, 1991, no. 1.

HOW DO WE GET THERE?

11

Nikolai Shmelev

The First Phase of Economic Reform in Russia

What Can We Expect in the 1990s?

If the experience of the Russian economic reforms of 1992–93 has proved anything, it is that the most carefully crafted theoretical plans have a highly tenuous connection with life. Experience has also demonstrated that not one of the celebrated economic theories—classical Marxism, Keynesian economics, social market economics, or monetarism —has virtually any applicability to the conditions prevailing in Russia.

The realities of our daily life persuade us more and more that all we need today are the four rules of arithmetic and basic peasant common sense. If we lack anything, it is neither theories nor inspired strategic plans spanning a decade or even a century, but just a simple under-standing of the mundane everyday rules of life: Act not according to a theory but according to the rule of reason and specific circumstances, weighing every side of the issue, measuring results against efforts, and trying not to force life, but to conform and adapt to it.

What we need in Russia today is not an elegant, complete theory of reform but the utmost pragmatism, an eclecticism that corresponds to our specific Russian conditions, acknowledges what is expedient and possible under these conditions, and obeys only one paramount criterion: the utilization of the entire creative potential of society, whether visible or not.

Now that the early euphoria resulting from such a radical turn toward democracy, the market, and a civil society is wearing off, the sobering realities—our whole legacy of the past seventy and more years —become increasingly clear. On all the evidence, what we have undertaken will require not just a few years or even decades but no less than two or even three generations. If we understand our present crisis in terms not of our nation's death but of its rebirth, we can see that the crisis will be chronic and permanent for a long time to come. Russia will have to learn to live for more than one decade under conditions of this permanent crisis.

Long-Term Goals

Russia's movement toward a normal market economy has begun. Judging from all the evidence, and no matter what turn events may take, this movement has on the whole become irreversible. This conclusion does not, of course, exclude the possibility that this movement may slow down or even come to a halt for short periods. Given our historical legacy, Russia's future economy will probably continue to have a relatively heavy proportion of state-controlled industry, but it will undoubtedly be market-oriented and structured along the same lines as the rest of the industrial world.

The fundamental modernization of the Russian economy in accordance with market criteria cannot occur, however, without a solution to six strategic tasks extending in importance far beyond the present decade:

The *first* task is to change the predominant type of property ownership from public to private and establish a highly developed market infrastructure, including stock exchanges, an equities market, an extensive network of commercial banks, pension and investment funds, commodities exchanges, an insurance industry, mediation and legal services, and facilities for extending consumer credits. In rudimentary form all these exist already, but considering the scale of capital accumulation that will be needed and the sheer difficulty of organizing these institutions, we cannot expect rapid success.

The *second* task is to reconstruct our entire productive capacity, which for decades was geared to everything except the needs of human beings, including the thoroughgoing conversion of the defense industry to civilian production, the closing or gradual retooling of obsolete or inefficient plants (those producing raw materials and energy resources, as well as many in the metallurgical, machine-building, chemical, construction, and wood-processing industries), the widespread introduction of energy-efficient technologies, and a sharp reduction in the number of environmentally destructive industries. Tasks of this scale, affecting as they do at least half and as much as two-thirds of the country's enormous industrial capacity, require massive investments. Here, too, we are talking in terms of decades.

The *third* task is to restore agriculture, which was almost destroyed during the years of Soviet rule. Most of the collective and state farms, which have demonstrated their inefficiency and utter historical pointlessness, will undergo a process of slow, nonviolent death, to be gradually replaced by an economy of private farming. Here also, at least one generation will be required, and more likely two.

The *fourth* task is to unlock the country's enormous hidden manpower reserves and provide useful, productive employment. By many estimates, from one-fourth to one-third of the industrial workers employed today are redundant even by our technological standards. Naturally, given the social ramifications, this problem cannot be solved by using surgical methods, as it were. But in principle it *can* be solved: in Russia today about two-thirds of the work force is employed in production and only one-third in the service industries, whereas in all the industrialized countries the opposite ratio prevails. Clearly the redirection of manpower from production to service industries cannot be undertaken in one fell swoop; here again the task must be reckoned in decades.

Fifth, a market economy for so vast a country as Russia cannot be efficient without a well-developed road and rail system as well as extensive communications, telecommunications, and information systems. These, too, will require much capital investment and many years to establish.

And, *sixth*, Russia must gradually open its doors to foreign competition, in order to attract foreign investment capital; its economy must participate actively in world trade and the hard currency financial system. The Russian producer is not yet accustomed to fighting for his niche in international economic transactions; the Russian consumer is still not used to considering alternative products offered by the foreign market; and Russian society still looks askance at any foreign investor, viewing him as a curiosity rather than the norm. Although in this respect the Russian mind-set is changing with astonishing speed, I find no grounds for supposing that protectionism, in all of its many manifestations, will soon disappear.

For these reasons the 1990s may be viewed as a kind of preparatory stage, when the most serious effects of the prolonged domination of purely administrative relationships in our economy should be removed and the foundations laid for an accelerated movement toward a market economy.

The following tasks appear to have the greatest importance for the 1990s:

- restoring the full functioning of money and establishing fiscal equilibrium;
- introducing an effective system of taxation;
- privatizing most state-owned property and removing institutional and other barriers to private initiative;
- beginning to restructure industrial capacity and winding down loss-making industries;
- halting the decline in the production of consumer goods and then spurring its growth, meanwhile promoting the service sector;
- restoring an integrated economic space within the borders of most of the former Soviet Union;
- creating conditions so that foreign investment capital can begin to flow vigorously into the country.

Results of the First Stage of Reform

The first eighteen months of radical economic reform have been difficult, harsh, and inconsistent, but they have unquestionably yielded tangible, positive results in a number of important respects. Leaving aside the cost of achieving these results, certain fundamental changes in our economic life have occurred:

- In a country that had almost returned to the "stone age" of general barter, money—thanks to the lifting of price controls—has once again begun to function (even if sluggishly and unevenly).

- An awkward, agonizing, but vigorous process of privatizing state property has begun, and private initiative, primarily at the lowest and most primitive level of small-scale street peddling, has begun to take hold.
- Perhaps most important, the public mind-set has rapidly begun to change at the top as well as the bottom of society. The more socially active and influential members of society, especially the directors of large industrial enterprises, have finally begun to experience a taste for the market, a taste for independence. Together with this new interest has come the realization that reforms are serious, that there can be no turning back, whatever the lurches and spasms along the way toward a market economy.

Nonetheless, we cannot help but notice that from the outset, our reformers made a number of major mistakes that have had far-reaching consequences. Perhaps the most serious mistake was the excessively abrupt manner in which price controls were lifted, as a result of which the population and most enterprises for all practical purposes lost 99 percent of the savings they had accumulated as of January 1, 1992. By one means or another, the government should have honored the promises it made at the start of the reform. It should have provided at least some measure of compensation for the loss of these savings. But it did not. People do not soon forget such things, if at all. In the final analysis it is the people's trust in government that is the most important guarantee that reforms will succeed. In any event, this trust is the main reason why the public will agree to endure the inevitable hardships to come.

In my view, another mistake the team of reformers made was that it did not decide to decontrol the price of energy at the same time as prices were freed on all other types of production. In the spring of 1992, this step would of course have intensified the general shock from price liberalization, but not in any fundamental way; by the end of the year undoubtedly the public as well as the economy as a whole could have adapted to the new price levels for energy by one means or another. Once you have made up your mind to cut off the cat's tail, you must do so immediately, not bit by bit.

The third mistake—or rather, a case of plain bad luck—was that the reformers' nerves turned out to be weaker than those of the plant directors. The reaction of most of our directors to the freeing of prices was completely primitive, but, given all our traditions, it was absolutely understandable. Raise prices ten- or a hundredfold; produce goods not to be placed on the market but in warehouses; and wait until the state either buys your output at the new, higher price (which in most cases is a monopoly price) or writes off the indebtedness that bankrupt purchasers owe their suppliers through the use of budget subsidies and preferential credits.

If in the summer and fall of 1992 the government and the Central Bank had stood firm and permitted the least efficient plants to go bankrupt, the budget deficit and the inflation rate would unquestionably not have assumed the threatening proportions that they acquired in the second half of 1992.

Another fundamental flaw in the new reform strategy has been that, not by accident but by design, it paid insufficient attention to the potential represented by private entrepreneurial activity. While concentrating on the creation of joint-stock corporations and the privatization of the enormous state sector (a problem requiring many years to resolve effectively), the government has done practically nothing to encourage private initiative in production. In some ways it has even made things more difficult for those who had started or intended to open their own businesses. In dealing with new businesses, bureaucrats have clung stubbornly to the "permission principle" instead of the "registration principle." Rather than simply registering a new enterprise under relevant provisions of the law, officials deliberate at length among themselves over whether a given enterprise should be permitted or prohibited. The results: a monstrous scale of bureaucratic corruption in the country; a virtually prohibitive level of taxation; the impossibility of receiving long-term bank credits for investment; and a host of other problems.

Finally, some of the most important aspects of the reformers' foreign trade policy have had very painful results: exporters have been forced to sell half of their hard currency profits for rubles under conditions of galloping inflation (20–25 percent per month); hard currency accounts of many plants and individuals have been frozen as a result of the failure of Vneshekonombank (Bank for Foreign Economic Affairs)[1] in December 1991; and the regulations governing exports and hard currency transactions are marked by various unnatural restrictions. The result: a massive flight of the capital that Russia so badly needs today, in amounts far exceeding the incoming capital flow.

The main factor delaying the progress of the reforms during their first stage, it is generally believed, was fear—first, fear of a social explosion once prices were freed and most of the population was immediately impoverished; then fear of massive bankruptcies and the inevitable sharp growth of unemployment. Fortunately for the reformers, however, Russian society showed extraordinary calm and patience during the price liberalization, apparently having in mind the bitter experience of violence after 1917. The social explosion never came. But the fear of massive bankruptcies and high unemployment levels continues to prevail, and in my view this fear is now the main reason that the country's current leadership cannot find within itself the strength to reduce the budget deficit, to stop inflation, and to begin radical restructuring of the economy.

Fear, of course, is not the only thing that blocks reform. The most serious obstacles include the entrenched interests of the old bureaucratic structures in city and countryside alike; the public's residual hostility to the private sector; the peasantry's deep-seated distrust of change in any form (an understandable reaction in light of the betrayals it suffered so often in the past); the egalitarian, parasitic traditions of our entire society; the scale of government corruption and of organized crime; the paralysis of central authority; the explosion of narrow regional or local interests; and finally, the plain incompetence of many of those piloting the ship of state today.

In one respect, however, we see grounds for hope: all the diverse forces and interests in Russian society are still moving in a distinctly positive direction—toward democracy and the market.

Immediate Tasks

Without any question, Russia's dominant problem today is inflation, which for the last year and a half has at times hovered close to hyperinflation (defined as 50 percent a month or more).

There are those in our society who acknowledge the destructive role of galloping inflation but who nevertheless feel that its cause lies neither in monetary policy nor in the size of the current budget deficit but in the fact that the government permitted a decline of about one-third in Russia's gross domestic product during the 1990s. Closer analysis, however, makes clear that out of the overall 32–33 percent drop in production, at least 10 percent should be ascribed to the disruption of the economic links established under the now-defunct framework of COMECON (Council for Mutual Economic Assistance). Another 15 percent, approximately, should be attributed to the severance or reduction of production relationships among the former Soviet republics after the collapse of the USSR.

Thus 7–8 percent of Russia's current average decline in production derives from the inevitable difficulties that any program of serious economic reform would face, taken together with whatever decisions the government made. This percentage must be acknowledged as an entirely acceptable cost for making the transition from one economic system to another and for introducing such profound changes as, for example, sharp cutbacks in the bloated weapons industry. Moreover, since a significant portion of our industry requires basic reorganization, it is likely that some of the outmoded branches will see their production continue to fall for some years to come. In the meantime, it is a fact that the decline of consumer goods production has stopped. In my view this rebound can serve as a point of departure for a broader recovery, which in turn would signal that the economic crisis in its traditional sense has finally hit bottom in Russia.

Inflation

The drop in production is not the reason for the current level of inflation: under ordinary market conditions a decline in production is actually a powerful anti-inflationary factor. The primary reasons for inflation are the budget subsidies and preferential credits that are still being granted to an enormous number of unprofitable enterprises in industry and collective agriculture. A significant share of imported consumer goods receives subsidies as well.

Second, inflation is caused by the uncivilized, nonmarket behavior of our numerous monopolistic enterprises, which are artificially inflating prices without regard for the consumers' ability to pay, thus triggering a chronic crisis of mutual nonpayment among factories. Our sluggish banking system aggravates the problem.

Third, inflation is caused by the populist policy of both the legislative and executive branches of government, whose officials constantly make irresponsible, politically motivated promises to various sectors of the economy and society—promises that can be kept only by increasing the budget deficit.

Finally, inflation is brought about by Russia's continuing to subsidize the former Soviet republics through preferential prices and credits that for all practical purposes are not recovered. In this way, as much as 9–10 percent of Russia's gross national product is irretrievably lost each year.

Can the government halt galloping inflation in the next two or three years, before it completely destroys every incentive for normal work, for savings, and for anything resembling a normal investment process in the country? The government cannot stop inflation completely, I believe, because that task would require a much longer period of time, during which we must finish restructuring our economic base (at least in its general outlines); rid ourselves of most of the nonviable plants; and make sure that the hidden manpower reserves find useful employment, principally by stimulating the growth of private enterprise. Nevertheless, I think that in the next few years we can reduce the annual inflation rate to a more or less acceptable level of 20–25 percent monthly—provided, of course, that the government displays a sufficient degree of resolve and tenacity.

The loss-making enterprises and sectors of our economy must realize that the time for government subsidies and preferential financing of their inefficient operations is coming to an end. In the next two or three years they will be thrown entirely on their own resources, forced to sink or swim in the market. The government must finally bring itself (at least for purely instructional purposes at the start) to let loose a chain of bankruptcies in the least viable and most monopolized sectors. Nothing except the real threat of bankruptcy, it would seem, can change the myopic, irresponsible behavior of some of our managers, who are still convinced that even under market conditions the government will somehow pay the bill for their economic feebleness or their monopolistic appetites.

A strict monetary policy is inseparably linked with the government's need to practice utmost restraint in anything it says publicly, avoiding politically motivated promises. It follows that the parliament as well as the government must withdraw their promises of spring 1993 to compensate the public with "live money" for the savings that evaporated during the reform. If any compensation at all is feasible, it should only take the form of compensation in kind, not in cash.

Some of the government's recent anti-inflationary measures, together with its stated intentions, give grounds for hoping that inflation will be brought under control if not this year, then next. I have in mind primarily a kind of "anti-inflationary compact" between the government and the Central Bank that envisages definite limits on the size of the budget deficit, a tightening of the Central Bank's credit policy with respect to financing government expenditures as well as providing credit to commercial banks, an increase in the level of interest rates, substantial reductions in subsidies given to the "near abroad," and measures to increase infusions of hard currency to the domestic market. In addition, I would advise the decontrol of coal prices, steps to cut back coal and agriculture subsidies, curbs on the subsidies of imports, and restrictions on budget financing.

Even here, though, we should have no illusions. These measures constitute only the beginning of a serious anti-inflationary policy. Considering the extent of the populist promises already made by the government, there is no guarantee that we will not have to undergo another steep inflationary surge. Until the government breaks with the practice of keeping afloat our unprofitable industries as well as the economies of our closest neighbors, and until we can manage to establish an attractive interest rate that is the same for all types of borrowers, inflation with all its destructive consequences will undoubtedly continue.

Privatization and Private Enterprise

Another very important problem for the present stage of economic reform is to make headway in privatizing state property and creating conditions conducive to free private initiative. If we look at just one aspect of this dual task, we do see progress. The first, basically formal stage of the privatization of state property can be more or less completed in the next two or three years. But as for private enterprise in the deeper, classic sense, I detect no serious, positive moves. Furthermore, the recently enacted regulation requiring that any entrepreneurial activity be subject to government licensing authority means that the "permission principle" will only be applied more severely, and this application in turn will spread corruption further.

We can only hope that ultimately the logic of events will force the government to make concessions. For example, how, other than by using the private sector, can employment be assured for the millions of workers who will inevitably be discharged in the course of economic restructuring?

I am convinced that in a certain sense the government's attitude toward private entrepreneurial activity will be the key issue for the 1990s. Either we will have moved toward the market in earnest, or we will go on deceiving ourselves with various bureaucratic schemes like the current voucher game.

Ruble Convertibility

Although all price controls may be lifted in the next year or two (including those on petroleum, gas, electricity, and public utilities), price liberalization alone is not enough to restore the market to a relatively stable balance. In order for money to become both the end and the means of healthy competition, a convertible ruble must be the first priority. There is no hope for the existing highly inflationary, declining ruble; this conclusion is borne out by the absolutely unrealistic, purely psychological exchange rate in relation to the dollar.

Sometimes it seems to me, I admit, that the government and the Central Bank are deliberately trying to finish off the existing ruble, in order to eliminate the current national debt and the savings accounts of all ruble holders both in Russia and in the "near abroad," no matter what the cost, so that at some point they can issue a new, sound Russian ruble that will be convertible at a single fixed rate as soon as it is issued and that through free quotation will rapidly squeeze the old, "sick" ruble from the market.

If my suspicions are right, then I can only say one thing: better late than never. Without a *chervonets*, or hard convertible ruble, there will be no real opportunity to revive the investment process in the country, force producers to lower prices and compete for consumers, create a functioning system of labor incentives, and finally open up the economy and attract a serious flow of foreign investment capital, including our own capital that has fled abroad.

Tax Distribution

Chief among the tasks for the near future is to decentralize Russian finances and our entire system of economic management. For well-known historical reasons this problem has always been profoundly underestimated in our country. I am convinced that at the root of all the manifestations of separatism at the republic, regional, and district levels, there is the desire to receive at last their fair share of tax revenues based on the income generated in a given territory. If the ratio of tax distribution between Moscow and the autonomous subjects of the federation is not quickly established by law at approximately the average world level of 40 : 60 in favor of the localities, the latter will take arbitrary and unilateral measures to set the ratio at this level or at a level far less favorable for Moscow. Some members of the Russian Federation have already done just that.

One thing is clear: the tax ratio will be the subject of hard constitutional bargaining. In any event, the formula should favor the autonomous regions, but by the same token the major share of government spending should be transferred from the center to the localities as well. Such a trend should be viewed as no misfortune. Although the process is extremely strange to us, it is natural and beneficial. And if it should resist this trend, the Russian government will merely repeat the mistake made by perestroika's initiators.

The Predicament of Russia's Science and Research Potential

I am convinced that because of the reformist team's deeply flawed and inexplicable policies, the rapid destruction of our scientific and technological capacity (especially in the basic sciences)—which was perhaps our only indisputable national achievement in the last seven decades—has become the most grievous problem over the past year and a half. Two or three more years of such a policy, which actually has turned researchers and university professors into the lowest-paid members of society, and the damage, including that done to our defense research capacity, will become irreparable.

What assets do we intend to take with us into the twenty-first century? Even under normal conditions we will need at least two generations to recover from the damage that has been done. This suicidal policy, I am certain, must be stopped not in the coming years, but in the coming months. Otherwise we as a nation will revert for decades and generations to the backwoods of world history.

Unemployment

During the first stage of reform, the government's inflationary policy allowed it to keep unemployment at 1 percent of the whole working population. Obviously this level can no longer be maintained, otherwise all talk about the need for a sweeping reorganization of Russia's economic capacity will remain empty words.

It is understandable that our government and our whole society should fear serious levels of unemployment, on the order of 6–7 percent, should an effective anti-inflationary and organizational policy finally begin to be implemented. For a country that has not known unemployment for three generations now, having several million people out of work does indeed represent a great danger to society. But in actual fact we have no other choice.

That is precisely why the creation of a strong social safety net may be the single most important domestic priority of the 1990s. This safety net would mean in the first instance establishing a system of unemployment benefits, a program of public works, and a large-scale program for retraining discharged workers. Even at the present early stage of unemployment, retraining programs cover no more than 1–2 percent of actual requirements. Beyond that, however, I am profoundly convinced that a safety net would also mean above all the creation of highly favorable opportunities for the growth of small and medium-sized private enterprise in every area of industry, agriculture, and services. It is the private sector that in the near future will become the principal employer both of workers who have been laid off and of those who are entering the labor market for the first time.

An Internal Common Market

The breakup of the Soviet Union has made it morally unjustifiable and economically inexpedient for Russia to continue its traditional policy of subsidizing other republics with preferential prices and unrecoverable credits. In 1989–90 this "resources drain" cost Russia approximately $50 billion annually; in 1992 it fell to around $17 billion; and in 1993 and 1994, if the Russian government displays the necessary resolve, the loss could be reduced even further.

Meanwhile, after the euphoria following the Soviet Union's collapse and after many extremely painful economic setbacks, most of the former Soviet republics have begun to express interest in restoring a single economic region and reestablishing what once was a highly integrated economic relationship. This restoration, to be sure, should depend not on Russia's artificial support of its partners in the "near abroad" but on natural and mutually beneficial economic interests.

Today people say that in the 1990s a unified economic region or market over the greater part of the former Soviet Union will be restored, one way or another. But if it is to work, the reintegrated market area should have:

- a single, supranational hard currency, or at least an appropriate number of national but freely convertible currencies;
- a unified banking system with a common emission and payments center;
- a unified system of customs, border, and tariff regulations;
- a common infrastructure, including primarily electric power, transportation, highways, and communications;
- a common budget, however modest. Thus far, the republics have not embraced this concept, but I am sure that time is pressing them in this direction—and very swiftly at that.

The International Context

Further progress in our economic reforms is intimately connected with foreign economic factors. How successfully can Russia use its new opportunities for international cooperation?

Here not everything depends on what we do. But we should not count on making headway if Russia continues its policies of virtually discouraging rather than stimulating exports, maintaining strict export quotas, and levying inordinately high customs duties, which average 30–50 percent of world prices. Intolerable, too, is the requirement that 100 percent of export profits must be taken in rubles at the very time when the ruble remains nonconvertible and continues to fall. Is it of no consequence to us that billions of dollars have fled abroad as a result? The current tendency to increase import tariffs constantly on most imports, combined with the artificially low ruble exchange rate, constitutes an almost prohibitive tariff for many commodities.

Under existing conditions we can have no reason to hope for a serious flow of private investment capital from abroad. Despite all Russia's potential appeal as an investment market, serious private investors are frightened away by the political instability, the constant devaluation of the ruble, the lack of a stable legal framework, and the absence of a taxation system that would level the playing field for the domestic and foreign investor. If these obstacles are not removed, the 1990s may be counted as lost years.

Taking into consideration only the economic aspects of reform in Russia, and leaving aside the political dimension, there is little reason to hope that in the 1990s our leading Western partners will take decisive joint action to support us. Here the most that can probably be expected—and this step would in itself be extremely important—is continued deferral of debt servicing. The $6 billion ruble stabilization credit of the International Monetary Fund (IMF) could be most important, provided the Russian government succeeds in curbing inflation or finally makes up its mind to issue a convertible gold-based ruble parallel to the existing one. In my view, the notion of reducing to a minimum the customary government credits for investment and other purposes is exceptionally promising. We could shift to a normal credit system managed by Russian commercial banks functioning under market conditions. Since the Russian government has no funds for bank guarantees, nor it is likely to have them in the near future, Western governments would have to back this measure. Specifically designated credit funds, notably to assist small and medium-sized enterprises and to support Russian science, would be highly beneficial.

At the same time, there is reason to hope that during the 1990s the last vestiges of trade discrimination against Russia in Western markets will disappear. Certainly this is the most important precondition for Russia to play an active role as a full-fledged member of the world trade and financial system and of the leading intergovernmental organizations.

Recently, the media have discussed a plan under which a specially negotiated international agreement would exchange Russia's debt to the West—about $85 billion—for the debts owed Russia by other countries —about $145 billion. Although politically and technically extremely difficult, this idea is unquestionably attractive.

Another idea, which is equally unconventional but may be more feasible, is to have the West provide credits to some of the former Soviet republics in order to purchase petroleum and other energy resources from Russia at world prices. Without such outside support, these new states may not be able to survive the inevitable transition to world prices in their dealings with Russia.

Conclusion

During "the events" of October 3–4, 1993, the Russian government probably reached its greatest point of instability. After these events, the threat of a total civil war has subsided, although a period of aggravation of turmoil is possible, and even quite inevitable, at the level of the individual autonomous republics, regions, branches of industry, and social groups. With the ratification of the Constitution on December 12, 1993, we can expect that a distinctive type of semiauthoritarian, semi-democratic government will be installed in Russia. This regime will be fairly severe, but nonetheless it will maintain a policy of observing basic human rights and moving toward the market.

Obviously, the events of the last two years demonstrate that the collapse of the Soviet Union—at least in economic terms—was a temporary phenomenon. Left to their own devices, with Russia's subsidies sharply reduced, all fourteen of the former Soviet republics have proved to be economically nonviable. Even those republics with a certain economic stability, such as Turkmenistan, have accomplished this objective primarily through Russian aid or, like the Baltics, through aid from both Russia and the West. Given all the political and psychological complexities of this process, the restoration of an integrated economic region on the scale of the former Soviet Union (with the possible exception of the Baltics) is only a matter of time, perhaps only a few years.

The long-term interests of the West or of the world community as a whole would not appear to be served by obstructing the processes of reintegration within the boundaries of the former Soviet Union, particularly given all the military, political, and economic ramifications were such obstructionist measures to be taken. Instead, the West would see its long-term interests better served by encouraging the emergence of some kind of new, free, and democratic Confederation of Former Soviet Republics. The republics would be oriented toward their own problems, but at the same time they would be organically included in the entire fabric of contemporary international relations.

It is becoming increasingly clear that in the near future the West should stop altogether any current or investment credits to the *government* of Russia (except those earmarked for financial stabilization purposes).

The main issue today is to provide an effective stimulus to the Russian private sector and greater incentives for private foreign investors. First, opportunities must be expanded for Russian entrepreneurs to receive long-term investment credit at commercial banks. Second, foreign investors in Russia must be insured from various types of risks. Neither of these goals can be achieved through the Russian government's resources alone. Therefore a definite change is needed in the West's credit policy. Except for the fiscal credits, all other credits must go directly to Russian commercial banks or enterprises. Unlike the customary commercial practice, these must be backed by Western government institutions.

Of course, the West should no longer provide unconditional assistance to reforms in Russia. But the nature of the conditions, including those set by the IMF, should be substantially altered. Judging from recent events, such changes are warranted: Russia is unlikely to endure a second round of shock therapy without any sort of social "anesthesia."

Today we have every reason for both despair and hope. How matters will evolve depends primarily on the degree of common sense that we as a nation and as a society have been able to preserve. This injunction may apply to the government at every level more than it does to the man in the street. But much depends on members of the general public as well: first and foremost, how strongly life has convinced them that there is no turning back.

Translated by Catherine A. Fitzpatrick

Note

1. As of January 1994, Vneshekonombank's frozen private accounts were being transferred to other banks able to conduct transactions in hard currency. —H.I.

12

Emil Payin

Separatism and Federalism in Contemporary Russia

Following the breakup of the USSR, the question whether Russia will follow the path of the Soviet Union has become anything but rhetorical. Gloomy scenarios describing the disintegration of the Russian Federation, accompanied by ethnic and regional conflicts, have begun to appear in abundance in mass-circulation newspapers, magazines, and academic publications. Certain of these forecasts lack any degree of empirical analysis and are being used by the communist opposition to frighten Russians with the problems caused by the government of the "antinational," "mercenary," "Yeltsin mafia." Most forecasts of Russia's disintegration, however, are based on an assessment of the actual threats to the federation as well as of the crises that have afflicted Russia's economy and sociopolitical life in the early 1990s.[1]

What Do the Regions Want?

When the Russian Federation declared its state sovereignty in 1991 it included three-quarters of the former USSR's territory and two-thirds of its population. A unitary state, just as the Soviet Union had been, Russia was ruled from a single center, with Moscow closely controlling every

185

action throughout the vast territory that the regional authorities took. The money earned by the most developed oblasts—in Central Russia, the Urals, and the Volga region—as well as the exorbitant profits from the oil-producing Tiumen region in western Siberia, went into the national treasury. Only a small portion of the profits earned by each region was returned to it, and the size of that portion bore no relationship with the region's productivity. The largest recipients of state subsidies were the showcases of socialism—the capital cities of Moscow and Leningrad.

The inefficiency of this kind of administration had become obvious long before Mikhail Gorbachev's perestroika began, and after the breakup of the Soviet Union in December 1991 it became an anachronism. Existing economic ties between regions were destroyed, the centralized system of administration was diluted, and control over all economic activities became concentrated in the hands of local authorities, even though in legal terms they still had no formal powers of control. The central authorities were still able to collect taxes from the regions but were increasingly less able to provide them assistance. The regions became increasingly dissatisfied.

At first, the demands made by regions to the federal authorities took the form of constructive local initiatives. At the beginning of 1992 more than 150 Russian administrative units (oblasts, administrative regions, and even individual cities) applied to the federal authorities with requests to set up so-called free economic zones on their territory. Local authorities assumed that by offering tax privileges in such zones they would be able to stimulate the flow of investments into their regions.[2]

This venture soon met with failure, because only a few of the cities and regions turned out to be attractive to investors. However, this "zone fever" demonstrated that the regions were seeking and would continue to seek various means by which to acquire economic independence.

The federal authorities had to respond to these processes in some way. In October 1992 President Boris Yeltsin made a statement about the need to review the concept of economic reform and to shift its center of gravity to the Russian regions. The percentage of regional budgets in the newly consolidated budget of the Russian Federation was to be increased from 18 percent in 1992 to 40 percent in 1993, and the rights of all regions in the area of foreign trade were broadened.[3]

These inconsistent and half-hearted measures, however, did nothing to moderate the regions' dissatisfaction with federal authorities. Indeed these measures could not have done so, given the fact that different regions wanted different things from the authorities. Regions rich in raw materials (mostly those producing oil, gas, and nonferrous metals) sought greater independence, especially in foreign trade. Poor agrarian regions wanted more protectionism: higher state procurement prices for agricultural production, credit privileges for the purchase of chemical fertilizers and agricultural machinery and for payment for fuel, and limitations on imports. Different political parties began to represent the interests of different regions. The Civic Union took it upon itself to defend the interests of industrial regions, and the interests of agrarian regions were taken up by the agrarian faction of the Supreme Soviet of the Russian Federation, and, from 1993, by the Agrarian Party.

However intense the conflicts between "rich" and "poor," agrarian and industrial regions, they in no way compared with the growing struggle between national-territorial units (autonomous republics, autonomous oblasts, and okrugs) and territorial-administrative units (krais and oblasts).[4]

The conflict between the autonomous national units and the Russian administrative regions was to a large degree a consequence of the centralized system of administration. Under socialism a principle was observed according to which the national income was redistributed for the benefit of the least-developed national regions, which received grants to develop their industry and their social infrastructure. However, all these benefits were canceled out by the inefficiency of the economy. As a result, the inhabitants of autonomous areas had no advantages in comparison with Russian regions, while the Russian regions felt a growing sense of being deprived of their fair share.

Moreover, the so-called aid given by the Union government to autonomous national areas was largely hypocritical and served as a cover for, among other things, the forcible Russification of the national regions of Russia. Outside the North Caucasus, only two of Russia's autonomous republics, Yakutia and Tataria, had secondary schools with instruction in their national languages, and both the numbers of titles and the press runs of books and periodicals in native languages were constantly declining. During the period of socialist industrialization, the rapidly growing cities were filled primarily with settlers from Russian oblasts. As a result, cities in national regions became predominantly Russian, and

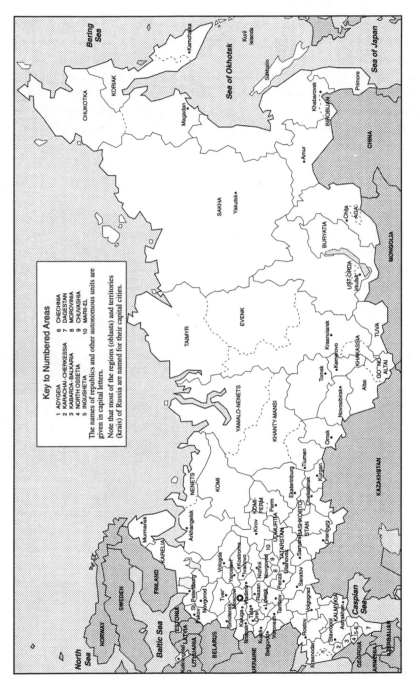

The Russian Federation

the proportion of indigenous people in them was two to four times lower than in rural areas.

The potential for conflict between autonomous and Russian regions was embedded in Stalin's 1936 Constitution, which combined two contradictory principles of state structure—the ethnic and the territorial. This Constitution divided peoples into "titular nations," which gave their names to their corresponding national-governmental units, and "nontitular" ones, which did not have their own territories. Most important, it granted unequal rights to different types of regions and, consequently, to their inhabitants. Thus, each national autonomous unit on the republic level had its own constitution, parliament, and even the right freely to secede from the federation. Krais and oblasts had no such rights.

This unbelievably complex and contradictory structure, based on a hierarchy of national and territorial regions, could not have existed for seventy years had it not been a transparent fiction. Regardless of whether a region was called a republic or an oblast, it was ruled by the head of the local division of the Communist Party directly subordinate to Moscow. Autonomous republics, just like krais and oblasts, did not possess the slightest degree of independence. When the communist regime collapsed, however, the republics suddenly "remembered" their rights and attempted to give genuine meaning to what had been purely declarative provisions in the Stalin-Brezhnev Constitution.

In 1990–92 all the republics passed declarations of sovereignty. The first to do so were Tatarstan, Yakutia, and Checheno-Ingushetia, which had become "pioneers" in the struggle for sovereignty as early as the Gorbachev period.

For example, the Constitution of the Republic of Tatarstan defines the republic as "a sovereign state, a subject of international law." In its relationship with the federal authorities Tatarstan insists that "constitutional-treaty relations" be established with Russia and that the Republic of Tatarstan be granted associate member status in the Russian Federation, a status that could serve as a precedent for withdrawing from the unitary political space of the federation. The constitutional laws adopted by Tatarstan attest to its intention to achieve full independence: the Law on Mineral Reserves hands over all state property on the territory of Tatarstan and its mineral reserves to the exclusive ownership of the republic. The Resolution on Military Duty and Military Service of Citizens of the Republic of Tatarstan requires citizens of the republic to carry out their military service only within the borders of Tatarstan.

The authorities of the Russian Federation, remembering the lessons of Mikhail Gorbachev's not very successful national policy, at first supported these declarations of sovereignty by republics. Nor did the federal center oppose changes in the status of ethnic regions or the creation, by some of them, of the institution of the presidency. The establishment of the Council of Heads of Republics chaired by Yeltsin, which dealt with key issues of federal policy, helped to increase the political influence of national regions.

It should be noted that the support of the center did have positive results. The Russian Federation has turned out to be probably the only multinational state that has succeeded in avoiding bloody ethnic conflicts on its territory. However, following the "parade of sovereignties" by the Russian republics, krais and oblasts also showed an uncontrollable urge to improve their status. First the Vologda and Sverdlovsk (Ekaterinburg) oblasts and then several other Russian regions announced their intention to proclaim themselves republics. In October 1993 the Sverdlovsk region made good on its threat and adopted a Constitution of the Ural Republic.

In my view, the idea of this Ural Republic constituted no danger for the integrity of Russia. In fact, the bases of its governmental structure strengthened the authority of Russia on its territory. The Ural Republic asserted no right to secede from Russia and did not plan to have an army, issue its own currency, or seek any other attributes of a sovereign state. The Constitution of the Ural Republic differs from the constitutions of the national republics in Russia in that it unconditionally recognizes the supremacy of Russian law and federal state authorities on its territory.[5] In addition, the fact that the highest official is called governor rather than president testifies to the absolute conformity of the new Ural formation with the conception of a single federative state. Most important, people living in the oblast (that is, the republic) were totally indifferent to the lobbying activities of the local authorities. It would have been possible to arouse the populace to support a republic only if the federal center had used force against them. This action would have incited them, purely out of a sense of protest, to consolidate around the notion of a local republic.

A much greater threat to the integrity of Russia is the growth of the political appetites of leaders of national republics in the federation, since it is they who have the opportunity to draw to their side large numbers of people by playing the "national card" in the struggle for political power. Two variants for a negative development of events are possible.

Under the first variant, the communist-Soviet elite existing in many republics scares the inhabitants of its republic with fears of a growing "dictatorship" by Moscow, and stirs up national feelings at the same time. The result is a political struggle fueled by aroused nationalism and separatism, a phenomenon that has become familiar from the examples of Nagorno-Karabakh, South Ossetia, and Abkhazia.

Under the second option, a radical nationalist opposition movement takes advantage of "anti-imperial" sentiment in order to come to power. This is what happened in Chechnia after the failure of the August 1991 coup, when the group led by General Djokhar Dudaev overthrew the chairman of the Supreme Soviet of the Chechen-Ingush Republic. We now know that the former communist leader, Doku Zavgaev, was much less of a nationalist and separatist than the current president of the Chechen Republic, General Dudaev, even though he proclaims his anticommunist opinions.

Thus, in Russian regions—both national and territorial—many clear reasons have arisen for dissatisfaction with the strict centralized system of state administration. Regions have been continually increasing their demands for greater administrative and economic independence. In Russian krais and oblasts these demands were purely economic in character and were aimed at turning a unitary state into a genuinely federative one. In autonomous national areas, on the other hand, the accumulating dissatisfaction with the unitary state led to different political demands. Economic and administrative independence was viewed by local political elites only as an intermediate step toward full independence— to secession from the federation. It can be said that in the Russian krais and oblasts the idea of federalism developed, whereas in autonomous national areas the idea of separatism developed. Both currents contributed to the formation of a new regional elite, which was destined to play an important role in the political struggle within Russia.

The "Third Force" in the War of Authority

The issue to examine here is the intensification of the struggle between the two branches of federal power—the legislative (the Congress of

People's Deputies and the Supreme Soviet) and the executive (the president and the Council of Ministers). This struggle took place in most of the newly independent states of the former Soviet Union but reached its peak in the Russian Federation in the spring of 1993 when the Ninth Congress of People's Deputies, held in March 1993, attempted to remove President Yeltsin from power. Although the attempt failed, it demonstrated that compromise between these two political antagonists was impossible. The stage was set for a crisis of federal power in Russia.

Both sides needed allies, and a tug-of-war began, with each side trying to draw regional authorities into its camp. Supreme Soviet Speaker Ruslan Khasbulatov staked his fate on the Russian regions, and during his trips to the Russian oblasts he constantly emphasized the need to raise their status. President Boris Yeltsin's policy was to seek closer contacts with the leaders of the autonomous national areas, with whom he regularly conferred before every "showdown," such as a congress or a referendum. It is by no means the case that the president had warmer feelings for the republics than for the krais and oblasts. He simply assumed that the chief executives in the Russian territorial entities, appointed by the president (and popularly referred to as governors), would side with him in any event and therefore that he should concentrate his greatest efforts on enlisting the support of the more independent political actors—the leaders of the autonomous national areas.

The regional leaders thus emerged as members of a "third force" that gained the greatest advantage from the struggle between the two branches of federal power because each branch cultivated them. The regional elites therefore adopted the tactic of allowing neither side in the conflict to gain a decisive edge and doing everything possible to prolong the crisis of federal power.

Until the April 1993 referendum the balance of power in the struggle for the regions was on the side of the legislature. The majority of regional councils supported the Supreme Soviet, and they were joined by some heads of executive authorities of the regions. According to official procedure, their appointment and dismissal was subject to approval by the Supreme Soviet, and this provision protected them from "punishment" by the president. Furthermore, to get rid of the governors who moved into Yeltsin's camp after the defeat of the August 1991 coup, the local councils decided to hold new elections for the heads of the executive power in several oblasts of southern and central Russia. The newly elected heads were members of the old Party nomenklatura who traditionally have had a strong base among the conservative-minded population of the agrarian oblasts of Russia. The conflict within the top echelons of power contained many dangers for the integrity of Russia. I will mention just two: first, the possibility that the "conflict of authority" would spread and that confrontation would intensify between the representative and executive powers in the republics, krais, and oblasts of the Russian Federation; and second, the danger that separatists in the constituent parts of the federation would take greater and greater advantage of the conflict between the president and the parliament in order to win more and more political privileges from each branch of power.

The second danger became particularly severe during the so-called gradual constitutional reform. Because Yeltsin could not get his draft Constitution approved by the Congress, he hoped to confer legitimacy on it through achieving a ratification of the basic law of Russia by the heads of the constituent parts of the federation. However, the regional political elites—and especially the leaders of the autonomous national areas—tried to turn the president's wishes to their own advantage. Indeed, it is hard to think of a better situation for them than one in which both the president and parliament needed their support. Aware of their own significance, the heads of the former Russian autonomous areas began to demand an ever greater price for their assent to drafts of the new Constitution, while it became increasingly clear that in fact they were interested in none of them.

As early as December 1992, the heads of the republics rejected the parliamentary draft, and in May 1993 they raised numerous objections to the presidential version. Among their main objections were the following:

- The draft did not express the right of nations to self-determination.
- The main body of the text did not completely correspond to the principles of the Federative Treaty.
- The draft was deficient in that it introduced a dramatic change in the balance of power by vesting supreme governmental power in the Russian president.
- The principle of the absolute supremacy of the federal Constitu-

tion and laws over the laws of the republics within the Russian Federation was unacceptable.[6]

However, the main objection raised was that the presidential draft had been adopted by "unconstitutional methods." Needless to say, the regional leaders were no more devoted to legality than the Russian president, but they had located the most vulnerable spot in Yeltsin's plan for constitutional reform: the absence of a legal method for adopting the Constitution in the event that the deputies sabotaged it.

As early as May 12, *Nezavisimaia gazeta* published a letter signed by eleven heads of republics protesting against the procedure proposed by the president for the adoption of the Russian Federation Constitution, which involved bypassing the Congress of People's Deputies. On May 27, the same paper published a letter dated May 25 signed by sixteen heads of republics (the only ones not to sign were the heads of Tatarstan, Udmurtia, Chuvashia, and the Karachai-Cherkess Republic). Under the eye-catching headline "The Heads of Republics Present a Constitutional Ultimatum to the President,"[7] the letter demanded that a law on the procedure for the preparation, discussion, and adoption of the new Constitution be passed within one month.

On the eve of the Constitutional Conference, in May 1993, Yeltsin was anxious to ensure himself of the support of regional leaders. At this very conference it was proposed that the new Constitution be ratified and that at the same time the Russian deputies be forced to present themselves for early parliamentary elections. To achieve that end, Yeltsin was ready to make major concessions to the most intransigent regional elites and leaders of the national autonomous areas.

Taking advantage of the weakness of federal power, four republics, Chechnia, Tatarstan, Bashkortostan, and Yakutia, stopped paying federal taxes. As a result, the more developed Russian regions had to bear the brunt of federal taxation. During 1992 the gap between the amount of federal taxes collected and the payments made from the federal budget per citizen in Moscow, the Samara oblast, the Nizhnii Novgorod oblast, other oblasts of Central Russia, the Volga region, and the Urals was 15,000–25,000 rubles. In the main oil-producing region, Tiumen oblast, it reached 60,000 rubles, more than double the average monthly wage earned by inhabitants of the "donor" regions.[8]

This glaring economic inequality is highlighted by comparing two members of the federation located in the same geographical zone (the Far East), the Primorskii krai and the Sakha Republic (Yakutia). The amounts each paid into the local budget per citizen differed by a factor of six. The citizens in the Russian region who duly paid taxes into the federal treasury were worse off than the citizens of the republic that was subsidized by the center.

Yakutia's President, Mikhail Nikolaev, who is well known for his pro-Yeltsin position, obtained permission for Yakutia to keep 25 percent of the diamonds it extracts and also gained a substantial increase in the republic's share of revenues from the sale of gold mined on its territory.[9]

While economic privileges were obtained illegally by the republics by soliciting them from the central government, their political privileges were reinforced by the new Constitution of the Russian Federation.

One of the early presidential drafts of the Constitution provided unprecedented political privileges for ethnic entities: they would receive the same number of seats in the upper chamber of the future parliament as the Russian krais and oblasts, although the latter were twice as numerous.

On May 26, during a meeting of the heads of republics, the president approved a statement to the effect that in addition to the Federative Treaty, the relations between the republics and the federal authorities could be regulated by bilateral agreements. Those republics that had not signed the Federative Treaty (Tatarstan, Bashkortostan, and Chechnia) had the option of conducting their relations with Moscow entirely by means of bilateral treaties, in the same way as foreign states.

Finally, in June, at the Constitutional Conference, the president agreed to the following formulation of Article 5 of the Constitution proposed by the heads of the republics: "A republic is a sovereign state within the Russian Federation." The president's political opponents leaped on this phrasing and accused him of being ready to sacrifice the integrity of Russia in order to force through his draft Constitution. The use of the concept "sovereign state," without clarifying what this term meant, opened the way for arbitrary interpretations of the powers of republics and for the emergence of bitter conflicts between the republics and Moscow. It also provoked the growth of separatism in the Russian regions.

Mikhail Gorbachev, during his rule, had tried to delay the disintegration of the USSR by making concessions to the republics, but these concessions from the center had led merely to an escalation of demands from the political elites in the republics. The leadership of Russia repeated many of the mistakes made by the Soviet government, but, luckily for them, the new political conditions softened the negative consequences of these mistakes and allowed the Russian leaders to correct them in time.

After the Constitutional Conference, on which the authorities had pinned such great hopes, failed to fulfill its mission and failed to enable President Yeltsin to work with the members of the federation in putting an end to dual power (*dvoevlastie*), the president shifted the emphasis of his relations with the regional elites. First, the president no longer relied primarily on the leaders of the ethnic republics, acknowledging the increased influence of the Russian territories. Second, having failed to find a legitimate means of ending the situation of dual power and the constitutional crisis, President Yeltsin resorted to force, announcing the dissolution of the Supreme Soviet and the calling of new parliamentary elections.

Yeltsin's celebrated decree of September 21, 1993, brought a new flare-up of conflict between the legislative and the executive powers in the Russian regions. Most local councils ruled that the President's action was unconstitutional and announced that the execution of his decree was suspended in their territories. The reaction of the authorities in the republics was particularly sharp. The only leader who supported Yeltsin was the president of Yakutia, Mikhail Nikolaev.

On the eve of the October revolt, the "third force" was surprisingly quick to organize itself. On the initiative of the chairman of the Constitutional Court, Valerii Zorkin, and the president of Kalmykia, Kirsan Iliumzhinov, a Council of Subjects of the Federation was established. The council's decision to cancel the presidential decree immediately and the subsequent decision of the recalcitrant congress to strip Yeltsin of his presidential powers and to return to the state of affairs before the issuance of the decree were highly favorable for the parliament and totally unacceptable for the president. Justifying its actions by the desire to avoid bloodshed, the "third force" in effect enabled the parliament to decide to fight to the end and to some extent provoked it to use armed force.

The August 1991 coup precipitated the breakup of the USSR. The question is often asked whether the October 1993 revolt will not have similar consequences for the Russian Federation.

Is Russia in Danger of Following
the Path of the USSR?

The political processes under way in Russia in many ways recall those that took place in the USSR on the eve of its disintegration. At the same time, certain features of Russia's political development distinguish Russia from the USSR and make it more likely that the state that marked the fourth anniversary of its independence on June 12, 1994, will preserve its territorial integrity.

First, the former Soviet central government found all of the republics of the former USSR arrayed against it in a united front. The situation in Russia today is very different. The krais and oblasts are becoming more and more dissatisfied with the political privileges enjoyed by the national entities. For their part, since the dissolution of the USSR the regions have become aware of the tremendous difficulties caused by the severing of traditional economic ties, the erection of political and customs barriers, and the sharp increase in the fares for transportation from one "independent" state to another.

The Russian Federation itself has been confronted with certain problems deriving from growing separatism in the autonomous national areas. Some of these (Kalmykia, Dagestan, and the Chechen Republic) have been making territorial claims on adjacent Russian regions. The territorial dispute between the North Ossetian and Ingush republics has led to armed conflict, although this was rapidly localized. The heads of Russian krais and oblasts have been advocating the equality of all the members of the federation and the preservation of its territorial integrity. They fought a fierce battle against the republics at the Constitutional Conference. Indeed, they forced the leaders of the republics to agree to include in the text of the Constitution a provision on the equality of all subjects of the federation. Also as a result of the efforts of the krais and oblasts, the final text of the Constitution included a whole series of articles prohibiting the secession of a state from the federation.[10]

The campaign waged by the leaders of Russian regions proved to be far more effective against separatist tendencies than if the federal authorities had made a similar attempt. All the same, the federal authorities retain many economic levers with which to prevail over antireformist, separatist forces within the regional elites. The federal authorities control railways, air space, pipelines, and power grids, not to speak of the forces of law and order. For instance, a republic that refuses to pay taxes can have all its accounts in banks on the territory of Russia frozen and the transport of its goods abroad banned.

A major reason why Moscow did not in fact use these powers earlier was that dual power prevented it from doing so. If one branch of government had decided to impose economic sanctions, say, against those who refused to pay taxes, the other branch would have immediately obstructed the imposition of these sanctions, seeking to gain political capital as well as recruit new allies.

After the October 1993 revolt was crushed, the situation changed dramatically. All the republican organs of power that had declared Yeltsin's decree of September 21 unconstitutional revoked those decisions immediately after the collapse of the coup. On the eve of the April referendum observers had questioned whether the republics would allow it to be held on their territories, but they raised no such questions with respect to the December referendum and early parliamentary elections. It was clear to all that the republics would not dare to launch an open attack on the federal authorities, not so much because they feared to do so as because they recognized that a fundamental change had transformed Russian politics.

A year before, if a republic had announced its withdrawal from Russia, that would have been considered a daring act. Today even Tatarstan, the wealthiest republic, which has advanced further than any other along the road of sovereignty, declares through its president, Mintimer Shaimiev, that not only has it no desire to leave the federation but that it wants to preserve its integrity. Of course, there is a difference between declarations and actions, but declarations are nonetheless significant: they are a measure of how unpopular the idea of a breakup of the Russian state has become.

Only the Chechen Republic, as early as 1991, actually seceded from the Russian Federation. But the other republics of Russia will hardly wish to follow its example. Today the Chechen Republic is crippled by the burden of its independence. National consolidation in Chechen society proved to be short-lived. As soon as fear of Russia as the foreign enemy disappeared, conflicts among various regional, clan, and ethnic communities within the republic emerged and intensified. Today three regions of the republic refuse to obey the Chechen leadership.

Even greater internal conflicts may appear in other autonomous national units, were they to leave Russia. For instance, in Kabardin-Balkaria two peoples, the Kabardins and the Balkars, are divided by irreconcilable territorial disputes, while in Dagestan a dozen ethnic components are making territorial claims on each other. Most of the leaders of national republics within Russia are well aware that internal conflicts could become dangerous if their autonomous units were to leave the federation. Unlike the USSR, the Russian Federation is quite homogeneous in its ethnic composition: Russians constitute 82.6 percent of its population, and they also make up a majority in most autonomous areas. Only in six autonomous units is the titular nationality more numerous than Russians. Four of these republics are in the North Caucasus (Dagestan, Ingushetia, Kabardin-Balkaria, and North Ossetia), one in the Volga region (Chuvashia), and one in Siberia (Tuva), and if any republics are likely to leave Russia, it will most likely be these. In fact, we should immediately drop North Ossetiia from this list because, as the only Christian autonomous area in the Muslim North Caucasus, it will not desire to leave Russia.

The Chuvash Republic should also be removed from this list. No political forces in the republic today have announced their intention to fight for its independence, and even if such forces were to appear, the likelihood of its withdrawing from the Russian Federation would be negligible. Chuvashia, like most of the other republics within Russia, has no independent borders with other states and thus could be completely blockaded by Russia. It would be easier for republics located along Russia's frontiers to withdraw, but at worst Russia would be "chipped off" around the edges; it could not be split up into parts.

When the predominance of Russians in the Russian Federation is cited as a factor strengthening the integrity of the federation, it is sometimes argued that the Russian communities in some national republics have supported aspirations for national autonomy. Indeed, it is true that the republics have attained a relatively privileged economic situation. For instance, republics pay less taxes to the federal treasury than they used to and thus maintain higher standards of living and influence public opinion to support greater autonomy. In Birobijan, the Jewish autonomous oblast where virtually no Jews have remained, it is the Russians who favor the preservation of the republic's autonomy. These relatively well-to-do "autonomous islands" in the sea of Russian misfortune are a temporary phenomenon, however; sooner or later living standards will equalize. Moreover, the fact that Russians support a wider degree of independence for the regions does not mean that they would support secession: the negative consequences of "departure" from Russia have become all too evident.

Another factor restraining Russian regions from leaving the Federation is the perception of external threat. For instance, in Siberia and the Far East worries have been growing about the territorial claims put forward by China and Japan. People in these regions understand that they will be defended from external threats only if they remain within a single and strong state. In addition, only such a state can protect them in conducting foreign trade relations.

A year ago, many publications wrote about the disintegration of Russia as inevitable, and even as a good thing. Today such opinions are out of the question. Time has passed, and the experience of bloodshed and of millions of refugees has had a sobering effect. Changes in the political climate of post-Soviet society have also caused the liberal intelligentsia to rethink its position. When the majority of Moscow and Leningrad residents voted against the preservation of the Soviet Union in the 1991 referendum, they were, of course, voting not against the preservation of the country's integrity but rather against the political regime that was at that time ruling it. They believed, not without good reason, that it was impossible to eliminate communism without breaking up the empire.

Today no one thinks that merely by destroying the Russian state can we avoid the danger of a restoration of communism. On the contrary, today communists are forming alliances with nationalists and separatists of all types.

It is for this reason that the struggle to preserve the integrity of Russia is at the same time a struggle against national communism.

Translated by Jonathan Edwards

Notes

1. D. Ol'shanskii, "Politicheskaia psikhologiia raspada," *Nezavisimaia gazeta,* January 16, 1992; Richard Pipes, "Russkii shans," *Stolitsa,* 1992, no. 27; L. Shevtsova, "Lovushka dlia prezidentov," *Literaturnaia gazeta,* June 30, 1993.

2. *Regionalizm kak novaia mirovaia tendentsiia: Sbornik nauchnykh trudov*

(Moscow: Institute of World Economic and Political Research, Russian Academy of Sciences, 1993), pp. 33–34.

3. Ibid., pp. 35–36.

4. There are 32 national-territorial units in the Russian Federation (including 21 republics, 10 autonomous okrugs, and 1 autonomous oblast); and 57 administrative-territorial units (including krais and oblasts and the cities of Moscow and St. Petersburg, which also have this status). Since spring 1992, when representatives of all of the above areas signed a treaty delineating authority between the regions and the federal authorities (the so-called Federative Treaty), they have been referred to as "the subjects of the federation." Two republics, Tatarstan and Chechnia, refused to sign the Federative Treaty.

The differences between autonomous entities (republics, autonomous oblasts, and okrugis) were mainly determined from their population size: the republics are those areas with the greatest population, and the okrugi are those with the smallest, but these differences are more theoretical than real, and it is not a coincidence that most autonomous oblasts and okrugis proclaimed themselves republics in 1992. See *Chislennost' naseleniia RF* (Moscow: Information and Publishing Center, 1992).

5. "Konstitutsiia Ural'skoi Respubliki," *Oblastnaia gazeta* (Ekaterinburg), October 30, 1993.

6. *Nezavisimaia gazeta,* May 12, 1993.

7. *Nezavisimaia gazeta,* May 27, 1993.

8. N.V. Zubarevich, "Rol' regional'nykh elit v politicheskoi zhizni Rossii" (Moscow: Center for Ethnopolitical Research, 1993).

9. Ibid.

10. *Konstitutsiia Russkoi Federatsii* (Constitution of the Russian Federation), draft submitted for the referendum of December 12, 1993 (Moscow: "Izvestiia" Publishing House, 1993).

13

Arkadii Vaksberg

Fitting the Punishment to the Crime, and Politics Too

In the former Soviet Union, crime was on the decline; in post-Soviet Russia, crime gets worse every day: according to conventional wisdom in Russia, both propositions are beyond dispute, the lamentable effects of the social and political changes that have swept the country. Paradoxically, neither of these assertions—not even the second—can be accepted without qualification and analysis, and, above all, without first giving a specific definition of what is meant by crime and its increase. However straightforward and elementary both these notions may seem, they are far from that under the conditions prevailing in Russia today, and they need to be deciphered.

Beginning in 1973 or 1974 and until the end of 1991 I was able, as a correspondent for *Literaturnaia gazeta*, to attend all except perhaps one or two of the closed sessions of the USSR Supreme Court, which were held four times a year. Those in charge of the highest court in the land very much wanted to project a public image of themselves as genuine liberals dedicated to truth and legality, and they chose me for the job because they considered me better equipped for this task than anybody else. Why? To explain the unique role that *Literaturnaia gazeta* played in our society during the Brezhnev era would require a separate article. Be that as it may, the fact that for a long time I had access to the zealously guarded holy of holies, the very top rung of the Soviet judicial hierarchy, enabled me to observe the simple mechanics of "window dressing," prompted by the best of intentions.

At least once a year the USSR Supreme Court convened in plenary session to hear a report on the "Crime Situation and the Role of Law Courts in Controlling It." The prosecutor general and the minister of internal affairs of the USSR invariably took part in these sessions, with occasionally a deputy chairman of the KGB also present. These officials spoke with a degree of candor that they permitted themselves to use only among close colleagues. Invariably, the picture was depressing. The growth of crime, especially the rise in serious crimes (homicide, armed robbery, burglaries, gang rape) far exceeded the average levels reported over many years by the developed and even by the less-developed countries. The statistics of death sentences passed and executed were particularly horrifying.

The press release issued after each session contained no hint of the depressing facts aired by the speakers. I was astonished—right after what I had heard in that very chamber—to hear, and then to read in the papers, that crime was constantly going down, that it was being successfully brought under control, although of course "certain shortcomings" still had to be overcome. Accordingly, the courts were urged "to intensify their struggle"—which, translated from "officialese," meant only one thing: to hand down even harsher sentences. To report each session in such a way as to get clearance from the Supreme Court (nothing could be printed without the chairman's signature), and yet not to debase oneself by lying, required one not only to look for the right euphemisms but to wage an exhausting battle with the censors and use all one's diplomatic cunning.

These pages of our recent history would not be worth recalling were it not for one fact: crime today is being used in precisely the same way, as a card in the great game of politics, although under different conditions and for different purposes. The real state of affairs is far different from (though not necessarily opposite to) the way it is reflected in official documents, statements of government leaders, and media reports. Truth lies in the eye of the beholder.

This phenomenon is hard not only for an outsider to grasp but even for somebody who has been following developments from inside and has access to factual material and purportedly authentic statistics.

Least of all should one trust public opinion. The man in the street has always been more afraid of crimes that threaten him (murders, violence, theft) than of crimes against society as a whole (embezzlement, corruption, contraband). This was so in the past, when crime was "steadily declining," and it is still the case today when crime is "steadily growing." Whatever the real facts, people have always complained that "you can't go out into the street," that there is wanton killing everywhere, and the like. Such complaints are no guide to the true state of affairs.

Unfortunately, statistics are even less reliable. Whereas in the period before perestroika all statistics on crime were classified and strictly held as state secrets, today they are open to public scrutiny and easily accessible, or so it would seem. In fact, this is an illusion. The publication of highly selective and carefully sifted statistics under Mikhail Gorbachev was replaced under Boris Yeltsin by the presentation of equally selective and carefully sifted statistics at press briefings organized by the Ministry of Internal Affairs and some of its regional directorates, notably in the Moscow region.

These publications and statements have no basis in fact. The figures are random and incompatible. For instance, what conclusion can be drawn from the statement that the number of murders (even if the figure is accompanied with a qualifier: "murder for material gain") has increased by so many percentage points in Moscow during the first half year of 1993, compared with the same period of the previous year? Moscow has become a place where criminal groups based in distant regions of Russia and even in other countries (the former republics of the USSR) settle scores with one another. That fact alone calls for so many radical adjustments to the statistics that comparisons are impossible.

Take another example. How does one compare the growth of crime under the rubric "embezzlement on a particularly large scale"? The notions of "large" and "particularly large" have always been arbitrary and unscientific, especially after the liberalization of prices and the ensuing hyperinflation, which no price indexing can correct. Basic changes in the social and economic structure and altered economic relationships derived from the new position of law and private property in the economy are among the many factors that make it impossible to compare figures that may, on their face, appear to be comparable.

Thus, in analyzing the present criminological situation and its social and political impact, it is best to put aside statistics as well as meaningless comparisons and trends in crime and concentrate instead on the factors that engender or contribute to crime. When viewed from this standpoint, the situation is indeed alarming, reflecting as it does all the dramatic contradictions of the long and tortured process of emerging from under the rubble of a system that has collapsed.

Reports of blood-curdling murders carried in the daily press do not necessarily mean that such crime has dramatically increased in number, only that such information is no longer taboo. Judging from the materials that I received at the USSR Supreme Court, grisly murders have always been committed, but now it is the motives that have changed. The primary motive these days is not "a fatal attraction," which attested at least to strong feelings or to depression caused by domestic conflicts (although life has by no means become easier or more pleasant), but eliminating a competitor, settling accounts, sparring "for a place in the sun," blackmail, envy, and sheer hatred, often with no discernible cause. The life of a human being has lost any value. It is much simpler to destroy a person one dislikes than to wage a prolonged war of maneuver with him.

What makes murder even simpler is that the danger of punishment is not great and in most cases does not exist at all. One can bribe one's way out of any punishment or evade it either with or without resort to blackmail. Any police detective or government prosecutor knows well what his fate will be if he goes about his job with too high a degree of professional zeal. This threat is no longer something imagined by the fainthearted. Every day brings fresh proof of its reality.

A sense of impunity encourages any would-be criminal, but especially a murderer. Even the most ruthless and cynical criminal is apt to think twice before taking the life of another, but such restraints no longer seem to apply. Murders are committed everywhere and at the slightest provocation. They have become practically a daily affair. After all, there is no official state of war in the North Caucasus, Transcaucasia, or Central Asia; thus every violent death that occurs there is a crime. But of course nobody goes on trial. Murder is accepted as a sad inevitability. It is striking that nobody thinks about these events in terms of criminal law. The more people become accustomed to seeing violent death all around them, the more killers are produced.

In light of this violence, it is not surprising to see the proliferation of quasi-legal companies flimsily disguised as "service firms" along with completely illegal organizations that, among many other services, provide hired gunmen ready to carry out on short notice the most "delicate" assignments. The fee is affordable; the risk of undesirable consequences slight.

It serves no useful purpose to judge this phenomenon by moral criteria. Social cataclysms have always provoked explosions of violence, often in the most savage and horrifying forms. The phenomenon of liberty, which has never had a tradition in Russia, does not manifest itself in freedom of word and thought, awareness of one's own human rights, or the desire for closer ties with world civilization. For some people—alas for many people—it brings a feeling of freedom *from* the law, the rules of human community, and respect for the prerogatives and freedoms of others. In Russia, the paralysis of executive and legislative power encourages the wave of violence termed, in the current slang, *bespredel*—"anything goes." The maxim that the deterrent effect of punishment depends not on its severity but on its inevitability (for decades ascribed to Lenin but actually originated by West European philosophers in the eighteenth century) has often been proved true, but never more vividly than in our country in recent years. The crime detection rate has never been high in this country, although it was statistically camouflaged to look higher than it was. Many ways exist (and have been often described) for creating the illusion of a successful struggle against crime. The padding of statistics on crime was just as staggering as that on production or, say, housing construction. I myself once was the victim of these manipulations after burglars broke into my summer house. Although the investigation was directly supervised by the USSR minister of internal affairs, the Moscow sleuths, with astonishing cynicism, turned an unsolved crime into a closed case and triumphantly reported their success to their superiors. Can one imagine the plight of those who are timid or have no connections in high places?

Because realistic or reliable statistics do not exist, it is hard to say whether crime detection became still worse during and after perestroika or remained at the same level. In any case, it is safe to say that the detection rate is extremely low. The only difference is that now the authorities impassively acknowledge it and do not conceal it as before. The most shocking and scandalous crimes are promptly reported in the press; readers are always informed that an investigation has begun; but as a rule no further information is offered. Time is on the side of those who are unable or unwilling to uncover anything: fresh and still more shocking reports (crime after grisly crime is committed every day) eclipse the "outdated" reports. Nobody asks the responsible officials even for interim reports about the status of the investigation. This continuing state of affairs in itself contributes to its escalation, far from being a deterrent to violence.

The foregoing observations, of course, apply not only to crimes of violence but to all types of crimes. In the minds of most people concerned about the problem (whether Russians or foreigners), crime in present-day Russia is associated with the ubiquitous and nearly invincible mafia, which allegedly penetrates all levels of society, as well as the government. Until recently the mafia was thought to be a characteristic of "the Western way of life" and was associated with Sicily or Chicago. But it has now spread swiftly all over Russia. The press must get the credit for building up this image of Russian crime in the last decade of the twentieth century. We need to define the term "mafia" more clearly. With the blessing of lawyers and journalists, it is now loosely applied to anything: street vendors who are in league with each other to keep the prices of tomatoes and meat high, taxi drivers who charge a visiting foreign businessman three times the normal fare (and take only hard currency), government bureaucrats who are lining their pockets in the process of privatization of state property (that is, property nobody owns).

Given such latitude in the use of the word, the line is blurred between the real mafia, on the one hand, which is a serious threat to democracy and, consequently, to the future of Russia and, on the other hand, the equally dangerous but conventional forms of organized crime, which is nothing new and has not caught society unawares. This blurring of distinctions between two interconnected but separate phenomena plays into the hands of the true mafia, which skillfully hides behind numerous other criminals.

And yet the existence of the mafia in the postperestroika society is not a myth but a reality. We are witnessing something more than simply a merger of the criminal world and governmental structures (already well known in the West). A fierce struggle for power is taking place, involving the use of criminal groups and criminal methods, on the one hand, and, on the other, the attempts of criminal groups to put their own people in command positions where true and not token power lies. These interconnected and coordinated processes are taking place before our eyes. No force in society today can stop it with the help of law, within the law, and by legal methods.

Not that the relevant laws are lacking, not that the enabling mechanism is lacking, but the levers that could set this mechanism in motion are immobilized. Fear, apathy, and most often a pathological growth of an acquisitive instinct no longer restrained by morality or elementary professional honor have opened all the doors to the mafia, turning its potential opponents into hostages and drawing them into mutual support groups.

In October 1993, Minister of Internal Affairs Viktor Erin informed the public that Russia now has about 150 powerful mafia organizations, comprising more than 3,000 criminal gangs. The question arises: if this is no longer a secret for Ministry of Internal Affairs officials, if they know which mafia groups operate, and where, and what they do, if they know many of the mafia members by name, what stops them from putting a halt to mafia activities, in accordance with the law?

The question is rhetorical. The answer is obvious, but it will never be provided. Lamentable though it may be, the situation is controlled, not by the bodies that by tradition are still called law-enforcement agencies but by the 150 (or 3,000) groups, associations, or gangs that have divided up their turf and have infiltrated those power structures where they have reliable support. The "law enforcement bodies," whether composed of honest professionals or of cynics wearing militia uniforms who have been bought (sometimes on the cheap) by mafia bosses, can only record the alignment of mafia forces, collecting some dividends in the process.

If the government were to admit the gravity of the situation, instead of doling out the syrupy optimism to which our fellow citizens have been treated, it would inspire respect and make one trust information coming from that source. It would highlight the vital role that law enforcement agencies play in heroically taking on a powerful and dangerous enemy that threatens each of us. It would provide convincing arguments in favor of larger expenditures to provide our guardians and protectors with modern technology—which they badly need. Most important, it would buttress their standing in national politics, because the subject of crime—its dangers and the need to protect society—has become a trump card used by politicians across the political spectrum.

Criminal dossiers, briefcases, and entire suitcases containing documents designed to compromise this or that politician, whether authentic or not, have a way of popping open at the right moment. These sensational "revelations" have nothing to do with the real struggle against crime. They merely promote the political ambitions of yet another champion of the "popular good" who hopes to score points in the struggle for political power. How lawyers react to such charges depends entirely on whom they want to please and whom they want to trip up; it has nothing to do with their professional duties. But the social background against which scheming politicians weave their intrigues is no figment of their imagination. It is a tragic reality of our times. More accurately, this is a cancerous growth which has metastasized throughout the organism. Even surgery will not help.

The word "corruption" has joined the postperestroika vocabulary as easily as the words "democracy," "pluralism," and "constitutionality." Now we have caught up with the West, we have both democracy and corruption, a sure sign that we are moving toward capitalism. It is true that corruption is international and no political system is immune to it. But our corruption has two distinctive features. First, it has spread across the nation with lightning speed like an epidemic (pandemic is perhaps a more accurate term) that blights every sphere of activity and penetrates every pore of society to the point that it has become the rule rather than the exception in business relations.

Second, the main carriers of the virus have been the former apparatchiks, members of the nomenklatura at various levels, who for years had instructed us in right living and had exacted compliance with the rules of Party ethics. The Red-Brown opposition of communists and extreme nationalists likes to blame the reformers for plunging the country into corruption and destroying a "society of law, order, and justice." But the former functionaries, once appointed by the Party to be "captains of industry," hold all the key positions in the central and regional administrations and in the economy generally. The former secretaries of regional, city, and district Party committees, who now call themselves presidents and general directors of various foundations, associations, and firms, or who have remained heads of local councils, municipalities, or departments, are precisely those people who are carrying out what has come to be called "nomenklatura privatization."

It is these former functionaries who have full control of real estate; they sell, allocate, and lease land and buildings for bribes that may be in money, assets, or reciprocal favors. It is they who illegally export to the West raw materials, metals, and other valuable commodities that bring enormous profits. Why is it that nobody (certainly not at the official level) has ever attempted to trace the antecedents of those who are involved in the largest and most repellent scandals? Why has nobody probed into the recent past of all these confidence men and speculators? Such probes would have answered many questions.

Those who have something to offer in return for bribes—for example, managers of assets that they have the right to sell—are for the most part the middle ranks of the former Party nomenklatura who have learned the modern market jargon and have prudently burned their Party cards (both literally and figuratively). The fact that these people have been able to keep their heads above water and even get promoted is a testimony not only to their skillful mimicry but to their genuine professional skills and expertise—qualities that turn out to be useful even in these troubled times. Another reason for the resilience of the former apparatchiks is the popular fear of security screening (*lustratsiia*), background checks of Party or KGB affiliations that the more radical democrats have been demanding. By using some simple demagogic techniques, the opponents of the democrats have managed to mislead the public so that the possibility of security screening has come to be regarded as a threat not just to Party apparatchiks and professional policemen (in uniforms or in plain clothes), but to *all* former Party members and their families. No advocate of screening has ever dreamed of suggesting an inquiry on such a scale.

As history has often shown, those who yesterday strangled liberty are quick to remember all about freedom whenever their own freedom comes under the slightest threat. Nobody clamors so hysterically and aggressively for human rights as deposed tyrants who violated the rights of millions of people. It is one of the weaknesses (or perhaps strengths) of democracy that such complaints are taken seriously. Indeed, it is not becoming for democrats to use the same methods as their opponents. The time-honored maxim "No freedom for the enemies of freedom" has once again suffered a crushing defeat.

The resulting situation has at least one redeeming element: it has brought home to everyone the Party elite's prodigious capacity to adapt itself to dramatically changing circumstances. What is more, everybody has seen its astonishing, disheartening cynicism. The facility with which these people have become integrated into the new system and have renounced and trampled upon their former "ideals" has come as a surprise to many people. Come to think of it, there is no reason to be surprised. After all, these people have plundered the country for decades, only they had a different name for it: they described it as "legitimate privileges," which they had earned by their Herculean efforts in trying to improve the people's well-being. For fairness's sake one must add to the hordes of "has-beens" the rapidly proliferating "new elite," the strident advocates of reform who have quickly filled the vacuum formed in the old and new offices and have set about their main task: getting rich at any cost. They do not, of course, neglect the flood of gold that has obligingly turned toward them: there are always more people willing to give bribes than those who are ready to take them. Today, however, their numbers seem to have become equal.

As attested by the classic works of its literature, bribe taking has been Russia's eternal curse. It seemed to have reached its peak in the times of Leonid Brezhnev. How wrong we were! Actually, we were a long way from the peak. How can one talk about a peak in these times of escalating venality? Bribery has always been a crime with the highest level of latency: how many bribes and "favors" have been documented? Those who have been caught red-handed represent only the tip of the iceberg. Their numbers do not begin to tell us about the true scope of the national disaster. Today bribes (for everything) are given and taken right and left, but how many prosecutions have been started and how many have been followed through?

Impressions of daily life should not be used as a basis for reaching sweeping conclusions, but in this case they seem to reflect the true state of affairs accurately. I recite a few facts that I myself witnessed or learned about from my close friends: A customs officer at an international air terminal suggests to a foreign visitor that he should pay fifty dollars to avoid paying four times that sum as a fine for some infraction. A middle-level bureaucrat tells a caller to pay one thousand dollars for arranging an appointment with a chief who could instantly resolve the caller's problem. Another bureaucrat, with equally disarming frankness, advises you not to begrudge five thousand dollars in exchange for getting five of the nine critical signatures on a document authorizing the privatization of office space. If this kind of thing can take place at the lower or middle levels of administration and business, one can imagine the scale and the cynicism of the bargaining going on at high, very high, and even at the highest levels of power.

One of the many reflexes stimulating this process is a sense of uncertainty about the security of one's position. Unlike their predecessors, who had come to power during the stable Brezhnev era, the current rulers at any level feel themselves to be birds of passage who have drifted by chance into the corridors of power. Their insecurity accounts for their near pathological greed, aggressiveness, and lack of moral scruple. For them it is a race against the clock. The threat to their positions may in fact be less immediate than they imagine, but that feeling of insecurity spurs them on and makes them grab what they can—for tomorrow it may be too late.

This race creates an atmosphere of extreme nervousness that involves more and more people, so that criminal behavior becomes part of a person's everyday life or even part of his basic attitude toward life.

Nobody can prove that the pandemic of corruption sweeping Russia exceeds in scale that which existed in the good old days under Comrade Brezhnev. The people who took bribes then were different, and bribes have assumed new forms. In those days they were called "overstatement of profits," which were shared equally by those who did the "overstating" and those who shut their eyes to it. In the Brezhnev days, there were "gifts presented from the bottom of the heart" on the anniversaries of the Bolshevik Revolution or for the birthday of a distant relative. In those days, bribes and favors were euphemistically called "solicitude" and "reciprocal solicitude." In the immortal vernacular: "I'm for you and you're for me."

Nowadays people have no time for euphemisms and etiquette. They simply ask, "How much?" This bluntness saves much time and effort, but the substance is the same, and the number of such "deals" may not have increased as much as some people would have us believe. Those who use bribery charges as cards in their political games know very well how such accusations can affect ordinary people. The thief who shouts "Stop thief!" reflects behavior known since time immemorial.

How long will the present situation continue? Are there any glimmerings of hope that it will change? Social forecasts are a dangerous business in general, but especially in this case. The level and structure of crime are influenced not by political factors alone, which do lend themselves to a measure of forecasting. I have not here touched upon many key factors that contribute directly to the escalation of various kinds of crime. These factors include the open borders among the fourteen former republics, now sovereign states; huge holes and breathtaking contradictions in criminal law and regulation; ethnic conflicts that all too often disguise mafialike feuds between clans, presenting them as sacred crusades of patriots defending their motherland; the social vulnerability of many segments of the population who have been marginalized in the prime of their lives, for example demobilized servicemen and officers who have been ejected from their comfortable homes without having a civilian skill or any prospects for the future; the hundreds of thousands of refugees, who have been victims of the mad, ill-considered race among republics to gain sovereignty, as well as victims of aggressive nationalism. All of them rightly feel that fate has done them a deep injustice. In their state of desperation they are ready to do whatever it takes to survive.

Paradoxically, the trend to internationalize dangerous crimes that were hardly ever known in Russia, such as the narcotics industry, smuggling, terrorism, and other by-products of the changes sweeping the country, may help to combat these crimes. Cooperation with Western professionals, who have great experience tackling these universal evils, is inevitable. Significant change, however, can occur only after the social, political, and economic situation in the country has changed dramatically. When the time of troubles, with all the cataclysms accompanying a period of transition, is succeeded by a new phase in the development of state and society, a system of law will be established that will not promise to achieve the utopian goal of "liquidating" crime. Such a system will put in place all the mechanisms necessary to protect society against criminals. This process will be long and arduous; it will demand many sacrifices along the way. Will society be able to resist the temptation of "accelerating" this process, of jumping over the abyss instead of patiently building bridges and destroying the roots of crime, and not just its evil fruits?

Who can tell? In any case, the yearning for a government with an "iron hand," one that would use traditional formulas to restore "order and discipline" is very much alive. It attracts more supporters every day, even among intelligent, thoughtful persons and among practically all the political groups that competed in the December 1993 elections for a new parliament. For the foreseeable future, crime will continue to be a critical variable determining Russia's future.

Translated by the Federal News Service

14

Alexander M. Yakovlev

The Presidency in Russia

Evolution and Prospects

> *King James I: Do you think that there is anything above the King?*
> *Chief Justice Coke: The King should be under no man, but he is under God and the Law.*

The President of the USSR: Shift of Powers

The creation of the office of the presidency was an unprecedented event in the history of the Russian and the Soviet state. The one-man rule, autocratic principle of Russian statehood had been established at the outset of the empire, serving as a basis for the absolute monarchy in Russia, and it survived the October 1917 Bolshevik Revolution. The political slogan "All power to the Soviets" first was used by the Bolsheviks to disband the Russian democratic Provisional Government in 1917 and later on was used to legalize the Communist Party's dictatorial rule.

After the Revolution the autocracy principle was successively embodied in Lenin, Stalin, Khrushchev, Brezhnev, and others, all of whom possessed one decisive characteristic: they were the leaders of the Communist Party, the organization conceived, created, developed, and functioning as a party of uncompromising one-man rule.

The legal origins of the presidency in the Russian Federation may be traced to the period of the Soviet Union's constitutional development that preceded perestroika. At this time the Presidium of the USSR Supreme Soviet, which was considered to be the office of the "collective president" invested with both legislative and executive functions, was described in Article 119 of the USSR Constitution as "a standing body of the Supreme Soviet of the USSR, accountable to it for all its work and exercising the functions of the highest body of the state authority of the USSR." Article 120 stated that "the Presidium of the Supreme Soviet shall be elected from the deputies and shall consist of a Chairman, First Vice-Chairman," and so on. Accordingly, Soviet state structure was constructed as a pyramidal one crowned by one figure, the chairman of the Presidium of the Supreme Soviet of the USSR. Until 1989, this position was primarily ceremonial (real power being exercised by the Party). During the Stalin period (from 1938 to 1946) the chairman was Mikhail Kalinin—a man whose wife Stalin sent to a labor camp, a man who served his master while trembling for his own life.

The election in 1989 of the Congress of People's Deputies of the USSR and the ensuing election of the Supreme Soviet of the USSR marked the beginning of the transformation of power in Russia. More and more important decisions were being made not by the Politburo but by the Supreme Soviet or the Congress of People's Deputies. The secretary general of the Communist Party of the Soviet Union, Mikhail Gorbachev, spent most of his time not in the Central Committee building at Staraia Ploshchad' but in the Kremlin, at the Supreme Soviet sessions held in the Palace of Congresses.

A simple but fundamental change had taken place: elected representatives began openly, under the watchful eyes of a nation extensively served by television, to discuss the issues, publicly debating them, freely voting their decisions. Now Party directives were not automatically applicable. The Party could no longer dictate; it had to ask the Supreme Soviet to adopt its directives. These procedures, which sound elementary and which in a democratic society would have long ago been taken for granted, endowed the Supreme Soviet with the power to decide significant matters of state.

The functions and the structure of the Presidium of the Supreme Soviet were also changed: its chairman now became the chairman of the Supreme Soviet (and the head of the Presidium as well). The architect of perestroika, Mikhail Gorbachev, secretary general of the Communist Party of the Soviet Union (CPSU), was elected a people's deputy and the chairman of the Supreme Soviet of the USSR. This previously ceremonial position acquired new significance; it was occupied by the political leader of the (only) ruling party. The 1989 elections provided the two newly constituted bodies with legitimacy, while the chairman of the Supreme Soviet acquired new authority as "the highest official of the USSR" (Art. 112). Under the amended Constitution he could conduct foreign policy negotiations, head the Defense Council, recommend appointments for top government positions, and address the Supreme Soviet on the state of the nation and other important issues.

The real meaning of this development was to shift as much power as possible from the Communist Party apparatus to the Congress and the Supreme Soviet. But the powers of the chairman of the Supreme Soviet reflected the other side of this process: the unity of powers principle (as opposed to that of the separation of powers) was maintained. Gorbachev (remaining the secretary general of the CPSU) as the chairman of the Supreme Soviet became the head of state with the customary executive powers and functioned simultaneously as chairman of the legislative body.

In March 1990, at the extraordinary Third Congress of People's Deputies of the USSR, a proposal to institute the office of the presidency was submitted. At this session of the Congress I had the opportunity to open the debate.

> Now we have reached a stage of our development where we are obliged to answer very simple, but basic questions. One was put to me recently: Aren't you fed up with adopting more and more new laws which nobody bothers to carry out? As this simple question shows, the mere enactment of laws, without the instruments to execute them, gives one the terrible sensation of being involved in ethereal, fictitious activities. If even the perfect laws (or sometimes less than perfect ones) that we adopt remain "suspended in empty air," the very idea of the state based on law is undermined. The very idea of perestroika—to exchange the domination of man over man for the dominance of the law over everybody—becomes hollow and insubstantial. Because of this I understand and share the ideas which are forming now in society—to create certain institutions which would permit us to implement the laws. Let us also ask ourselves some simple questions: What do we need? Do we need a strong state power? I answer this question in the negative. What we need is a strong *executive*

power. Wherein lies the strength of this power? It executes. What does this power execute? This power executes the laws. For me, therefore, a strong executive power is one which implements the will expressed by a strong *legislative* power. Another point. The demarcation of competence, the separation of legislative and executive powers, must be supported by reestablishing an independent, influential *judicial* power. All the endless and inevitable questions about competence, the interrelations between the norms of law and the realities of life must be considered and decided by the judicial power, not by the legislative or executive authorities.

There is nothing new in all of this: it is the age-old, venerated idea of the equality and independence of the three branches of power. That is the central problem we now face. In an attempt to strengthen state power God forbid we forget that what we need is not just any kind of order but order based on law. Order can take many different forms: the order of a prison or the gulag is not the kind of order that we need.

The institution of the presidency of the USSR brought a new dimension to the political power process. The chairman of the Supreme Soviet was deprived of all executive powers and his position reduced to the easily recognizable one of the Speaker of parliament. The definition of "the highest official" was transferred to the newly established post of the president of the USSR (and Gorbachev was elected by the Congress of People's Deputies of the USSR to that post). Also transferred was a whole list of executive functions. He became "the head of state" and the head of the cabinet of ministers without the legal authority to rule over the legislative bodies—the Congress and the Supreme Soviet.

In his acceptance speech President Gorbachev said:

Fears have been expressed that the presidency could pose a threat of the usurpation of power. There are no grounds for such fears. This is guaranteed by the Constitution itself, and the Constitution is protected now by the powerful supreme representative bodies of state power that have genuine rights, the Congress of People's Deputies and the Supreme Soviet. It is guaranteed by a serious, carefully thought out set of checks and balances that rule out the possibility of development in the direction of an autocracy. . . . The principle of the separation of powers assumes a clear demarcation of functions.

The basis for the separation of powers was established. Soon after that the end of the Soviet Union aborted this process.

The President of the Russian Federation:
A Bipolar System of Power

Within the Russian Federation the same processes were observed: the concentration of all powers in the hands of the chairman of the Supreme Soviet of the Russian Federation at the early stage of amending the Constitution and the subsequent institution of the presidency. The same kind of political logic was present there: Boris Yeltsin, the most influential person in Russian politics, was elected to the position of chairman of the Supreme Soviet of the Russian Federation and accordingly embodied all powers pertaining to the Congress of People's Deputies and to the Supreme Soviet of the Russian Federation as well as executive powers. Soon after that, Yeltsin was elected by popular ballot to be the president of the Russian Federation.

At that point in the process, however, there was one significant difference in comparison to the same process on the all-Union level. Although the title "the highest official of the Russian Federation" was transferred to the president as well as the title "the head of executive power," nonetheless he was not given the title of "head of state." The Congress of People's Deputies of the Russian Federation was described in the Constitution as "the highest agency of state power of the Russian Federation" (Art. 104). The Congress of People's Deputies and the Supreme Soviet were adamant in guarding the Bolshevik principle, "All power to the Soviets."

Soon the person elected by the Congress of People's Deputies as the chairman of the Supreme Soviet of the Russian Federation (following Yeltsin's election as the president) emerged as an influential political figure (Ruslan Khasbulatov). All the powers accorded to Yeltsin as the chairman of the Supreme Soviet were now granted to Khasbulatov. Article 115 of the Constitution remained unchanged, endowing the chairman of the Supreme Soviet with the functions pertaining to the chief executive and the head of state, parallel to that of the president of the Russian Federation. All powers provided in the Constitution for the Congress and the Supreme Soviet remained unchanged. The only possibility of curbing the powers of the Congress of People's Deputies was to amend the Constitution. But the only body capable of amending the Constitution was the Congress itself.

As a result, instead of the separation of executive from legislative power, which could have been expected with the institution of the presidency in the Russian Federation, there emerged a bipolar system of state power: the chairman of the Supreme Soviet (the Congress of People's Deputies and the Supreme Soviet) versus the president of the Russian Federation.

Checks and Balances

To assess the institution of the presidency at this juncture in the formation of the Russian Federation as a state, it is useful to single out some specific points in regard to government structures generally. Theoretically it is possible to make a distinction between the two "ideal types" of a democratic state structure: parliamentary and presidential republics.

In both these types the state power is based on the popular will, but in presidential republics the popular mandate is given not only to the legislature but also to the popularly elected president. In this situation the separation of the legislative from the executive power becomes institutionalized, forming a structural duality (the president *and* the parliament), under which the president serves as head of state and chief executive officer. (In a parliamentarian republic the chief executive —the prime minister—is elected by the parliament).

In both types of republics the legislative and the executive powers interact and counterbalance each other:

- The right of parliament to a no-confidence vote (requiring the resignation of the government) is balanced by the right of the prime minister to dissolve parliament and hold early elections.
- The right of the president to promulgate or veto a law adopted by the parliament is balanced by the right of the legislature to override that veto.
- The right of the president to nominate the highest government officials is balanced by the right of parliament to confirm or withhold confirmation.
- The right of parliament to adopt laws is balanced by the right of the president to change laws through the referenda he is empowered to conduct.

Applying this analytical framework to the 1992 version of the Constitution of the Russian Federation, it can be said that:

- The Congress of People's Deputies and the Supreme Soviet were empowered to compel the government's resignation through the use of a no-confidence vote and to impeach the president for any "violation of the Constitution" (Art. 121.10), but the president did not have the power to dissolve the Congress or the Supreme Soviet and hold early parliamentary elections (when at the final session of the Congress the president and the chairman of the Supreme Soviet proposed early elections for both the Congress and the president, the outraged deputies voted to remove the president from office and only seventy-two votes saved him).
- The right of the president to promulgate (or not to do so) the legislative acts of the Supreme Soviet could be overridden by a simple majority in the Supreme Soviet; this provision therefore deprived the presidential veto of any real significance.
- The right to nominate the judges of the Supreme Court of the Russian Federation and the Supreme Arbitration Court belonged not to the president but to the chairman of the Supreme Soviet.
- The president's right to address the Congress of People's Deputies on the most important questions of socioeconomic development, on foreign and domestic policy, was duplicated by the chairman of the Supreme Soviet's having the same right.
- The president did not possess the right to conduct referenda; this was entirely the prerogative of the Congress of People's Deputies and the Supreme Soviet.

As a result, the bipolar system of government had an asymmetrical character: the predominance of power resided in the Supreme Soviet and the Congress of People's Deputies.

The new Constitution of the Russian Federation that was adopted by the referendum of December 12, 1993, radically changed this balance. The new Constitution assigns the title of "head of state" to the president of the Russian Federation (Art. 80). Executive power "is exercised by the Government of the Russian Federation" (Art. 110). The chairman of the government of the Russian Federation "defines the basic guidelines for the activity of the government of the Russian Federation and organizes its work" (Art. 113). Neither the chairman of the Council of Ministers nor the president is given the title of " highest official," but many provisions in the new Constitution permit one to consider the president to be the chief executive as well as the head of state.

With the consent of the State Duma, the lower chamber of the Federal Assembly, the president can appoint the chairman of the Council of Ministers (the government). He has the right to chair sessions of the government; adopt (or not) decisions on the dismissal of the government, appoint and remove from office members of government such as the deputy premiers and federal ministers (upon the proposal of the chairman of the Council of Ministers), and submit to the Federal Assembly candidates for appointment as judges of the Supreme Court and the Supreme Arbitration Court, the general prosecutor, and justices of the federal courts (Art. 85). The president is the commander in chief of the armed forces.

The new Constitution empowers the president to submit draft laws to the State Duma, to sign and promulgate laws (his veto can be overridden only by a qualified majority of the State Duma), and to dissolve the State Duma if that body rejects his candidates for chairman of the Council of Ministers three times. Should the State Duma pass a no-confidence vote for a second time within a three-month period, the president may dissolve it, although not within the first year after parliamentary elections. The State Duma cannot be dissolved when martial law is declared or a state of emergency is in effect on the whole territory of the Russian Federation, or within a six-month period preceding the expiration of the president's term of office, or from the moment the State Duma files charges against the president with the intention of removing him from office until the adoption of a corresponding decision by the Federation Council (during a three-month period). The president sets the date for the new elections so as to ensure that the newly elected State Duma will convene no later than four months from the date of its dissolution.

The Separation of Powers versus the "Father of Nations"

As the head of state and chief executive, the president is also endowed by the Constitution with the power to legislate, to issue edicts (ukases) (Art. 90). The government must be guided by "the Constitution of the

Russian Federation, federal laws and the normative edicts of the President of the Russian Federation" (Art. 115). In prerevolutionary Russia the emperor was also empowered to issue edicts of a normative character, thereby stripping the Code of Laws of the Russian Empire of any real significance. Nobody was particularly concerned with the Code of Laws, and the country lived, not under the protection of a stable, predictable shield of well-known, definite laws, but from one ukase to the next.

The concept of edicts or decrees survived the 1917 Revolution. The USSR Constitution gave the Presidium of the Supreme Soviet the right to issue decrees of a normative character between sessions of the Supreme Soviet, although they had to be confirmed at the next session of the Supreme Soviet or they did not become law. The Supreme Soviet obediently approved all these decrees because they constituted Party directives clothed in legal form. Under amendments to the USSR Constitution passed in 1990, however, the Presidium of the Supreme Soviet was deprived of the right to pass decrees. Thus it would be logical to expect that no further provision to enact edicts would be made for any branch of government.

But such was not the case. Article 127.7 of the USSR Constitution this time allowed the president of the USSR to issue decrees "on the basis of and in fulfillment of the USSR Constitution and USSR laws." This definition was ambiguous. An edict adopted "on the basis" of the Constitution could very well be just another piece of legislation, while a decree adopted "in fulfillment" of the Constitution and USSR laws could be a specific act of an executive nature, since it was not on the normative level of law. Immediately after the passage of that article, President Gorbachev issued decrees of a normative character, thus continuing the practice of the Presidium of the Supreme Soviet, but this time without the obligation to obtain the subsequent approval of the Supreme Soviet itself.

The same situation can be observed in the new Constitution of the Russian Federation. The right of the president to issue decrees of a normative character means that he can exercise both legislative and executive powers. The Federation Council, the upper chamber of the Federal Assembly, can confirm (or not) only those presidential decrees that relate to the introduction of martial law and a state of emergency (Art. 102).

The validity of the separation of powers principle was recognized in the prerevolutionary period. Professor N.M. Korkunov, in his classic text on Russian state law, commented that Aristotle in his polity distinguished between these branches of power, although for Aristotle this was not the principal matter but rather a useful distinction for a more convenient classification of powers. Korkunov contended that John Locke, who elaborated the separation of powers notion, shared Aristotle's view.[1] Only Montesquieu in *Esprit des lois* linked the separation of powers principle with the preservation of freedom, guarantees of legality, and the negation of tyranny. From a simple classification used as a convenient way to describe the structure of a government, the separation of powers became, in Korkunov's words, "the main condition of any legitimate political organization, the main guarantee against the arbitrary restriction of liberty."

But how could the vital separation of powers principle be reconciled with the autocratic Russian empire, with the power of an emperor described as an "absolute [*samoderzhavnyi*] and unrestricted" monarch? The answer to this question is very instructive. Korkunov argued that the separation of powers is nothing more than "a particular instance of the more general mode of correlation between the functions of power, namely, the *combination* of powers as they are specifically applied."[2] As a result it was the combination of powers that was defined as the main, essential feature of the state, while the *separation* of powers was depicted as subordinate, less significant and less decisive.

But how is it possible to avoid tyranny under the "combination of powers as they are specifically applied"? How can abuses of power be prevented? Abuses can be prevented, argued Korkunov, if separate and equal organs of power, similar in type, perform the same functions (for example, the Roman consuls), or if a specific function is vested jointly in several persons in such a manner that each of them possesses the same power as the others. As an example, Korkunov referred to the Roman *magistrates collegiarius*. This approach to the separation of powers principle reduces it to a subordinate position in governmental organization (the dominant principle being the combination of powers) and, first, reinterprets it as the problem of separation of power *functions* (not the separation of *powers*) and, second, describes collegiality in political decision making as the guarantee against abuses of power. This later concept survived the 1917 Revolution. In his Secret Speech of

February 1956 describing Stalin's absolute power as the general secretary of the CPSU and his terrible abuses of this power, Khrushchev proposed that the decisive guarantee against the personal dictatorship of the secretary general be the adherence to the "collective leadership" of the party.

The separation of powers, in Friedrich Engels's view, is nothing more than "the prosaic division of labor as applied to a state mechanism for the sake of simplification and control."[3] Soviet theory of state and law held that "the existence in the socialist state of organs of power with different competence means that simultaneously with the realization in reality of the unity of powers principle, it is necessary to have some degree of separation in the application of the state power functions."[4]

Not the separation but the "combination" or "unity" of state powers, not the separation of *powers* but the separation of state *functions*—these are the common theoretical positions of the Russian empire's legal theorist and of the Soviet theory of state and law.

This similarity could be observed in political realities as well. Peter the Great established many collegia in the state apparatus. As early as 1809 the Imperial State Council was instituted. None of these collegia were able to diminish the absolute power of the tsar. The republic of Soviets was declared to be the principal form of the Soviet socialist state. The term *soviet* is the Russian word meaning "council," the collective ruling body. The Soviets were pictured as collective bodies of state power performing all necessary functions, legislative as well as executive. None of these bodies were able to diminish the absolute power of the Party, and no single collective body of the Party was able to diminish the absolute power of the secretary general.

In the Russian Federation Constitution, in 1992, as amended, Article 1 declared that "the sovereignty of the people, federalism, a republican form of rule, and the separation of powers are unshakable foundations of the constitutional system of Russia." Article 3 stated: "The system of state power in the Russian Federation is based on the principles of the separation of legislative, executive, and judicial powers." These were the same amendments included in the Constitution of the Russian Soviet Socialist Republic, a Constitution that conformed to the 1936 Stalin Constitution. Of course, the Stalin Constitution never mentioned the separation of powers. Contrary to that principle, Article 2 stated: "All power in the USSR belongs to the people. The people exercise state power through the Soviets of People's Deputies, which constitute the political foundation of the USSR." The incompatibility of these two principles was evident: either all state power belongs to the Soviets or the state powers are separated. Nonetheless, in the 1992 revision of Russia's Constitution these principles were both presented side by side.

In the August 1993 draft of the new Constitution of the Russian Federation, Article 10 stated that "state power in the Russian Federation is exercised on the basis of the separation of legislative, executive, and judicial powers. Bodies of legislative, executive, and judicial power are independent." This general principle was supplemented with a specific norm in Article 97: "Deputies of the State Duma work on a full-time professional basis. Deputies of the State Duma cannot be in state service or engage in any other paid activity, apart from teaching, scientific, or other creative activity." On October 11, 1993, the president issued Decree 1623, "On Amendments and Supplements to Regulations of the Federal Bodies of Power for the Transitional Period," in which the same formula was repeated: "Deputies cannot be in state service." This decree was published in the official newspaper, *Rossiiskii vestnik.* One week later, the same newspaper reprinted this decree with the same date of adoption, the same title, and the same official number. But this time the relevant norm was phrased differently. Now it said: "Deputies of the State Duma work on a full-time professional basis *with the exception of deputies who are the members of the Council of Ministers—the Government of the Russian Federation.* Deputies of the State Duma cannot be in state service or engage in any other paid activity, apart from teaching, scientific, or other creative activity *with the exception of deputies who are the members of the Council of Ministers—the Government of the Russian Federation*" (emphasis added).

On October 28, 1993, the same official newspaper carried an editorial explaining this point: "Let us not forget that the separation of powers does not suppose that they exist in absolute autonomy." And further:

> The separation of powers—it is no more (and no less) than the mechanism that does not permit the mixing up of functions, not the functions of a person but those of state bodies. Legislative bodies have one kind of competence, executive organs have another. If there is no mixing of these functions, there will be no encroachment by one branch of power upon the other—thus we need not fear losing the separation of powers principle.

Of course the point in question is debatable, but it is hard to get rid of the impression that this position is much closer to that of Korkunov, Engels, and the Soviet *Juridical Encyclopedic Dictionary* than it is to Montesquieu's *Esprit des lois.*

On November 3, 1993, the same official newspaper published the president's report on the prospects for constitutional development in Russia. The president said:

> I am astonished that at the present time some people have begun to doubt the separation of powers principle. I consider this a grave political mistake. Only recently we survived a tragedy. The deepest cause of this tragedy was exactly the distortion of this very principle in the present Constitution. Let us not forget it.

On December 12, 1993, the new Constitution of the Russian Federation was adopted. This Constitution made no provision for the possibility that members of the executive branch (the Council of Ministers) could simultaneously serve as members of the legislative branch (the State Duma). Only the "concluding and the transitional provisions" stated that "a deputy of the *first State Duma* can simultaneously be a member of the government of the Russian Federation" (italics added). As Russians often say, however, "The most stable things in Russia are those which are proclaimed to be temporary."

The Outlook

The prospects for the presidency in Russia will be heavily influenced by several factors, notably the personality factor, the institutional factor, and historic-cultural factors. It would be impossible to ignore the role played in the history of Russian constitutional development by the personal traits of certain historical figures. Alexander II, the Tsar Liberator, is the most outstanding example. The personal adherence of President Yeltsin to the development of democracy in Russia is evident; it plays (and will play) a significant role in shaping the future of the presidency in this country.

No less significant will be the role played by the state institutions that the new Constitution establishes, the role of the new bicameral legislature, the Federal Assembly, being crucial. It can be said without exaggeration that an independent, influential legislative branch, an authoritative parliament that adequately expresses the will of the people and enjoys the support of the majority, constitutes the *conditio sine qua non* of the separation of powers and of democracy as a whole.

Will the newly elected Federal Assembly be inspired to respond adequately to this historic calling? Will an independent, authoritative judiciary provide an orderly mechanism for conflict resolution and the protection of the people's rights and freedoms? To a significant extent the answers to these questions will depend on historic and cultural factors, two of which can be singled out as potentially dangerous for the development of democracy in Russia.

The first may be called the "outrage factor." Any democracy inevitably has to deal with the discussions and debates necessary for the reconciliation of diverse interests and different approaches. It is a time-consuming process. It may look cumbersome and seem not the most effective form of government. Sometimes the apparently endless debates can irritate the public ("the country is just going to hell and all they do is debate"). In this situation, the eventual benefits of democracy can be lost from view, particularly if those with special political agendas inflame public irritation to the point of outrage.

Will the people of Russia prove susceptible to this kind of anti-democratic propaganda or will they not? Will they or will they not succumb to the temptation to try to achieve miraculous results through "the strong hand, no nonsense" approach of dictatorship? Presidencies in many countries have lent themselves precisely to such sentiments.

The second danger for democracy, deriving from Russian history, may be called the "*paterfamilias* factor." During hundreds of years Russia was predominantly a peasant society. A traditional peasant family is entirely subordinated to the father. The head of the family and the provider, the guardian of safety, the legislator and the judge—for centuries they were the father in the family and the tsar on the throne. Many things have changed in Russia. A previously illiterate population is now in full possession of a wide range of information through the print, audiovisual, and other media. Russia is now an industrialized, urban society. Two-thirds of the population are urban dwellers with a dispersed family structure.

To what extent have the peasant, patriarchal sociocultural stereotypes survived? Can they influence political behavior to such an extent that in an intolerable economic situation people will ask, "Where is our father? Let us ask the president to be him!" The consultative body that Peter the Great instituted, the Senate, granted the tsar the honorary title of "Father of the Nation."

Or will the belief that God and the Law are above the president prevail?

This chapter was written in English by the author

Notes

1. N.M. Korkunov, *Russkoe gosudarstvennoe pravo* (Russian State Law) (St. Petersburg: Tip. M.M. Stasiulevicha, 1913–14), p. 211.

2. Ibid., p. 378.

3. Karl Marx and Friedrich Engels, *Sochineniia* (Works), 2d ed. (Moscow: Gosudarstvennoe izd-vo polit. lit-ry, 1956), 5:203.

4. *Iuridicheskii entsiklopedicheskii slovar'* (Juridical Encyclopedic Dictionary) (Moscow: Sovetskaia entsiklopedii, 1984), pp. 313–14.

15

Protopresbyter Vitalii Borovoi

The Religious and Spiritual Factor in the Making of a New Russia

Introductory Remarks

In the birth pangs accompanying the emergence of a new Russia, a particular historical role will be played (and is being played) by the spiritual factor—especially the Orthodox Church, although, of course, this does not exclude the possibility that other religions and confessions of the Russian Federation may influence the course of events.

Here we must understand and keep in mind that the church known, historically and traditionally, as the Russian Orthodox Church (Moscow Patriarchate) is the Church of All Rus—that is, the Church in Russia, Ukraine, Belarus, Moldova, the Baltic lands, and farther, beyond the Urals, in the expanses of Eurasia. This church was a great missionary church, traversing, in order to preach Christianity, vast expanses of Eastern Europe, Siberia, and Asia (going as far as Korea, China, and Japan and in North America, extending from Alaska in the north to California in the south).

This church brought into being many local Orthodox churches, which have now become either autocephalous—independent—or autonomous and self-governing under patriarchal jurisdiction. Orthodox churches exist in Poland, the Czech and Slovak republics, Finland, Latvia, Estonia, Lithuania, Japan, and the United States. A significant Russian, Ukrainian, Carpathian-Ruthenian, and Belorussian diaspora has launched churches in North America, Western Europe, and Australia.

The whole of this diaspora, even those which do not recognize the jurisdiction of the Moscow Patriarchate, historically comes within the scope of the traditional conception of the Church of All Rus, for all of them have their primary canonical, historical, and spiritual origins in the Russian Orthodox Church.

From this bare listing it is clear what significance the Orthodox factor can and should have in the making of a new Russia.

The Ecumenical Nature of Early Christianity in Rus

Historically and geopolitically, Rus was located in the center and on the crossroads of influences and borrowings among the cultures of Byzantium, the East, and the West (Hellenism, the Slavic world, the European world, and Eurasia).

The penetration and spread of Christianity in Rus were characterized by its heterogeneity and its fundamentally ecumenical nature. It was confined to no single ethnic group but rather extended far beyond its original bounds to cover the whole of Eastern Europe and, from there, to include the countries and peoples of Eurasia.

There is a profound geopolitical and historical truth in our ancient tales and legends about the beginnings of Christianity in Rus (the legends of the Apostle Andrei Pervozvannyi, of the Kherson bishops, of Kii (the legendary founder of Kiev), of Black Sea–Azov Rus (the "third center of Rus"), of Christianity in Khazaria, and of "the calling of the Varangians" (that is, of the western Scandinavian factor in the Christianization of Russia). These legends demonstrate the fundamentally ecumenical, but nevertheless synthesizing, universal quality that brought Rus and Eastern Europe within the bounds of the entire Christian *universum*, thus becoming an organic part of the Universal Church.

The centuries-long history of the Church of All Rus evolved in a dialectical fashion, assimilating and recasting the spiritual values and the heritage of both Byzantine (Eastern) and European (Western) culture with the aim of producing a specifically Orthodox synthesis, an integral culture that would be a creative reflection of the spiritual essence and truth of Orthodoxy. What were these attempts to express the Orthodox synthesis of truth, culture, and society?

They were the Kievan (primary) synthesis, the Muscovite (messianic) synthesis, and the Petersburg (imperial) synthesis.

The Kievan (Primary) Orthodox Synthesis

At the time of Prince Vladimir, Rus was closer to Bulgaria, the Czech lands, Poland, and Western and Northwestern Europe than to faraway Byzantium. To develop the famous route "from the Varangians to the Greeks" required an intense concentration of energy, while Central Europe and Northwestern Europe were closely tied together and familiar with each other. It was here that Western Christianity spread. The Czech lands, Poland, Denmark, Norway, and Sweden all accepted Western Christianity. Rus may have accepted it as well; indeed, the papacy energetically tried to spread its influence in Rus. Nevertheless, Rus accepted Christianity from Byzantium and assimilated the Eastern Orthodox heritage of Saints Kirill and Methodius. The tale of the "choice of faith" made by Saint Vladimir at his baptism has a deep historical significance.

This choice was undoubtedly influenced by the fact that at that time Byzantium was at the peak of culture and education, whereas the West was at an immeasurably lower level of development.

To accept Christianity from Byzantium was to attach oneself to the treasures of Byzantine and world culture. At the same time Rus received a wealth of Slavonic Christian culture from Bulgaria, conveyed in a comprehensible, Slavonic language (Holy Scripture, liturgies, the heritage of Saints Kirill and Methodius and their disciples, and a rich collection of literature and other writings, either translated from the Greek or written originally in Slavonic). At that time there was nothing in the West on a comparable cultural level. The language of the church became the common language of all Rus, the language of "the people." A single Christian Orthodox culture covering the whole of Rus began to develop.

The continual interaction of this culture with the peoples of Southern and Central Europe (Bulgarians, Czechs, and Poles), as well as with the peoples of Western and Northwestern Europe (Germany and Scandinavia), created favorable ecumenical conditions for the development and flourishing of the culture of Rus. These contacts also formed the basis for the development of the Kievan (primary) Orthodox synthesis.

This process was interrupted by the invasion of the Tatars and the imposition of the burdensome Tatar (Mongol) yoke.

The Muscovite (Messianic) Orthodox Synthesis

The Tatar yoke was a time of painful trial for the Russian church. Not only did the church bear and survive this trial; it was also enriched with new historical experience and new creative spiritual energies.

Kiev fell, but Christian culture did not disappear. It was preserved by the church, which became for the people the custodian of their spiritual values and their source of support in the disasters that befell them. The main reason for the defeat of Rus and for the imposition of the Tatar yoke had been the political disunity of the individual princes, their internecine strife and continual quarrels. This painful lesson was not taken in vain, and the church employed all its efforts and strength to achieve a unified state of all Rus.

This devotion to the unity of Rus and the growing realization of the need for unity by the people of the princedoms, appanages, and military units of Rus lay at the core of the entire life and history of the Muscovite period of the Russian Orthodox Church. These ideas also became the driving force of the Muscovite princedom (later tsardom) in its struggle for the creation of a strong, centralized, Russian (Muscovite) state, capable of uniting all of Rus and of becoming the custodian of Orthodoxy and the holy protector of all the Orthodox peoples from outside threats to their faith and nationality.

The Muscovite state was very conscious of its responsibility for "all Rus," for "all Orthodoxy." This consciousness, inspired by the church and accepted by Muscovite Rus as its holy duty, was the source of the Muscovite state's inner strength and enabled it to emerge as the victor from all the challenges it faced, to emerge with new strengths and plans for the future.

Devotion to holy duty enabled Muscovy to survive and overcome the Tatar yoke and to emerge from it onto the wide expanses of Eastern, Trans-Volga, steppe Europe, going beyond the Urals and into Siberia and vast areas of future Eurasia. It also enabled Muscovy to repel the crusading aggression in the Baltic region and subsequently to break through to the Baltic Sea. It enabled Muscovy as well to deal with the protracted struggle with the grand principality of Lithuania and with

Poland for the unification of all the lands of Rus—Ukraine and Belarus—around Moscow and with Moscow. Moscow's victory made it possible to create a "Great Rus," successor and heir to the Christian cultural mission of Kievan Rus in the Eastern Orthodox ecumenicity. Finally, devotion to holy duty also enabled the Orthodox peoples of Ukraine and Belarus to stand their ground, notwithstanding the onslaught of the ecclesiastical union, Polonization, and other assaults on their nationality.

Beyond serving as the principal unifying force and spiritual center for all Rus, the Russian church during the period of Muscovite Rus also allowed the Russian people to see themselves as a great power.

The union of the Greek Orthodox Church with the papacy on terms proposed by the See of Constantinople at a council held in Florence (1439–43), and later rejected by the Orthodox, and the betrayal of Orthodoxy by the Byzantine emperor as well as the Constantinian-Polish patriarch and metropolitan, Isidor the Greek, ended the Russians' belief in the sacred power of the Byzantine ecclesiastical authorities. Russians could no longer believe that the Constantinian-Polish patriarchs and the Greek metropolitans whom they sent to Rus were loyal to Orthodoxy. In Moscow the church authorities decided it was necessary to "save Orthodoxy" and that this was now the sacred duty of the Muscovite prince and the Russian church. They expelled Isidor and elected as the metropolitan of all Rus their own Russian Orthodox candidate. Thus the Russian church became independent from Constantinople, and the Muscovite prince became the defender and custodian of the whole of Orthodoxy.

The conquest of Constantinople by the Turks in 1453 and the disappearance of the "Holy Empire of the New, Second Rome" was interpreted in Rus as an eschatological sign of the coming of "hard times," a period of decline and deviation.

Now the Russian church and its metropolitan (later patriarch) became the custodian of the Orthodox faith, and the defender and holy protector of all Orthodox people was to be the Muscovite grand prince (later tsar), the heir and successor to the Byzantine emperors. This eschatological sense of responsibility led to the belief in the world mission of Moscow, as the "Third Rome," as "Holy Rus." These messianic and eschatological beliefs made up the Muscovite Orthodox synthesis.

Such claims of the Muscovite state were ended by a deep crisis and an explosion of radical reform under Peter the Great. Here begins the Petersburg (imperial) period in the history of Russia and of the Russian church.

The Petersburg (Imperial) Orthodox Synthesis

The radical reforms of Peter the Great were most painful for the church and for Russian society. The Orthodox ideal of "bringing the world within the grace of the Church" was violently replaced from above by the authoritarian and harsh reality of state secularization. The structure of the church was broken up and was reconstituted according to the Protestant model. The patriarchate was abolished, and a synod, the Ecclesiastical College, headed by the state's chief procurator, was established. The church was transformed into the Department of Orthodox Faith. The centuries-old foundations of Orthodoxy and Holy Rus were displaced, to be turned toward the West. In essence, the ecclesiastical regulations of Peter were, in their own way, the proclamation of a Russian Reformation.

As we know, Peter's project did not succeed. The synod did not become a Protestant chief consistory. The regulations remained a mere document of state legislation, devoid of any canonical value, an alien document signifying the Babylonian captivity of the Russian church.

From the reign of Peter the Great, the Orthodox Church and Russian society were threatened for long periods by a kind of ideological, cultural, and religious-confessional "enslavement" to the West. The threat came from the two main orientations of Western life—Protestantism and Catholicism—which, with varying degrees of success and turns of fortune, fought for influence over the cultural and religious life of Russian society. The main object and goal of this struggle, however, was the church.

During the reign of Peter and of his immediate successors, the Protestant orientation held sway, while under Catherine the Great, Paul, and Alexander I the Catholic orientation had the upper hand. Enslaved to Western influences and passions, much of the governmental, aristocratic, and gentry-landowner society came to be historically and socially divorced from the people, to whom they seemed foreign.

Nonetheless, all the efforts of the Protestant and Catholic hierarchy to subordinate the Russian church to them, to weaken its influence on the people, and to use it for government purposes were in the end unsuccessful. The church and the Orthodox common people endured and overcame the dangers threatening their faith and nationality.

The enormous influence and the enthusiasm for the West manifested in some sections of Russian society aroused a natural reaction within other parts of society, especially among people who were patriotically inclined and who loved their Orthodox Church. This reaction is known as Slavophilism and *pochvennichestvo* ("back to the soil" movement), and in its later form it is also known as Eurasianism. The Slavophiles knew and loved the West, but they also saw the faults of Western culture and wanted Russia to avoid what they saw as the mistakes of the West. They developed the idea of a synthesis of Christian Western culture with Orthodoxy, the idea of *sobornost'* in ecclesiastical and social affairs—the responsibility of all for each within an organic and harmonious community. Both sets of Slavophile ideas were developed by Aleksei Khomiakov and Iurii Samarin and were taken further by Fyodor Dostoevsky, Vladimir Solov'ev, Prince Nikolai Trubetskoi, Nikolai Fedorov, and, in their own way, Nikolai Gogol and Fedor Tiutchev. Their struggle against the exhaustion and rationalism of Western theology, philosophy, and life as a whole was carried out in the name of the integral unity of culture in one's outlook on the world as well as one's daily life. The Slavophiles aspired to reconcile the East and the West on the basis of Orthodox, Slavonic, Russian culture and to create a synthesis from the creative originality and well-rounded development of the Russian church and Russian society.

Of particular significance in this synthesis was the prophetic faith of Dostoevsky, who with brilliant genius expressed in his Pushkin Speech of June 8, 1880, at the unveiling of the Aleksandr Pushkin memorial in Moscow, the significance of the Russian people's "gift of universal humanity." The purpose of the Russian in this world, Dostoevsky said, is clearly all-European, universal: "To become truly Russian, fully Russian, can only be and can only mean to become the brother of all people, to become a universal man." The task of Russia is "to utter the word of great, universal harmony, of the brotherly and everlasting concord of all peoples." Dostoevsky's passionate faith in the gift of universal humanity is his solemn ordinance to the Russian people for centuries to come. Dostoevsky's Pushkin Speech can be considered the finest expression of the ideals of the Petersburg (imperial) Orthodox synthesis.

This synthesis in the history of Russia and the Orthodox Church was tragically interrupted, however, by the Revolution of 1917–18.

The 1917 Revolution and the Break with the Imperial Orthodox Synthesis

After the 1917–18 Revolution, Russia became a testing ground, a raw materials base, and a labor reserve for the international experiment of a Marxist, atheist society and state.

This was a time when the ideology of militant communism dominated. In the process of its implementation, the ideology was transformed into a totalitarian system of utopian maximalism and repressive party dictatorship.

The Revolution in Russia was welcomed by some in the West with joy and with the hope that the fall of the tsarist regime and the disintegration of the Russian empire would once and for all remove the danger that the Slavic peoples would unite under the leadership of Russia, an alliance that would turn Russia into the superpower of Europe and Asia. Many in the West (including the Vatican) had been afraid of this danger.

The liberal and left-wing circles of the Western intelligentsia and the powerful labor union movement throughout the world, for their part, warmly supported and welcomed the Bolshevik Revolution in Russia and the new Soviet regime, which skillfully manipulated Western public opinion. The "Soviet experiment" was interpreted as the creation of a new, just, socialist society of workers and peasants, a process that should not be hindered and the "mistakes," "exaggerations," radicalism, and even brutality of which could be pardoned.

In ecstasy from such hopes and illusions, many people did not notice (or, more precisely, did not wish to notice) *how* this experiment was being conducted, *what* its ultimate goals and its consequences for the West were, or *what price* the experiment exacted. Even the testimonies of refugees and victims of the totalitarian Soviet system encountered disbelief and suspicion.

It was only the martyrdom of the church that proved beyond doubt that the very essence of the ruling party system was aimed at actually negating and repressing all freedom and aspired to destroy and uproot all religious belief. Everyone knew that the Russian Orthodox Church at the time of Patriarch Tikhon and Metropolitan Sergei in the early 1920s was more than loyal to the Soviet authorities and that it submissively, silently removed all limitations, restrictions, and controls that it had had over the organs of state power.

Nonetheless, the Russian church suffered more than all other religions and faiths. Systematically and deliberately (out of purely ideological, atheist motives), the Communist Party subjected the Russian church to destruction, with the result that it was completely uprooted from the consciousness, the life, and the history of our people.

And this action was taken against our traditional, historical Russian church, a loyal and obedient servant of the state, which had demonstrated its selfless devotion and its self-sacrificing faithfulness to its people during times of peaceful construction as well as during bloody wars. The martyrdom of the Russian church opened the eyes of the West to the fact that, if the Soviet Union were to become dominant on a world scale, such a fate awaited the West also.

The proliferation of revolutionary movements and communist parties in the West and in the countries of the Third World finally convinced the West that Soviet ideology and influence had already extended too far beyond the former borders of Russia and that the Soviet experiment would also be performed on the West as the next victim. And since Western democracy also came to be threatened by the revanchist expansionism of German nazism and Italian fascism, the best way out of this dual Soviet and Nazi threat, many thought, was for these two antidemocratic, totalitarian systems to confront and destroy each other. This confrontation indeed happened: in 1939 the Second World War began and in June 1941 German troops invaded the territory of the Soviet Union.

The Second World War and the Russian Orthodox Church

The German troops occupied all of the Baltic states, surrounded Leningrad, and took Belarus and Ukraine. In central Russia they reached as far as Moscow and Stalingrad, in the south as far as the Caucasus, and they were preparing to celebrate their final victory in Moscow. Adolf Hitler and the West, however, failed to take into account the power of the awakening of national consciousness and the strength of universal Russian opposition in the face of German enslavement and genocide. Here the Russian church played a key role in the defeat of the enemy by becoming the strongest factor in the task of awakening Orthodox national patriotism among the Russian people.

Josef Stalin skillfully used this patriotic Orthodox stimulus to mobilize and organize the united forces of the people for the defense of the fatherland and for its ultimate victory over the aggressor. The universal significance of this victory and the very liberation of Europe from Nazi occupation owe much to the moral strength and national self-sacrifice displayed by the Russian Orthodox Church. As a result of the victory, the preconditions were established for the founding of the United Nations, the development of the ecumenical movement, and the establishment of the World Council of Churches in 1948.

After overcoming a series of difficulties, the Russian church (together with its sister Orthodox churches) became a member of the World Council of Churches in 1961. Our church undertook active dialogues with the Roman Catholic Church, the churches of the United States, England, Germany, and Finland, the confessional organizations and associations of the Lutheran Church, and the Reformed Church. In Moscow, the Russian church conducted conferences involving representatives from all religions and confessions and organized round tables of scholars and theologians, which had a considerable impact on the international community.

All this ecumenical activity took place under the vigilant, ubiquitous, and all-embracing control of the Soviet state (the Council on Religious Affairs and other governmental organs) that often caused the church to be compromised both within the Soviet Union and in the eyes of Western public opinion. Many people did not understand the real goals and the nature of the Russian church's participation in the ecumenical movement; they thought that the church was merely carrying out the orders of the Soviet government. However, the reality was different and more complicated than it appeared.

It is true that during the time of brutal repression (under V.I. Lenin, Josef Stalin, and later Nikita Khrushchev) the church was forced to compromise and to make concessions in political and social matters, but *never* and *in no way* did it do so in questions of faith, doctrinal teaching, and truth to Christ and to his Gospels. Its loyalty is demonstrated by the martyrdom of the church and its silent profession of the deepest truths of Orthodoxy, which it preserved and protected.

After the West had officially recognized the Soviet regime and Soviet propaganda had begun to have an impact on Western public opinion and in Third World countries, the Russian church had been left alone, in complete isolation, to withstand the entire force of a totalitarian, repressive system. The church had no choice but to adapt to the brutal conditions of a fight for survival—to maneuver, avoiding direct attack by the authorities, keeping itself from complete devastation and destruction, at the price of sacrifices and humiliations, and to preserve itself as an organized, canonical, religious community (a church) until such time as its martyrdom should ease in intensity. The consciousness of this mission gave the church the confidence to make temporary, necessary concessions and adaptations to the yoke of the authorities. The apparently enslaved church held out and remained alive inside, ready to "resurrect" itself again and awaiting the historical events that would make renewal possible.

After the moral victory of the church during World War II and Stalin's postwar ersatz "thaw" (exploiting the moral and patriotic authority of the church), in 1956 Nikita Khrushchev exposed the crimes of Stalinism and permitted a temporary "pro-Western thaw." But before attacks on the church resumed (this time directed by Khrushchev), the Russian church hastened to take advantage of the altered political circumstances after Stalin's death to approach Western churches, hoping thereby to escape the state of isolation in which its tragic history had unfolded since the Revolution. Membership in the World Council of Churches, as noted above, together with the ability to cooperate with the entire Christian world, gave us confidence in the solidarity and support of the world ecumenical movement of all Christian churches.

And here the roles of church and state in Russia were reversed. It was *not that we were used* for the purposes of Soviet foreign policy in the West (we were too weak, insignificant, and ineffective an element in the international game for this role), but that *we used* those who wished to use us. And, in the final analysis, we used them (as can be seen today) with great success for the church. These tactics helped the church to survive and to hold out until its *second moral victory*, this time a victory not over an external enemy of our people but over the totalitarian system of atheist dictatorship that had ruled the country and endeavored to destroy the church since the Revolution of 1917–18.

As a result of the deep crisis of the totalitarian systems of Eastern Europe, a crisis that led to the breakup of the Soviet Union, new, complicated, and very difficult problems arose to confront the Russian Orthodox Church.

The Russian Orthodox Church after the Breakup of the Soviet Union

Within the church, schisms have arisen because of the nationality policies of the new states that emerged from the territory of the former Soviet Union. Under pressure from republic governments and nationalist parties or movements, church schisms have taken place in Ukraine and Moldova.

The schisms in Ukraine are particularly serious. The Moscow Patriarchate has granted the Orthodox Church of Ukraine full autonomy and self-government. The Kievan metropolitan of all Ukraine has a synod, a council of Ukrainian bishops, and a council of the whole Ukrainian Church. The election of the metropolitan, the appointment of bishops and clergy, and all issues of church administration fall entirely under the Ukrainian Church's canonical jurisdiction. All that remains is the canonical tie between the Kievan metropolitan and the Moscow patriarch. Even so, groups of nationalist Ukrainian politicians wanted the complete separation of the Ukrainian Church from the church in Moscow and pressed for full autocephaly.

The Moscow Patriarchate, however, cannot at present grant full autocephaly, because the questions of *who* is to grant this status and *how* have become a disputed issue that can only be settled at the next meeting of the All-Orthodox Council. Until the council convenes, it is vital, in order that the unity of Orthodoxy not be destroyed, that everyone refrain from making pronouncements and from recognizing the autocephaly of any group. In the meantime, the Ukrainian Church can continue to enjoy full autonomy and full self-government.

The Ukrainian political and church extremists, however, desired a political and religious break between Ukraine and Russia, and they set out to split Orthodoxy into two mutually hostile parts (Ukrainian and Russian). They issued a self-styled proclamation of autocephaly and of a Kievan Patriarchate opposed to the Moscow Patriarchate.

Even though the overwhelming majority of Orthodox Ukrainian bishops, clergy, and believers oppose this forcible split and deplore the hostility among Orthodox people it has engendered, the government of

Ukraine has supported those demanding a break with Moscow. As a result, chaos and lawlessness reign within the church in Ukraine. Already three Ukrainian Orthodox Churches exist and are fighting among themselves. One is canonically tied to the Moscow Patriarchate, while the other two claim their autocephaly, and one of them calls itself the Kievan Patriarchate.

Aside from the problems in Ukraine, the Russian Orthodox Church is contending with schisms, dissonant voices, and calamities in church life within Russia itself. Schismatic groups (parishes) of the so-called Russian Church Abroad, hostile to the Moscow Patriarchate, have appeared. In Ukraine and Belarus, Orthodox believers have come under attack or have encountered proselytism from the Uniates and the Catholics. A large number of Protestant missionaries and representatives of sects from the West have appeared. Besides the Baptists, evangelists, and Pentecostalists, groups unfamiliar to Russians, such as the Mormons, the "Moonies," and the Jehovah's Witnesses have come as well. Propagandists from Eastern religious faiths and mystical esoteric cults have proliferated.

Within Russia itself, a large number of strange and extremely destructive groups and movements have emerged, such as the Bogorodichnyi Tsentr (Virgin Center), the Beloe Bratstvo (White Brotherhood), and all kinds of adventurers, pseudobishops, and pseudoprophets, impostors from the groups calling themselves "catacomb" or free churches.

The church now has the difficult task of restoring normal church life in the eparchies and parishes—a new Christianization, catechization, and evangelization, spiritually enlightening the people of Russia and the new states of the former Soviet Union who believe in the Russian Orthodox Church.

It is very important that the church not lose its way, that it understand the signs of the times as the difficult but vital transformation of the former totalitarian ideological, political, and socioeconomic system takes place. The church should welcome this challenge with hope and joy, for new opportunities for Christian witness and service are opening up. Moreover, we should understand and know that everything that is happening to us is a divine call to the church to repent of all its past and present sins, a divine command to reform radically the whole of the church and society.

During our submissive, Soviet-era existence, many people were alienated by the silence of the church hierarchy and clergy in the face of the assaults directed by the atheist authorities. Many people accused individual hierarchs and the clergy of despicable obedience to the commands of the authorities and even of collusion with them.

Historically, our sins are twofold: our utopian maximalism resulted in a split between the ideals professed by the church and our sinful reality, thereby helping negate these ideals; our age-old obedience to state power frequently led us to render unto Caesar not only that which belonged to Caesar but also that which belonged to God. Both traits were the heritage of medieval Byzantine theocracy, which was characterized by utopian maximalism and based on the closest of unions between church and empire, the so-called symphony of powers. Indeed, Emperor Justinian clearly stated that the "priesthood and the kingdom" (that is, the church and the state) derive from the same source; they were created by God to aid each other, as body and soul, in one symphony.

From the very beginning, the Byzantine church tied its history to that of the Christian empire so as to form one complete historical process, in which the worldly, earthly principle would merge with the heavenly, grace-giving principle and "bring itself to grace" in order to transform "the kingdom of this world" into "the kingdom of Heaven."

It is hardly necessary to demonstrate here that this plan failed; theory was not translated into reality. The failure of Byzantine utopian maximalist theocracy is not only the central drama of Byzantinism; it is the tragedy of the whole Orthodox Church and of our Russian church as well.

Since we were the successors of Byzantium and considered ourselves to be "Holy Rus," the "Third Rome," this is our historic sin. This sin came down to us and was assimilated by us. Orthodoxy became predominantly a monastic-ascetic and liturgical-ritualistic piety of personal salvation. Humility and obedience were laid down as the foundation of man's spiritual journey. The church became a sort of medical institution to which individual souls could turn for treatment. Hence the suspicion of anything "worldly," of any form of socially creative activity, of organized structural change in social life.

By the same token, all responsibility for the structure of society was placed on the state and on state authorities. A dualism arose between the church and the world, between the church and culture.

Meanwhile, radical innovations in science, philosophy, art, government, and religious thought bypassed the church and often ran counter to it. Thus, Orthodox Christians began to live on two planes, representing two virtually incompatible aspects of their existence—the church and the world. On one level were the turbulent and creative developments in society, culture, science, and life in general; on the other was the relative immobility of the church and its attachment to the past. The church ceased to be the leader of its people and gradually became a minority with little influence on the dynamic impulses in society, culture, and government.

Only in the nineteenth century did a vigorous reaction against this state of affairs begin to emerge. At first spontaneous and individual, then widely organized, the movement for the revival and renewal of the church began on the very eve of the Revolution.

The Movement for Church Revival and Renewal

From the onset, the religious, social, ecclesiastical, and theological movement for the renewal of the church aroused widespread enthusiasm within the church and in society. The advocates of renewal contended that within the framework of a just ecclesiastical and social structure, the transformation of the church (and the world) could be achieved through a brotherly union of people in "holy *sobornost'*." Aleksei Khomiakov expanded the idea of "free *sobornost'*." as the essence of the historical mission of the Russian people. Vladimir Solov'ev developed a profound system of "Christian politics," which for him meant the social mission of the church. In defining the meaning of religion in the church and society, Solov'ev drew upon the doctrine of God-manhood, according to which man in society is not merely a passive observer of God's glory but God's active colleague in the building of his home. Religion is not the personal business of each one of us but the general business of us all. Christianity is not merely passive "God-contemplation"; it is also active "God-in-action."

According to Dostoevsky, the ultimate aim and desired outcome of all social activity was the Universal Church. Thus, Dostoevsky's "Russian Christian socialism" treats the church as a social ideal: true Christianity cannot be confined merely to the home or the church; it should be public and social.

In his *Philosophy of the Common Task* Nikolai Fedorov outlined his thesis that the world organism is one whole and that the task of man (of the Christian) is to draw together the fragmented multiplicity into a "multi-unity." Mankind is called upon to construct not only a new society but also a new universe. Men should be reunited so that the words "I" and "you" are replaced by the words "we" and "all." All men are brothers, all are connected, and no one is distant from others.

Similarly, Nikolai Berdiaev, the great herald of freedom and creativity, called on man to take part in building the world as a means of continuing the building of God's world.

The concept of Christianity's social nature and the goal of saving the world deeply marked Russian religious, philosophical, and social thought and found a strong resonance in the movement for church renewal, to the point of giving it at times an excessively revolutionary, radical cast. This tendency, in turn, produced reactions of alarm and distrust in the government as well as in the church hierarchy. Because of obstacles raised by the government and the conservative sector of the episcopate and the church bureaucracy, what little progress was made in church reform depended on heroic actions of a few. The stages in this movement are linked with the names of Archimandrite Fedor Bukharev (the inspector of the Kazan Spiritual Academy from 1860 to 1877); Professor V.I. Eksempliarskii (Kiev Spiritual Academy); and the Union of Enthusiasts for Church Reform headed by Metropolitan Antonii Vadskovskii and including Archimandrite Mikhail Semenov, Father Grigorii Petrov, Father Ivan Egorov, Professor A.V. Kartashev, Nikolai Berdiaev, Father Pavel Florenskii, V.E. Ern, and Sergei Bulgakov.

We should also note the religious-philosophical meetings in St. Petersburg (1901–3), the activities of the so-called Thirty-two group (1905), and the declaration of the Christian Politics group in the Duma (1906).

Issues relating to church renewal were also promoted by the so-called renewal movement of Aleksandr Vvedenskii, Father A. Boiarskii, and S. Kalinovskii during the first stage of that movement before it adopted, in the 1920s and 1930s, extremist and revolutionary views and took radical, antichurch, and uncanonical actions to attain its goals.

The drive to renew the church existed in parallel to efforts to reform society and state. Political and ecclesiastical motives frequently became intertwined, at times to the detriment of church reform, as the following examples illustrate:

- the proclamation by Sergei Bulgakov (the future Father Sergei Bulgakov) of the founding of a Christian political party;
- the program of the Russian Christian Socialists announced by Archimandrite Mikhail Semenov, professor at the St. Petersburg Spiritual Academy;
- the Union of Democratic Clergy and Laity founded in St. Petersburg in 1917;
- the Christian Brotherhood of Combat established by Valentin Pavlovich Sventsitskii (1901–7).

From 1905 to 1907, a precouncil office began preparing for the convocation of a General Council of the Russian Orthodox Church. The office worked intensively to prepare for a fundamental, radical renewal of the life, activities, and administrative structures of the church. The General Council did not meet, however, until 1917, and then issued a number of decrees outlining the general course of reform and the landmarks along the path of renewal. But it was already too late. The Revolution came, and following it great destruction, a bloody civil war, famine, and the worst trials both for the common people and for the church. In 1918, the General Council was forced to cease its work on church renewal.

Only now, in the new, renewed life of Russia, has the prospect of a genuine renewal (from head to toe) opened up for the church and society.

A serious obstacle in the path of renewal derives from the tragic events of the 1920s and 1930s, involving the "renewal schism" and numerous other splits in the church in the postrevolutionary period. The Communist Party and atheist propaganda took advantage of these schisms to weaken and demoralize the church from within, according to the principle "divide and rule." As a result, within the church hierarchy, clergy, and the broad mass of Orthodox believers there arose an extremely hostile attitude toward the ideas of the renewal movement, an intense allergy to any mention of the renewers and of renewal within the church.

This reaction coincided with the introduction of perestroika and with its failure; the invasion of Western influences; the breakup and disintegration of the country; chaos and the explosion of nationalisms and ethnic chauvinisms; and the pauperization and the drop in the standard of living of the masses. The country and the church were swept by a wave of antiecumenical feeling, reactionary ultrachauvinism, and Islamic religious fundamentalism.

Although the extremism and political adventurism of the renewers was rightly condemned by the church and will serve as a bitter lesson, a tragic experience that must not be repeated, the problem of a genuine renewal of the church from head to toe has not left us.

Church Renewal—A Strategy

The strategy for church renewal should in my view include three central elements:

- *truth to the fathers;*
- *free contact* with the West;
- *sobriety of spirit* in dialogue and cooperation with society.

Truth to the fathers involves drawing creatively upon:

- the heritage of the church revival movement of the nineteenth and twentieth centuries;
- the rich materials of the precouncil office (1905–7);
- the acts and decrees of the General Council (1917–18);
- the heritage of the theologians and religious thinkers of the Russian diaspora of the twentieth century, especially Nikolai Berdiaev, Father Sergei Bulgakov, Semen Frank, N.O. Losskii, Father Georgii Florovskii, Father N. Afanas'ev, Georgii Fedotov, and Ivan Il'in.

Free contact with the West implies using creatively the experience of renewal among the Western churches within the context of our own church's wrenching crisis and decline. For example, the activities and practices of the Roman Catholic Church in the Middle Ages stood in glaring contradiction to the ideal of a unified Catholic civilization in the form of an absolute papal theocracy, an ideal proclaimed and forcibly imposed upon the peoples of Western Europe. This dichotomy led to widespread discontent and to demands for the reform of the church from head to toe and ended in the explosion of the Reformation, the decline of the authority of the church, and public loss of trust in it. Unbelief, anticlericalism, and, finally, "enlightened atheism" appeared. Then the era of revolutions began.

Faced with revolutions, the spread of unbelief, the growth of secularization, and indifference to faith, the churches of the West (particularly the Catholic Church) understood the summons of the times and deliberately undertook a process of purification involving repentance and renewal. At the same time, the churches of the West endeavored actively to participate in the task of reforming society and in developing democracy, freedom, and the equality of all persons before the law. The churches affirmed within their societies the importance of human rights and the primacy of universal human values over national and ideological exclusivity.

As a result, the concepts of democracy and the freedom of man in society were so strongly anchored in the West that they survived many a severe threat from totalitarian systems, and today they provide Western culture and civilization with relative stability and good prospects for economic and social development. The Western churches in their respective countries have now become full partners in the construction of a new, more just society, of which they are an indivisible part and on whose development they are having a very favorable influence. The church in Russia (and, more widely, in Eastern Europe) should now draw upon the experience of the renewed Western churches in order to attain a comparable level of influence in society.

Sobriety of spirit and specificity in dialogue and cooperation with society implies that a precondition for church renewal is a decisive rejection of any sort of utopian maximalism in our programs and goals.

Utopian maximalism is always divorced from reality, and in the event of its failure it leads to stagnation, ossification, and withdrawal into an illusory world of external form and stylized decoration that covers up the ugliness of reality.

An illustration of this truth is the medieval papacy, the tragedy of Byzantium, and the stagnation that occurred in the Orthodox world after the failure of the holy Byzantine theocracy. Another shameful illustration is the tragic disgrace of our society and our church in the postrevolutionary epoch of our history.

Of course, our goals should include the continuation of the church renewal movement of the nineteenth and twentieth centuries and constitute a logical sequel to the renewal plan outlined by the General Council in 1917–18 and interrupted by the Revolution. Today's goals and programs, however, should be specific and understandable to parish clergy and believers; they should be socially up-to-date and attractive to the media; and, finally, at each stage of their implementation, they should take into account our particular situation and opportunities.

A New Synthesis, a New Mission

The peoples of Eastern Europe and their churches (and also the peoples of the Russian Federation and the Russian Orthodox Church) stand on the threshold of a new millennium in their Christian history. A thousand years of the history of our country and church demonstrate that it is difficult to interpret our past, but it is still more difficult to understand our present and to predict our future.

Berdiaev expressed this difficulty in these words: "The Russian people is an extremely polarized people; it is a combination of paradoxes."[1]

Tiutchev was right to state that "Russia cannot be understood by the mind, Russia cannot be measured by the common *arshin*; Russia has its own character. One can only believe in Russia." Our whole history, and the closely linked history of the Russian Orthodox Church, is rich in contradictory manifestations that develop in a dialectical fashion, resembling theses and antitheses in the dynamic historical destiny of the Russian people and their church. The highly contradictory nature of our history derives from these conflicts and their often very serious and violent clashes.

With the aim of overcoming this tragic dialectic, the Russian people were subjected to an enormous expenditure of energy. This is why the history of the Russian people is one of the world's most "tortuous histories."[2] This is also why Russian history is characterized by its discontinuity.[3]

This discontinuity, however, never represented a break, or an end, of Russia's history. Father Georgii Florovskii was correct when he stated: "The historic path has not yet been traveled. The history of the church is not yet over. The Russian path has not yet come to a dead end."[4] Whenever our country entered a period of conflict and the clash of centrifugal forces led to "discontinuity," our people consistently found in themselves the strength necessary to overcome any form of break.

The clashes of theses and antitheses that occurred in each epoch were reworked in the crucible of our history into a new synthesis combining the best creative elements from the conflicts of the past, in order to form new values and to create a new stage in our existence. Seeing this latent and providential significance in our history gives us hope for the future.

The key elements in this synthesis will be the principles of nationality articulated by the Slavophiles, the "free *sobornost'* " of Khomiakov, Solov'ev's concept of "all-unity," and Fedorov's doctrine of "multiunity" and active "God-in-action." The devotion of the Orthodox Church to its people will actively contribute to this synthesis, reconciling and uniting all men. The core of this synthesis should be Dostoevsky's "prophetic faith" in the "universal openness and responsiveness" of the Russians and of Russian culture. Nonetheless, we must understand that such a destiny for Russia is not so much a given as a task.

It will become the holy mission of a renewed Orthodox Church to aid in bringing about this all-European, universal openness and responsiveness of a new Russia. The mistakes and failures of the past should not be obscured. The harsh trials our church is now undergoing, in redeeming its past sins and cleansing itself from the disgraceful filth of recent years, will become for us a model of rebirth and renewal.

And then once again, as was the case at the time of Kievan Rus, Muscovite Rus, and the Petersburg empire of Russia, the church and its witness to Christ and to the moral values of Christianity will aid in the formation of a new Orthodox synthesis. And the church will become a universally accepted, positive, and creative factor in the future history of the peoples of a new Russia and the peoples of a new Eastern Europe.

"The grass withereth, the flower faded: but the word of our God shall stand forever" (Isa. 40:8).

Translated by Jonathan Edwards

Notes

1. Nikolai Berdiaev, *Russkaia Mysl'* (Paris: YMCA Press, 1971), p. 5.
2. Ibid., p. 9.
3. Ibid., p. 7.
4. Georgii Florovskii, *Puti russkogo bogosloviia* (Paris, 1983), p. 520.

16

Iurii Afanas'ev

Reviving the Humanities in Modern Russia

A Humanistic World View for a Civilization in Crisis

The departing twentieth century, marked by triumphant peaks and tragic valleys, sums up the achievements as well as the errors of humanity. And once again, as at the end of the nineteenth century, futurologists and prophets, skeptics and romantics, scientists and mystics, are talking about the end of modern civilization, or at least of its profound crisis.

This emotional conclusion rests not only on the scale of the changes we are undergoing but on the tendency, characteristic for the entire century, to deny the humanities their proper place in the world. In this respect, the technocratic and technological twentieth century has done its work well. However, the "physicists" are not crowding out the "lyricists" as energetically as they had in the middle of the century. The tragedies attendant upon the conquest of atomic energy and the development of lethal new weapons systems, the Chernobyl explosion and its consequences—these and many others have diminished public enthusiasm about the omnipotence of engineering thought. The energy of the "conquerors" is being replaced by the rationality and pragmatism of co-existence. However, the five years left in the final decade are more than enough for the military-industrial complex to regain its hold and to arrange matters so that only "trickle-down" financing is left for the "unproductive" areas of human knowledge and creativity.

Although the developed countries of the West have created relatively stable and materially comfortable conditions for those who work in the humanities, society as a whole is frequently indifferent to what the humanities have accomplished. As a rule, interest in the humanities is limited to small groups of the intelligentsia. The rest of society has learned to accept calmly the "strange fact" that these disciplines are needed for some reason, even though people assume that what real life needs is "practical" knowledge. Yet the West's acceptance of diversity allows what is obviously strange and not manifestly necessary to exist and permits humanist scholars to pursue their expensive studies in comparative material and spiritual comfort, to teach in schools and universities.

The twentieth century began with Oswald Spengler's bleak vision of a Europe in decline, afflicted by an inner crisis. And again the century is coming to an end with increasing talk, once again, about the crisis in European–North American civilization. However, because crisis in societal and historical processes has never been an element of decline only, a new stage in the development of civilization is emerging.

The division of the world into friends and enemies, characteristic of the culture and traditions of the twentieth century, is receding into the past. It is becoming obvious that the twenty-first century will either become the century of a more unified humanity or elicit an unprecedented catastrophe. This recognition has motivated the Maastricht treaties, the desires of former socialist countries to join the North Atlantic Treaty Organization, and the support of the European and world community for the new government in Russia. Political realities merely reflect deeper and more profound historical processes. Of course, even in the most developed countries, things are not proceeding smoothly. Most people retain the traditional twentieth-century attitudes of seeking new enemies, preserving their accustomed view of the world as one of polar opposites. But today, instead of an "evil empire," there are many smaller "principalities of bondage." Some observers forecast that Islamic fundamentalism or the developing world in general will be the new threat to world order, while others see nationalist movements and aggressive fragments of the former USSR as the real or potential enemies.

But for all the real or imagined threats, the habit of viewing neighbors as potential enemies is beginning to yield to the necessity of accepting the world as a single whole.

This shift in worldview must put humankind at the center of history and politics. Until now, that was the place held by national, regional, group, or class interests, and not only in countries with totalitarian regimes. This tendency occurs throughout the world, because the polarized worldview remains. The polarity holds true for revolutionary as well as conservative thinkers and even for classic liberals, who would seem to hold the individual as the center of the world. Only a comparatively small circle of humanist intellectuals propound a different worldview, one that requires a fundamentally new system of values.

A technocratic approach to culture, with an orientation to the mass consumer, has contributed to a unified global culture. Not surprisingly, in the traditional competition between European and American mass culture, the winner has been the more standardized, established, and accessible American version. This outcome does not preclude but even presupposes that the components of "mass" and "elite" culture can exist side by side.

The tendency toward cultural unification often has encountered powerful resistance. The outbreaks of nationalism in Germany, the growth in popularity of extreme rightists in France, the desire of most developed countries in Europe to defend themselves from immigration from both the South and the East, are evidence that the traditional perceptions of beleaguered national identity and hostile neighbors remain very much alive. There is need for a new level of cooperation in the humanities, which will be based not on concerns about individual sociopolitical priorities but on a conviction that humanity is the center of the historical process as its subject and highest value.

In countries where a totalitarian regime has been the norm, the condition of the liberal arts is even more complex and dramatic. In these countries the best manifestations of education and spirituality always managed to break through the political carapace of totalitarianism. History and literature, like the other humanist studies, were not so much branches of pure scholarship as a means of expressing nonconformist and revolutionary ideas. This tendency made them enormously popular. At the same time, the efforts of the totalitarian state to suppress free thought did great damage to the development of the humanities.

Consider the forced implantation of dogmatic Marxism in Russia under the Soviet regime. Not only were the natural historical processes of the development of democracy, the economy, social relations, political movements, culture, and personality violated, but they did not become the subjects of scholarly analysis or the sources of social experience. It can be said without exaggeration that the blows dealt to the liberal arts were perhaps even more terrible than those inflicted on genetics, cybernetics, and computer sciences. It is difficult to know how much was lost. Entire branches of scholarship ceased to exist. The country became isolated from the world's thinking in the realm of the humanities.

This political line eventually led in Russia to a society that was illiterate in the humanities. At the same time, even the liberal arts became instruments of the repressive regime. As was typical under a totalitarian regime, this transformation was not random but planned and supported by state policy and the new ideological dogmas churned out by the Soviet-style institutions of the humanities.

Therefore it was politically quite natural not to guarantee a legal, constitutional relationship between state and society but to encourage a "love affair." Only one side, however—society—was required to do the loving and take care of "its" state and its leaders. The social structure of the USSR assumed the primacy of the collective, "choral" principle rather than the broad development of citizens' rights and liberties, and in this emphasis it had antecedents in Russian history.

Nineteenth-century thinkers began to talk to mankind and about mankind in the language of G.W.F. Hegel and Karl Marx. Rejecting many convictions held by their predecessors, they changed the general view of man, denying him freedom of choice and a wholeness. The free man, the active subject of the historical process, was being turned into the object acted upon by so-called objective laws of nature and society. Therefore the purpose of the study of people and society began to change qualitatively. The social sciences were forced to shift their focus from understanding people and their world to interpreting the objective laws of development.

Marx's ideas were not radical, and many of his fundamental conclusions are not even original. The idea of a society without rich and poor occurs in the Bible and the Koran. Although nineteenth-century historical methodology asserted the incrementally progressive nature of social development, adherents of Marxism unequivocally declared that the meaning of history is determined by the fact that after capitalism comes communism, and certainly not the other way around or any other way.

But their opponents, for all their criticism of the basic tenets of Marxism, insisted on recognizing progressivism as the linchpin in the development of civilization. This emphasis inevitably led to a decrease in the role and significance of real people as compared to the ideal models of the abstract future.

And finally, the nineteenth century, with its turbulent technological development and growing differentiation in science, inevitably led to the loss of wholeness in the study of humankind, to a growing specialization among the disciplines, and to the gradual weakening of the very idea of humanism as the motivating force for the study of social sciences.

The twentieth century increased that differentiation and, because of the political splintering of the world, promoted a delimiting in the social sciences. United only in juxtaposition to the natural and technical scientific disciplines, the social sciences continued to lose their very essence as humanities. Under these conditions, the social sciences should have produced and developed concepts of so-called universal values and moved away from ideas of confrontation and dialogue. However, even civilized countries have not yet achieved this shift.

Speaking today of a crisis in civilization, we should be addressing the depletion of the foundations of twentieth-century civilization and the sources of twenty-first-century civilization. Receding, along with the twentieth century, are polarity and extreme judgments born in the nineteenth century. It is becoming ever clearer that the basic sociopolitical doctrines —conservative, liberal, and revolutionary—have many more elements in common than elements that divide them. Even more obvious is the fallacy of perceiving the world not as a unified whole but as a space divided up by impassable barriers.

Principles of Modern Social Sciences

The development of principles for modern social sciences, much less the consistent implementation of the principles, is no easy undertaking. The approach of a new age is making us look at previous efforts with an especially critical eye and analyze research traditions thoroughly. But more important, the humanities in Russia are burdened with additional difficulties, closely tied as they are with the Soviet type of thinking and culture.

In the past, a research project typically would be determined by essentially political means. This connection blurred objectivity, and the actual process of understanding no longer played a vital role in the formation of the perception of the object.

Marx's statement that "philosophers merely explain the world, whereas the point is to change it" became the operational leitmotif. An essential characteristic of the Marxist attitude toward other theories became the artificial distinction accorded to Marxist socialism as op- posed to all other concepts and theories. Only Marxist doctrine was considered scientific, the peak of human thought.

Such postulates inevitably led to the isolation of Marxism from other developments in the social sciences. (And this isolation in no way con- tradicts the oft-repeated statement by the founders of Marxist doctrine that Marx's theory needs further development and enrichment. The main source for further development and enrichment of the doctrine was supposed to be personal experience in revolutionary struggle, one prepared in a Marxist way at that.) All told, these traits led Marxism into self-absorption and monologism.

With other subjects, the dialogue turned into an argument, and only one side—Marxism—was granted the absolute and unquestionable right to the truth.

The danger inherent in the identification of social science with social policy was pointed out early by Aleksandr Bogdanov, who stressed that it would inevitably lead to authoritarianism in theoretical activity and promote the formation of authoritarian thought, in essence reviving the theological tradition of the Middle Ages.

The unassailable supremacy of Marxist doctrine as the theoretical basis for the development of the liberal arts and social sciences in the Soviet period led to a one-sided and excessive politicization of the sub- jects and their teaching. As a result, the problem of establishing a new university for the humanities oriented toward the acquisition of new knowledge in the social sciences has required us to think seriously about methodology.

The principle of unity, wholeness, and integrity is central to a mod- ern humanistic education. This idea developed simultaneously with civi- lization, which constantly revealed and confirmed that knowledge is comprehensive and systematic and includes not only scientific facts, theories, and hypotheses but also principles of a worldview, moral and ethical standards, and cultural traditions. Over the course of history, these had established the forms of interaction of human communities with one another and with nature.

This rather broad approach makes it clear that comprehensiveness cannot be regarded as a mechanical unification or the simple sum of accumulated information and traditions. Comprehensiveness must be perceived as a continuous mutual influencing, penetration, and regulation of the various components.

The intensifying development of the scientific worldview and accumulation of experience and tradition in science as a whole and in its individual branches reveal the essential elements that, to a great degree, determine the integrity of the system of knowledge. The most important element among them may be the need to combine the incompatible. The most vivid and typical example can be found in the differences in the left and right brain, with the left side responsible for reason, logic, and speech and the right for a unified perception of the world. This model of the brain leads us to look for an analogous dichotomy in human society, which would explain many facts in terms of right-sided or left-sided. In a sense, this same dichotomy appears in the categories of logical and historical, which are at the basis of any scientific knowledge.

Other examples, just as well known, are the co-existence of discreteness and continuousness in the theory of elementary particles and the principles of uncertainty and complementariness in quantum mechanics. There are so many examples of the co-existence of the incompatible that they require study, systematization, and analysis. D. Danin, who teaches a course on these problems at the Russian State University for the Humanities, has suggested introducing a special term, "centauristics," using the mythological centaur as a symbol for the concept.

In the last quarter of the twentieth century, new scholarly fields have developed on the borders of various disciplines. And as a rule, these new areas are the most promising and yield the greatest results. Chemical physics and genetic engineering are two such fields. Mathematical modeling is used not only in economics but in political science, history, sociology, and cultural studies. Computer science can fuse linguistics, philology, history, and archography, the study of archaeology and geography. Besides the education system, this process is also performed by the systems of information and communications, the significance and effectiveness of which are determined in great measure by the level of economic development and culture of a society because it is the cultural level that characterizes the information needs.

For both objective and subjective reasons, however, comprehensiveness of scientific knowledge as a fundamental principle and as a condition of its very existence has often been violated. The schism was seen most vividly in the division between the humanities and the natural sciences and their isolation from one another. The schism was brought on originally by purely objective historical preconditions, relating to the qualitatively new turn in the development of scientific thought at the end of the eighteenth century. Specialization and differentiation of the sciences in that period were powerful impulses for their gradual development and swift enrichment. (The scientific legacy of the Encyclopedists had shown the limits and exhaustibility of scientific universalism.) However, this quite natural specialization quickly led to a noticeable setting apart of the humanities from the natural sciences.

In the twentieth century, other factors had a powerful influence on the development of the sciences. They were most obvious in totalitarian states. These states usually supported the natural and technical sciences that were necessary for the creation of military power. The humanities and social sciences were usually stifled by the mono-ideology imposed by the state propaganda machine. Freedom of thought and inquiry in the humanities, as well as a critical analysis of reality, were unacceptable because they were a potential threat to the dogmas forced on society by the state.

In modern Russia, which is freeing itself from the stereotypes of totalitarian ideology, conditions are developing that will foster the renaissance of the humanities, for the re-creation of real history, for the mastery of sociology and political science, and for the comprehension of what twentieth-century philosophy has accomplished.

In seeking all possible support for this process, we must bear in mind two mutually connected tendencies that are clearly manifested in the development of civilization and that in significant measure determine the modern technology of receiving new scientific knowledge.

First, in the social sciences *mathematical methods* of data analysis and modeling of social and economic processes are becoming more standard. Mathematics became crucial in the natural sciences, beginning in midcentury with mechanics and physics, and today this discipline plays an increasingly important role in the humanities as well. Mathematical models are the lingua franca of science, emphasizing and supporting the comprehensiveness of scientific knowledge.

Second, the second half of the twentieth century is a transitional period for the most-developed countries from industrial societies to postindustrial, or informational societies, with the information industry as one of the main branches of their economies. The productivity of labor in this branch depends on the level of automation of mental, or intellectual, labor, which is being accomplished by new information technologies based on the broad use of computer technology, modern communications systems, and their software support. Computer systems can create new knowledge independently and thereby have a reverse influence on the human intellect that created them. Thus the support of the comprehensiveness of scientific knowledge is made possible not only through traditional scientific communication and the development of a common language of science but also through the creation of new means and methods for elaborating and disseminating information.

Thus the principle of integrity becomes a cornerstone of liberal arts education, closely tied to the contemporary information milieu in which the humanities function.

The next important principle is the principle of *dialogue*. The methodological bases of this principle, like the theory of dialogue itself, were developed and validated by Mikhail Bakhtin, whose work represents a seminal period in twentieth-century thought. B.S. Bibler, Bakhtin's interpreter and popularizer, called him "one of the intense concentrations of the real polyphony of humanistic thought of the twentieth century." Bakhtin considered the general pervasiveness of dialogue fundamental to the essence of human relations. "Relations in and through dialogue are almost universal phenomena permeating all human speech and all manifestations and relations in human life, of everything that has meaning and significance. . . . Where consciousness begins, there begins dialogue," he said.

The dialogue principle gives us a clear orientation for the organization of the learning process both in content and in form, so that students can examine all phenomena of private and public life through the prism of the dialogue. Dialogue is all the more important in education because it permits the formation of an essentially new type of thinking, a new type of culture.

Another important principle in education is *rationalism*. It may seem strange to call attention to things that should go without saying, but so much has been said about the twentieth century as the century of science, of reason, that rationalism has become a commonplace. It is forgotten that for lengthy periods of time entire regions, countries, and people devoted all their efforts, their human and natural resources, to service basically irrational, utopian ideas. The cult of reason that arose in the late eighteenth century quickly turned into its opposite.

But the past does not slip off the pages of European and world history without a trace. It creates the foundation for the assertion of a new humanistic worldview, which would be based on the following points:

- Theory is "deprofessionalized." It must cease being the property of a narrow circle of social sciences and become the basis of a new type of cultural and historical processes. Theory will then inevitably lose some of its self-imposed obscurity and rest on the more familiar elements of scholarship and rationalism.
- Humankind is at the center of this new worldview, but not as a simple repetition and re-creation of the European tradition of humanism. The new humanism will use the real person, not the ideal, as the true measure and essence of all things.
- This new worldview will speak in the language of dialogue and cooperation, the language of understanding and the search for meaning, the language of acceptance of differences of all the participants and ideas in the dialogue.

Russian Traditions and Western Thought

When we think about the ways to overcome the perversion and isolation of the humanities in the Soviet Union, which have been inherited in one degree or another by post-Soviet Russia, we must bear in mind an amazing paradox of history: the ancient Russian tradition is both the root of the efforts, natural for a totalitarian regime, to suppress free thought and also the source of some of the highest achievements of the humanities in Russia, achievements that led to qualitative changes in the world and in the West.

The bondage and subjugation characteristic of traditional societies are manifested in fetishism, mythologized thought, and collective and egalitarian strivings. A mythologized perception of the universe and consciousness that was either prehistorical or ahistorical were very important traits of Russian mass psychology in the early nineteenth century.

In 1917 Russia's social awareness remained irrational and premodern compared to most European countries in the early twentieth century. The Russian worldview retained many traits of peasant civilization along with a value system that was typical of closed peasant worlds. In this system patriarchal values were most esteemed and the surrounding world was seen as something potentially hostile and threatening. No less clearly manifest was the desire to suppress the personality in the name of collectivism. Petr Stolypin's agrarian reforms showed that the communal *mir* system resisted the creation of separate households. The peasants even tried to obtain land for the whole *mir* for collective land use.

The majority of Russians perceived state power in a traditionally egalitarian way, as a step on the ladder of divine hierarchy. This perception is the source of the belief in the exceptional role of leaders, who alone are capable of freeing the people and building a harmonious society with a plan that they themselves develop rationally.

A critical attitude toward Western concepts of autonomy and self-affirmation of the individual prevailed in Russia in the spiritual seeking of the later nineteenth and early twentieth centuries, and this attitude found consistent continuation and development by Bolshevik ideas and the Communist Party's practice of subordinating the individual to the collective. The Bolshevik conception easily absorbed Russia's traditional ideas of community, which precluded the possibility of political pluralism and dialogue and were oriented primarily toward suppressing dissident thought and factionalism as totally hostile to true national values and the interests of the majority.

The idea of world revolution was a perfect overlay for the traditional idea of Russia's special role in world history, an idea that goes back to pre-Petrine Rus. Similarly, the complex of ideas about Moscow as the Third Rome, with the Russian princes' right to rule inherited from the Roman emperors, was transformed into the idea of Russia's special role in liberating Christians from the Turkish yoke and then into the idea of uniting Slavs under Russia and promoting the voluntary membership of various ethnic groups in the empire. Similarly, in Soviet times the idea of proletarian messianism grew into the superpower complex.

Russian philosophers recognized the comprehensiveness of knowledge as a fundamental principle and made significant contributions to the humanities, but, paradoxically, their ideas took root and bore fruit in the West, not in Russia. Many fundamental ideas of modern humanities were born in Russia and developed in the United States and Europe. It would not be true to say that everything achieved in the social sciences has its roots and sources in Russia. But everything that was born in Russia in the first quarter of the nineteenth century was later developed under different conditions and on other soil. In the Soviet Union, barbaric methods put a stop to humanistic thought and work.

A perfect illustration is the development of the concept of comprehensiveness, of holistics, in the twentieth century. The humanities in Russia were formed as a comprehensive family of studies, not as an individual science or branch of knowledge, developing fruitfully and achieving visible results. As a family of sciences, a community of sciences, they created an atmosphere, a spiritual climate, that stimulated the development of each science individually. Almost the entire twentieth century was under the sign of holism. It was being developed in the late nineteenth century in several countries, in various disciplines, and they developed in parallel throughout the civilized world. Analogies are easy to draw between what the Russian scholar Pavel Miliukov and the Western scholar Henri Berr were doing in history. And the Russian sociologists George Gurvich and Pitirim Sorokin, expelled from the country in the early 1920s, easily fitted into the science in Europe and the United States and made a significant contribution to the direction of research in that field. The idea of holism in the research of Western historians flowed logically into the elaboration of the concept of global history in the works of Marc Bloch and Fernand Braudel. But in Russia this research was cut off.

Naturally, it cannot be said that the development of thought in Russia and the West moved in the same direction. On the one hand, the concept was formed of a multifaceted, whole, progressing, and stratified society, and attempts were made to measure the results of that development through categories of greater lengths of time. On the other hand, scholars tried to find the cell, the microcosm, that would reveal some of the general mechanisms of the development of human society.

On the whole, the liberal arts in the first quarter of the twentieth century took on a general rhythm and direction of development. Productive dialogue was possible because scholars from different countries were working on essentially the same question, even though approaching it in different ways. The great Russian scholar V.Ia. Propp, author of marvelous works devoted to finding historical roots in fairy tales, had discussions and dialogues on equal terms with the French ethnographer and sociologist Claude Levi-Strauss. The Russian scholar Mikhail Bakhtin had similarly fruitful creative dialogues with the French cultural scholar Lucien Fevre. They had different conclusions and interpretations of those conclusions, but dialogue was possible, and that is the most important thing.

The Russian school of culture, formed in 1920–40 by the work of Bakhtin, Propp, I.G. Frank-Kamenetskii, and O.M. Freidenberg, was in numerous ways ahead of world scholarship. They worked closely with Russian psychologists L.S. Vygotskii, A.N. Leont'ev, and A.R. Luriia, who were developing a cultural-historical theory of the human psyche. In turn, their work was based on the writing of the brilliant group of Russian philosophers of the Silver Age—Vladimir Solov'ev, Sergei Bulgakov, Pavel Florenskii, and Viacheslav Ivanov. We must not overlook V.I. Vernadskii, author of the idea that two tendencies—the natural-historical and the sociopolitical—would eventually form a single unified whole. And yet again, the full realization of this idea came not in Russia but in the works of the French Catholic philosopher Pierre Teilhard de Chardin.

And despite everything, the schism between Russian liberal arts today and Russian liberal arts at the turn of the century is not absolute. Numerous threads connect us to the earlier Russian school. An understanding of what Russia was in the humanities and how it happened that the Russian principles—which are also universal—were developed outside Russia will help us to understand how we will develop in the future.

The Russian State University for the Humanities in Russia's System of Liberal Arts Education

The significance of the founding of the University for the Humanities went far beyond the framework of the nationwide campaign of renaming institutes into academies and universities (often without the proper material base, without cardinal changes in the structures of these institutions, and without a review of their goals and aims). Over many decades, a society formed in the USSR in which elementary literacy was consciously passed off as education, in which a hatred for the intelligentsia was cultivated, and in which the physical destruction of the intelligentsia was reaching levels of genocide. Such a society easily falls into fanaticism, mysticism, and nationalism. Without appreciating the value of the individual as the basis of the commonweal, without turning declarations on human rights into a mechanism for the protection and guarantee of those rights, such a society hinders its own improvement. With all its landmarks—moral, ethical, aesthetic—gone, open to the influence of any informational flow, such a society readily absorbs the superficial flotsam of modern culture, from pornographic literature to third-rate film hits.

The mastery of the real achievements of human culture requires time, teachers, and spiritual mentors. One would think that when there is not enough daily bread (although Denis Diderot said that after food, education is the most important), millions of people live in ecologically disastrous conditions, and even minimal amounts of medicines and drugs are lacking, it would be impossible to find the means for creating a normal spiritual atmosphere. And it is almost impossible. But the word "almost" means that we must concentrate our efforts on realistic measures supported by faith in the spiritual healing ability of society to create support centers for culture and civilization.

We should remember that Albert Schweitzer's single mission in Africa lowered the mortality rate for a radius of a thousand kilometers. New information technologies permit us to exert enormous influence over significant expanses, and therefore centers of culture must first of all be information centers. Universities can be such centers.

Traditionally, in Russia, the word "university" stood for something slightly different from its meaning in Western countries. In Russia there were, and are, few universities, despite the renaming of many institutes as universities. In Russia a university education meant a multifaceted, universal education, a synthesis of the humanities and natural sciences as well as a higher theoretical level of education compared to other institutions. As a rule, universities attracted the most famous scholars, who formed schools in their fields, many of which were internationally acclaimed.

In the Soviet period, the traditions of university education were lost.

The number of universities dropped dramatically. The parallel existence of the state-supported Academy of Sciences, which did work primarily in classified areas, led to a rupture in the ties between scholarly
groups and the universities. While the natural sciences made great ad-
vances, the social sciences, in the vise of Marxist-Leninist methodology,
withered and degenerated. The ideological control over the universities
produced a split between the natural sciences and the liberal arts and
deprived the university education of its traditional comprehensiveness
and humanistic tendencies.

The history of the development of human civilization confirms the
integrity of the system of human knowledge that has two components:
natural sciences and liberal arts. The humanities include knowledge of
history and the tendencies and laws of development of human civilization. We could say that a knowledge of the humanities reflects the level
of reflection and self-knowledge of a society and at the same time characterizes the society's intellectual level.

In proposing to create a university for the humanities on the base of
the Moscow State History and Archives Institute, the institute took the
initiative to alter the course of the development of the humanities.
Transforming the institute into a university (Russian State University for
the Humanities, RSUH) involved high-level demands, goals, and principles, some of which are:

- the orientation of teaching, research, and production toward the
  support, revival, and development of political, economic, social,
  and cultural life in Russia;
- the integrity of the humanities in combination with specialized
  studies in a major field;
- the fundamental nature of the humanities and their derivation
  from the experience of society and individual;
- the development of unique research trends in the humanities;
- the integration of Russian humanities into world practice.

Such a university had to be a research and teaching center of a new
type that would affect the future development of the humanities in the
country.

For a university, three years is a tiny period, but we can already assess
some of its activities and evaluate its prospects. The RSUH can be classi-

fied as a nonclassical or neoclassical university, since many of its structural subdivisions or organizations—for example, the Institute of Higher Research in the Humanities or the Marc Bloch Russian-French Center of Historical Anthropology—do not exist in classical universities.

Forming a university in the late twentieth century has its drawbacks, but it also has a great advantage: the ability to orient itself toward the most advanced achievements of humanistic thought and to avoid blind copying. Even now we can conclude that the creation of the RSUH will have a serious influence on the preservation and revival of the traditions of the Russian humanities and on the development of liberal arts and social sciences in Russia.

Translated by Antonina W. Bouis

Epilogue

Andrei Voznesenskii

Of Easter Eggs, Black Holes, and Heroes

The Future of Russia?

Pavel Florenskii, our philosopher, who died in the camps, wrote: "Our names are prophesies of our fates and our biographies." This opinion is shared by astrologers and by the ancient Chinese. Thus, for example, Boris Pasternak's name encoded the Russian words prophesying his fate and his poetry: "country," "wound," "cross," "thorn" (crown of thorns), "anapest," and the English words "Easter," "star,"[1] and "past." The outline of the name "Moore" contains two prominent letter "o"s—the famous holes of Henry Moore's future sculptures.

And what comes to mind in the name "Russia"? Like a road marker in a snowstorm, the word "Poetry" shines through it in Latin letters. Poetry was indeed to be the future of Russia, for it became our national culture. The Russians know poems by heart, they are always buying books of verse, and they even come to hear poetry readings in stadiums. Yet our computers and our agriculture do not function. These are the pluses and minuses of the Russian mentality.

I wish above all for people to be satisfied, for them not to forget each other, and for the economy to stand on its feet. But if, all of a sudden, we become a normal contented country—and this is not likely to happen for the foreseeable future!—and poetry disappears from here, such a Russia, I think, would no longer be Russia. It would be of no use to humanity, and it would be of no interest to me.

"Because there is no hope, there is indeed hope," said the Apostle Paul. Today there is not the slightest bit of hope; therefore I am optimistic.

This feeling is shared by young poets. One year ago in Moscow there was a congress of palindromists. (A palindrome is a form of poem that can be read both from right to left and from left to right.) Velemir Khlebnikov, the father of our avant-garde, wrote a long poem called *Razin*, which can be read backwards. Well, these old women arrived at Kursk Station in Moscow and saw, to their enormous horror, a fast-moving sentence in neon lights running from left to right on top of a fourteen-story building. This was a prophecy of the future.

Looking inside history, I see the workings of the law of palindromes in the symmetry of certain events. Twentieth-century Russian history is arranged in the form of a palindrome. The black hole of the 1905–17 revolution, which began five years after the beginning of the century, is matched by a corresponding hole today (roughly from 1983–95), which ends five years before the end of the century. In accordance with the law of palindromes, Russia is now attempting to move backwards from the utopian goal of communism, back to the utopian capitalism of the nineteenth century.

We are tired of words and forecasts. Everyone talks away—the authorities, the opposition, crowds at political rallies—but no one works. People sell air; nothing is being done to create anything. I think the solution is for everyone to make something real and concrete. I will recount my own experience.

Last Easter I built an Egg of Poetry, five meters high, from plaster with a metal frame inside. On it we painted a globe with gold leaf and shining paint in the style of Russian Easter eggs. In the place of Russia we cut out a black hole, as if someone had broken the top of the shell in order to eat the egg. Around the meridians I wrote some lines of verse. On the squares formed by the intersection of the meridians and the lines of latitude we set up working television screens tuned to particular channels.

We worked on the Egg for about a month. Then the time came to worry about money. We received some from the "new Russians"—a bank headed by a man in his late thirties. This was the same bank that paid a fabulous price for the previously unknown *Square* by Konstantin

Malevich. The new businessmen respect art. For example, the Logovaz company has established a Triumph Prize of $100,000 for Russian litera-ture and art, and this money is coming not from *outside* but from *inside* our ravaged country! I know these people well, as I am a member of the jury for the prize. The president of Logovaz, Boris Berezovskii, is a talented man filled with initiative and energy. The jury is composed of independent artists, including two Americans, Vassily Aksyonov and Ernst Neizvestnyi. Last year, the winners included the composer Schnittke, who lives in Germany, the pianist Sviatoslav Richter, and the writers Bella Akhmadulina and Mikhail Zhvanetskii.

But let us return to the Egg. Helping me build it, practically free of charge, were some young architects from the Krikheli studio. We rented a huge studio in which people had once made sculptures of Josef Stalin and outer space satellites. Our workmen were being paid a lot of money, but they worked more from enthusiasm. I had an allergic reac-tion to the paint.

On the second day of Easter, April 20, 1993, we set up the Egg in the geographical center of Moscow, on Nezhdanov Street opposite the church. We organized a concert. Rock stars stood in the hole of the Egg and sang a program of rock music, which I wrote for the occasion, with the refrain "Russia Is Risen." There were fireworks. Despite the cold, some pantomimists came and performed. For the crowd of people there, including beggars, the elites, the young and the old, it was a source of joyful pleasure, free of charge. That Easter, many people did not have the money to buy traditional Easter eggs. The average monthly salary is fifty dollars, and what is more, living in Moscow is now even more expensive than living in New York. The whole event was broadcast live on television.

For six months after that, the Egg stood in the square, without offi-cial authorization. Children climbed up its exterior and looked out from the hole, lovers hid inside it from the rain, people drew graffiti all over its pedestal, and drunkards said prayers at its base. Its poems of plaster became a part of the city. It was a living book. Business had imposed a new form of censorship, and the high price of paper had caused many publications to cease, yet here we were offering poetry free of charge in the street. No one damaged the Egg, just during the attempted coup two bullets left marks on it and three passersby were killed by snipers nearby.

The Egg had its opponents. The conservative press accused us of committing a modernist sacrilege, a mockery of something holy. There was some foul language among the graffiti. But for me the most powerful thing was to see tears of joy in the eyes of Moscow beggars.

In October the Egg was removed to be installed in the Pushkin Museum. The Egg would not fit through the door of the museum, and we had to saw it into pieces. As a result I realized that, due to the narrow width of the door, all the great sculptures in the Pushkin Museum were brought there in pieces. You can still see the seams on Michelangelo's *Moses* and *David*. Once we got it inside the museum, we had to put it back together and repaint it, joining all the pieces with an electric welder (normally this is not allowed in the museum). After the exhibition we put the Egg in the courtyard outside the House of Film and decided to hold another concert there next Easter. Recently, the House of Film has become the site of liberal political rallies. Those who come to them, among them famous actors and writers, have to pass through a group of protesters blocking the entrance and shouting "You Jews! You've sold the country! Go back to Israel!" and so on.

A new Russia is being born, smashing the old stereotypes. Here, as in the past, there is a role for new, nonstandard poetry. Our country cannot be saved by logical means, only by surreal means. The Russian press realizes this. In the past, popular newspapers did not print full pages of verse. In 1994 the most widely read newspapers—the weekly *Argumenty i fakty* (circulation: 7 million), and the dailies *Moskovskii komsomolets* (circulation: 2 million) and *Izvestiia*—published two pages of my poems and crazy drawings. In an era of competition and struggle for readers and subscribers, this coverage indicates that poetry (even complicated poetry) is needed by people and is bought by them.

As a young man I once had a conversation with the philosopher Martin Heidegger. The transcript has been preserved in the Bavarian Academy. The first thing the German genius asked me was, "Is spirit capable of mastering technology?" We are trying.

There are shoots of hope. Recently the Logovaz company has created a new automobile firm called "AVVA" (All-Russian Automobile Alliance). "Avva" is how Russians pronounce and write the name of God the Father. The ancient Hebrew "B" (as in ABBA) becomes a "V" in Russian. Atheist Russia heard this name in a line of Pasternak:

Abba Father, if it be possible,
Let this cup pass from me!

"Hamlet"

For the time being, AVVA is the only company in Russia that will make anything, in this case the product being cars. Production will start in 1995. General Motors has invested some of the capital. I was the person who came up with the name AVVA for the company. Its logo AVVAWAVVA reads in a circle, like a wheel. When I thought of the name, I imagined that starting in 1995, on all the roads of Russia, in the fields and in the towns, car tires will be bearing the word AVVA. The roads will be offering up a prayer. This will be a genuine prayer of Russia, a prayer through action. "Prayer without action is dead!" In this sense I am an optimist.

And what has become of the Egg?

On the night of April 25, 1994, the day before Easter, it was smashed to pieces in the courtyard of the House of Film by unknown vandals. A couple of people without any tools could not have done this. There must have been a whole crowd of vandals, at least twenty people.

I walked among the fragments of the shell and thought that this is just like the fate of Russia itself. But there was no time for tears. It was not possible to restore the Egg, so now we are going to build a new one. If we have finished it, I will take it to New York in October, where I am giving a speech with Allan Ginsberg. I am an optimist.

And what about AVVA?

On June 7, in broad daylight, at the Mercedes–600 event, attended by the president of Logovaz and AVVA, a radio-operated device containing ball bearings exploded. A driver was killed, Berezovskii was wounded and burnt, a bodyguard was seriously hurt, and seven passersby were injured. It was one of a number of terrorist bombings carried out against Logovaz in June. The mafia? politics? competitors?

The new Russian businessmen are not only talented people; they are heroes. In this sense I am an optimist.

Translated by Jonathan Edwards

Note

1. "Easter Star" is the title of a poem from Boris Pasternak's novel *Doctor Zhivago*.

Appendix

Sergei Filatov and Liudmila Vorontsova

New Russia in Search of an Identity

The West has yet to realize that paralleling the peaceful political evolution of post-Soviet Russian society, the worldview (*mirovozrenie*) of the Russian people has undergone a change no less radical in scope than that caused by the 1917 Revolution. It has taken most Russians just a few years to cast aside values that traditionally have been regarded as inalienable features of their national mind-set: an omnipotent state possessing quasi-religious authority, disdain for wealth, egalitarian beliefs about property, conformity of opinion, collectivism, anti-Western attitudes, and the rejection of democracy and liberalism.

What makes this psychological revolution unique is its pervasive nihilism. Although every revolution contains some nihilistic elements, much more important are the specific goals and action programs that can rally a majority of the people under its banner. In Russia, society cast totalitarianism aside not as a result of a broad popular movement fueled by a new ideology but as a result of the utter decrepitude of the once-dominant communist system, which had outlived its time. Spontaneously rejected by the nation, the system died a natural death before it had hardly lived out the average human life span. What is happening in this country, therefore, is a repudiation of the old rather than a breakthrough toward the new.

The harsh nihilism that is supplanting communist ideology (and artificial versions thereof) results in many ways from the lack of a well-developed and structured world outlook. Leaders of society in Russia articulate their policy goals primarily through negation, using the rule of opposites. They define values as "antisomething": anticommunism, antitotalitarianism, and antistatism (occasionally carried to the point of complete asociality or destructive forms of national self-disparagement). One can hardly claim that these ideas were born overnight, in the brief perestroika years. They are rooted in the radical rejection of values that had been fostered over decades, values that turned out to be both utopian and short-lived. During the few years of perestroika, the vigorous growth of "new thinking" blotted out communist values from the public mind. But what is nihilistic about "new thinking"? What values does it reject? What does it offer instead?

Let us try to find answers to these questions by looking at the results of a nationwide public opinion poll taken in May 1992, involving 2,250 respondents in fifteen cities and towns of Russia and Kazakhstan on "The World Outlook of the Population of Russia After Perestroika: Religion, Politics, Culture, Moral Attitudes."[1] The conclusions of this poll are borne out by the findings of other sociological research services available to us.

All public opinion polls conducted in 1987–92, including those in which we took part (1990–92), point to a general collapse of communist ideology and a simultaneous upsurge of massive anticommunism. By 1992, public revulsion against communist ideology, symbols, and political organization had become widespread, while loyalty to communist values had diminished to infrequent forms of dissent. In every sector of the urban population, supporters of communist ideals numbered at most 5–10 percent on most issues. The idea of socialism was somewhat more palatable, evoking a positive response from 25 percent of Russia's urban dwellers. More than one-third of the respondents (36 percent) were adamant anticommunists who believed that "former Party functionaries cannot be trusted with important government posts." Anticommunist sentiment was strongest among the youth and among those who lived in large cities (the figure for Moscow was 42 percent).

Because communist ideology was the official symbol of Russian statehood for so many years, the collapse of communism sharpened nihilist attitudes toward all government agencies. Antistatism and asociality have many manifestations. One widespread example is public skepticism about the state's ability to cope with poverty. Only one-quarter of the people believe that the state can do anything about poverty, while one-tenth pin their hopes entirely on charitable institutions, thus demonstrating their complete disillusionment with the government's ability to intercede effectively in this field.

Another example is apathy about politics. Over half of Russians (56 percent) either do not believe in political parties and elections or do not know which party they would vote for. At most of the recent by-elections in different parts of Russia, voter turnout was less than 50 percent. Even the most popular political leaders still receive very low ratings in the polls (in the 7–21 percent range, while the "undecided" category, in one recent poll, numbers almost 40 percent). As a result of the anticommunist trend in public attitudes and the virtual absence of positive attitudes toward life, all forms of sociability are suspect. The very concept of personal social responsibility is being redefined. Those who do not believe that the state can solve social problems feel under no obligation to serve such a state. Long-established assumptions about duty to society as service to one's country and to socialist ideals have crumbled quickly and irreversibly over the past few years, to be supplanted by nihilistic indifference or self-centered irresponsibility.

The crisis of the "duty" concept, in the Soviet sense of the term, has brought about a cynical neglect of duty as such. "The communists made us attend meetings and rallies, take part in manifestations and elections, serve on Voluntary Law and Order brigades, join the Army and Navy Assistance Society, the Red Cross, the National Society for the Preservation of Cultural and Historical Monuments, or the teetotalers' movement. No more!"—such is the typical reasoning of an ordinary post-Soviet man when he tries to justify his apathy and social nihilism.

Less than half of the population (42 percent) sees military service as a matter of "duty and honor." Young people are particularly skeptical: less than one-third of them believe that military service is an honorable duty.

Dislike for the state spills over onto those who personify it. Positions that involve direct enforcement of the will of the state, such as the "bosses" (in government agencies, state-owned enterprises, or collective farms), law-enforcement officers, and politicians, have the lowest rating.

Antistatist attitudes foster the conviction (shared by 58 percent of the population) that "serving the homeland," although commendable, is not mandatory. Only 14 percent of the respondents have a sense of civic duty, and an equal percentage of inveterate "dodgers" take a negative attitude toward public life.

The rejection of communist ideals and the communist system has affected not only the government but even one's own people, leading to a form of ethnic nihilism or Russophobia. Perhaps unconsciously, the Russian people have assumed the blame for the sins of communism. Paradoxically, this attitude probably accounts for the weakness of Russian nationalism. People shun identification with this country and this nation. The feeling of national nihilism has contributed to the present wave of emigration: for many people, the important thing is to escape from "here," not what they are going to do "there." Contempt for one's own people, one's life-style, and even one's own person is aptly expressed in the new coinage, "We are all *sovki*" (a disparaging slang term for Soviet people, collectively and individually).

The desire to banish the communist past, however, has not been matched by any serious or original ideological effort. Russian consciousness today is a diffuse and amorphous grab bag of ideas, a zone of spiritual "entropy." A few values and authentic social emotions however, can emerge from this amorphous and eclectic state of mind.

Rejection of state coercion and control is one of these basic, strongly felt emotions. After years of brutal state control, the people, in an almost knee-jerk reaction, prefer anarchy to the government's lash. Again paradoxically, this attitude is an important guarantee of the preservation and strengthening of political freedoms and civil rights. Our surveys have shown that 74 percent of respondents advocate freedom of conscience and equality for all religious denominations, 42 percent support human rights, and 70 percent endorse freedom of expression —even for the widely detested communists.

These attitudes, however, are no more than social emotions that do not spring from a consistent worldview. Americans and Europeans can explain their adherence to democracy by citing the principles of Christianity as interpreted by Catholic and Protestant theologians or by referring to the logic of historical progress. Russians can do neither. Their history goes a long way to explain the apparently incongruous combination of widespread support for human rights with markedly less support for the rule of law (59 percent), parliamentary democracy and representative government (31 percent), and the separation of powers.

Another aspect of public opinion that explains the current situation in Russia is enthusiasm for "the market," which is the focus of very disparate ideological impulses. Behind the worship of the "market" are two simple ideas: "keeping up with the Joneses" by leading a "decent" life as seen in foreign films and during travel abroad, and repudiating Marxist-Leninist doctrine on private property ("It was drummed into our heads that private property is the source of all evil, but the truth is that it is the source of all good"). Two years of hardship experienced during the market reforms have not shaken either idea. In the April 1993 referendum, a significant majority of the urban population supported Boris Yeltsin's social and economic policies (as we had predicted they would). The no votes came mainly from old people and rural dwellers, the social strata that have not only suffered most under the reforms (although intellectuals in government service have been hit even harder) but have been least affected by the "revolution in worldview."

Moreover, despite all the recent hardships, less than 10 percent of those polled want a return to a planned economy. About one-quarter of the population supports radical economic reforms, whatever their social cost ("The market is the most effective economic system. A free market economy must be established as quickly as possible at any cost. Only then will we become a prosperous nation"). An equal proportion of the population believes that moral reservations about capitalism can be set aside in order to ensure the early attainment of a market economy ("Many people are getting rich by dishonest means. But their activities tend to promote the market. One has to come to terms with that. This is a transitional period. Things will eventually improve"). Among the youth and the better educated, the proportion of those holding such views increases from one-quarter to one-third. So thoroughly is the planned economy discredited that even among those people who say they will vote for the Communists at the next elections, only 35 percent favor a return to a planned economy (the rallying cry that does unite some Russians under the Red banner is the restoration of the USSR).

A vague commitment to freedom and an almost religious affinity for the "market" cannot fill the ideological vacuum, and a curious mixture of religion and the values fostered by classical Russian culture and the Soviet educational system has proved to be the only alternative system of standards and ideas on which Russians can rely.

A religious revival is occurring in a society where several generations had no connection with the institutional church or with Orthodox theology. Even attendance at church services did not involve people in real religious life and provided only a slight acquaintance with religious patterns of thought.

Opinion polls taken through 1988 reveal that 8–10 percent of the population professed to be religious, while in 1992, 40 percent of those surveyed said they were believers. This revival of religion, however, comes about as the result not of the testimony of the church but of the impact of our secular culture. Most people draw their religious views and beliefs from the mass media (39 percent) and from fictional literature (31 percent); only 9 percent of the respondents attribute them to the church.

A distinguishing feature of the Christian movement in Russia today is that priests are by no means the main influence in people's attitudes toward matters of faith, morals, and metaphysics. Instead, respondents cite as spiritual leaders the "intellectuals" and "thinkers" associated with traditional Russian culture, "old-fashioned" writers such as Aleksandr Solzhenitsyn (named by 15 percent of the respondents), the medieval historian Dmitrii Likhachev (14 percent), the physician A. Amosov (13 percent), the television journalist V. Molchanov (11 percent), and Patriarch Aleksii II (10 percent). The fact that the patriarch appears among the top five in this list is more likely to reflect his image as an "intellectual and thinker" than his ecclesiastical position.

If the role of spiritual fathers of the nation and prophets in our society is being undertaken by writers, scholars, and journalists, it is not surprising that when asked, "What does religion mean to you?" 32 percent of the respondents answered "morality," 20 percent "culture," 12 percent "serving other people," 10 percent "fidelity to national traditions," and only 9 percent "personal salvation." The fact that few persons identify religion with "loyalty to national traditions" casts doubt on the widespread notion that the Orthodox faith is perceived by most Russians as part of their national consciousness. More often than not, religion is seen as a universal cultural phenomenon rather than a national tradition.

Religious consciousness in Russia today is unstructured and amorphous. It has reservations about the institutional behavior of the Russian Orthodox Church and is uncertain about moral standards. When grappling with fundamental questions of faith and morals, most people do not automatically invoke Orthodox doctrines. When asked, "What can save mankind from evil and misfortunes?" respondents cite socialist faith in progress (38 percent) and belief in national traditions (18 percent). Only 12 percent of the respondents believe in the resurrection of Christ, and 4 percent believe in salvation by extraterrestrial civilizations or "humanoids."

Looking back over the past decade one can say that for much of the nation "nontraditional or alternative" religions have turned out to be traditional. About two-thirds of the population embraces nontraditional beliefs: 67 percent believe in evil spells, 66 percent in mental telepathy, 56 percent in astrology, and 46 percent in UFOs. More than one-third of the population believes in the Abominable Snowman, almost one-fourth in ESP, and about one-fifth follow Oriental beliefs (with elements of Buddhism, Krishnaism, and transmigration of souls). But proponents of nontraditional beliefs have not necessarily renounced traditional Orthodox Christianity. Even among the thinning ranks of atheists there is a substantial following for the nontraditional religions, including mental telepathy (almost one-half), astrology (about one-fourth), UFOs, the Abominable Snowman, ESP, Oriental wisdom, and the transmigration of souls. The denial of God does not mean the denial of all faith. The existence of a group of people who are believers and nonbelievers at the same time is a revealing phenomenon that attests to a loss of spiritual bearings.

In brief, one can describe the contemporary religious situation as the search for faith in a gray area between belief and nonbelief. According to public opinion surveys taken in 1991, atheists numbered between 10 and 25 percent of the population. In 1992, this proportion fell to a mere 2–11 percent. Atheism is receding into the past, superseded by other philosophies. A belief in God, though, has not won over the majority: in the cities surveyed, the number of those who believe in God ranges from 32 to 46 percent, while the proportion of people who believe in the supernatural varies from 20 to 49 percent, depending on the region.

Of those who believe in God, only one-quarter also believe in the existence of hell and paradise, and one-half believe in miracles, the devil, and life after death. At the same time, 16 percent of atheists do not deny that the soul survives the body, and 3–4 percent believe in magic and in the devil. This curious combination of apparently incompatible notions signals anything but a well-structured worldview.

This inchoate mentality is evident in the sphere of traditional religion as well. The Russian Orthodox tradition implies following certain practices and forms of worship: prayer, attending church service, receiving Holy Communion, fasting, and participating in church life. But most of those who profess a belief in God neglect the practices. As noted above, 40 percent of those polled say they believe in God. Nonetheless, only 8–10 percent pray every day or "frequently," and another 12 percent pray "infrequently"; the rest do not pray at all. Between 2 and 8 percent attend church services once a week or once a month, while the majority go to church only "on *holidays*" or "once a year." Only 17 percent of the respondents received the Eucharist in the last year or two, and only 7 percent observed the ritual of fasting. These figures show that adherence to traditional religion is actually much less widespread than the number of affirmative responses to the question "Do you believe in God?" would suggest. For most Russians, turning to traditional Christian faith is a form of metaphysical exploration "around the church" and classical Russian culture. Joining the traditional church community is not part of this spiritual quest. Only 2–3 percent of believers take the trouble to attend church services, work for the church, or educate themselves in religion. Significantly, however, many persons who are now outside the church would like to enter. Almost half of those who believe in God say they would like to take part in some form of church life. These responses suggest that there is still an enormous untapped potential for Christian missionary work, a real need for greater involvement with the church. The search for a new faith has thus far found no worthy outlet in church life. The Russian Orthodox Church has proved unprepared for "accepting within its bosom" the huge mass of people desiring to restore their faith. Many of those who attend church services come not to pray, communicate with God, or receive the sacraments but to enjoy the solemn beauty of the liturgy and escape the daily grind. People like going to church for aesthetic factors (beauty and solemnity of the church services was cited by 38 percent), while only 30 percent said they went to church for prayer, confession, or sacraments. Fourteen percent said they went to church to get away from humdrum reality; and 7 percent to satisfy their curiosity.

Another bewildering aspect of religious consciousness has to do with denominations and religious tolerance. The past three years have seen a dramatic increase in the number of people who call themselves

"Christians in general" (from 22 to 52 percent). The overall number of Christians (including "Christians in general," Orthodox Christians affiliated either with the Moscow Patriarchate or the Russian Free Church, Catholics, Protestants, and Old Believers) remained at the same level: 68 percent in 1990 and 68.5 percent in 1992. But the proportion of Orthodox believers (adherents of the Moscow Patriarchate as well as of the Russian Free Church) dropped by a factor of three, from 46 percent in 1990 to 15 percent in 1992.

Thus, although the total number of Christians remained at the same level, Orthodoxy has lost much ground. It is an amazing fact that in a country traditionally dominated by Orthodoxy, where Christians account for the bulk of the population (more than two-thirds), those affiliated with the official church account for less than 10 percent of the population (of the 15 percent Orthodox believers, 6 percent say they support the Russian Free Church). Who, then, is making inroads on Orthodoxy?

Adherents of other Christian denominations (Catholics, Protestants, and Old Believers) are not numerous—1 to 2 percent each. But 22 percent of the respondents consider themselves to be "something else" or have not made up their minds. The main challenge to Orthodoxy comes from the burgeoning group of people who identify themselves with no particular denomination, that is, "Christians in general." Holding less clearly defined religious views than the adherents of specific confessions, "Christians in general" are as a rule those who already believe in God or are on the way toward faith but who are not ready to enter the church unconditionally and observe church discipline (this finding accounts for the low percentage of people who observe Orthodox rituals). The rapid increase in the number of "Christians in general" at the expense of the number of Orthodox believers reflects a desire to revive Christianity, not in the Orthodox form that existed seventy years ago but in a more modern and universal form. Among those who call themselves "Christians in general" there are those who believe in God, those who waver between faith and nonfaith, those who believe in supernatural forces, and even atheists. It is astonishing how "Christians in general" can profess a "faith without boundaries." The phenomenon signals not only a high degree of religious tolerance but a kind of metaphysical eclecticism, the inability to shape a worldview in doctrinal terms. The growing number of people who formally profess Christianity and at the same time hold other religious beliefs characterizes many Western societies, particularly manifest among the young. Russia has not been left out of this world trend. In some ways we have even outstripped the West.

Another important indicator of our involvement in the world cultural and historical process is the level of religious tolerance. Most people, predictably, say they have sympathy for Orthodoxy. The second most popular religion is Catholicism. Considering that most Catholics today are young people, Catholicism has a good chance of spreading in our society.

On the whole, a high level of religious tolerance prevails with regard to all believers. Negative attitudes to any religion, in any region, never exceed 16 percent. Most people take a tolerant view of the conversion of their fellow citizens to Catholicism and the Baptist denominations, which are new to this country. The "confession" held in lowest esteem is atheism, with respect to which the negative assessments always exceed the positive.

In spite of growing public sympathy for diverse religious denominations, most of the population still pins its hopes for Russia's revival on Orthodoxy, at least as an idea and a tradition.

As to the Russian Orthodox Church and its institutions, however, critical judgments are often mixed. Only a fraction of the population has no reservations about the church; only 14 percent of the respondents consider that the Russian Orthodox Church is a "spiritually and morally robust force in our society," that is, carrying out its mission of being a moral and ideological shepherd. Forty-two percent of those polled believe that "during the Soviet period the Russian Orthodox Church developed many shortcomings, but on the whole it has not ceased to be a church and it will heal its wounds over the years." Eight percent of the respondents consider that the "Russian Orthodox Church is in an extreme phase of degeneration." These negative opinions must be attributed not only to the seventy-year Soviet period when the authorities tried to conceal and distort the role of the church in society but also to public dissatisfaction with the present condition and activities of the Russian Orthodox Church.

The results of opinion surveys in two small cities in the Pskov region, Pechory and Gdov, are highly revealing. In Pechory, a traditionally Orthodox city, only 11 percent of the respondents consider the Russian Orthodox Church to be a robust social force, while an equal number of people think that the church has sunk to an extreme degree of degradation. In Gdov, where the Orthodox community is just two years old, the corresponding figures are three times higher and three times lower, respectively. Paradoxically, the more the people are exposed to the Orthodox Church and the better they know it, the less they like it.

A guarded public attitude to the functions of the church is linked with a critical assessment of existing church structures. Respondents were very circumspect in their responses to statements that the church's involvement in every sphere of public life is necessarily favorable. Most people feel that the church contributes to a higher level of morality, and about half of the population thinks that the Russian Orthodox Church contributes to the development of culture and national self-consciousness. But despite the overall increase in religious affinity, a significant majority of the population disagrees with the statement that the church should contribute to democracy and governance. The church's involvement in political life encounters particular resentment.

Given such attitudes among Russians, how is the shaping of national identity and social relations likely to proceed? All the simple approaches tried by the peoples of the Commonwealth of Independent States and the other former communist countries have little or no relevance to Russia. There is no noticeable support in Russia for nationalism, which has traditionally been an essential if not the principal instrument for fostering a sense of national and state identity. It will take some time for the mood of national self-abasement, which has blighted us for almost ten years, to wear off; and when it does, it will not occur concurrently with society's search for solutions to ideological and social problems but as a result of such solutions. A restored sense of nationalism and national dignity will be a reward for achieving success in reconstructing Russia, not a factor in this process.

Most political leaders of whatever persuasion—from the reformer Sergei Shakhrai to the communist Gennadii Ziuganov—promote the age-old ideal of the "great Russian state" as a new supreme value. But demanding a commitment to a "powerful state," which is fast becoming an ideal of Russian politicians, actually tends to distance them from the people. It is beside the point for politicians to refer to the public opinion polls revealing that the people want law and order: after all, any normal person wants to be protected from street muggers and wants trains to run on schedule. If people demand that municipal services do their job properly, it does not follow that they are advocates of a "powerful state." The Russian state (as personified by its leaders) has yet to earn the elementary respect of Russians, to a degree comparable to the respect West Europeans have for their governments.

Nor is Orthodoxy likely to provide the rallying point for the reconstruction of Russia. Notwithstanding the explosion of religious feeling, it is precisely the unifying national function imputed to the Russian Orthodox Church that enjoys least public support. Patriarch Aleksii II and the Episcopate (like the political elite) seek a privileged position for the Orthodox Church as a "unifying force" enjoying broader rights in the nation than, say, Catholicism or Protestantism. But they speak only for a small group of "the church community" and political activists whose sentiments cannot be detected even by sociological surveys.

What, then, will be the ideological platform of the new Russia? At this point we can only speak about harbingers of the new.

While Soviet-era notions of civic duty as service to the motherland and to the socialist cause swiftly erode, a new sense of duty and responsibility is emerging, and without the aid of any propaganda efforts. The lowest number of "egoists" is found among senior citizens, most of whom believe that a person must serve his country and his people. The younger the age of the respondents, the less likely they are to think that a person's duty is to serve his country.

Over the long run, however, antistatist sentiments tend to produce a new, affirmative public morality. The crisis of the old Soviet sense of duty initially leads to a rejection of any sense of duty; only later does duty come to be perceived as service to society, justice, and God. In the scientific and humanistic professions the lowest number of "egoists" is found among secondary school and college students and among the intelligentsia. These Russians believe that one should serve not a "great power" or the nation but justice, charity, and solidarity (*sobornost'*), in the sense of a harmonious community where persons are accepted and helped as individuals rather than as means to serve utilitarian ends.

Because of the prevalence of antistatist and Russophobic sentiments, social activities on behalf of political parties or local organizations have been making slow headway. People remain skeptical of all politics. They are looking for forms of social self-expression that differentiate them from their social milieu rather than make them part of it. All the forms of social activity, such as they were, under the communist regime—the work collectives, the various Soviet-dominated ecological, cultural, and other groups—have discredited themselves and are falling to pieces.

This being so, the most promising associations for the future are those that are ideologically hostile both to the recent past and to the present: cultural, cultural-historical, and national-cultural interest groups and religious groups, as well as single-issue economic, charitable, and cultural groups.

Against the background of social apathy, Russians nonetheless give unexpectedly high marks to charitable organizations and say they are willing to make financial contributions to them. But the existing philanthropic agencies command little trust, and their potential support remains untapped. In the current atmosphere, religious and church organizations can play an important role. Thirty-nine percent of the urban population (57 percent of believers and 25–35 percent of nonbelievers) say they would like to take part in some form of church life, yet actual participation in any form of church life (barring cash donations, 34 percent) is just 2–3 percent, even among believers.

How does one account for such a sharp dichotomy? The Moscow Patriarchate, given its present organization and ideology, cannot provide an outlet for this gigantic potential. The very real conflict between the interests of believers and the structures of the church is a compelling argument for church reform, a reform that would invest church rituals with real and not imaginary substance.

The challenges facing Russia, which has no tradition or habits of a civil society and democracy, are formidable. Besides, our country has a way of choosing the most difficult paths, a tendency to reject simple solutions proposed by the political elite and the church bureaucrats, who have changed their ideology but not their "statist" way of thinking. If Russia stays its course it will be rewarded for its suffering and spiritual bereavement. The present ideological vacuum and moral decline may turn out to be a necessary way station along the road to Russia's future revival.

Translated by the Federal News Service

Note

1. The cities included Moscow, Pskov, Pechory, Gdov, Ufa, Omsk, Kamyshin, Stavropol, Ialutorovsk, Shatsk, Almaty, Uralsk, Aktiubinsk, Pavlodar, and Chimkent.

Chronology

Major Events of 1985–1993, from the Appointment of Mikhail Gorbachev to the December 1993 Elections

1985

March 10–13:   CPSU General Secretary Konstantin Chernenko dies of heart failure; Politburo member Mikhail S. Gorbachev is named to replace him; Vice President George Bush attends funeral.

June 11:   In major speech, Gorbachev deplores poor USSR economic performance and waste, urges broad new economic program.

October 15:   Gorbachev presents draft of new political, economic programs to guide nation to year 2000; economic plan aims to double national income and increase labor productivity up to 150 percent within fifteen years.

1986

February 25–March 6:   At Twenty-seventh Congress of the Communist Party of the Soviet Union, General Secretary Gorbachev calls for sweeping economic reforms; Congress confirms extensive changes in Central Committee membership and approves Gorbachev's October 15 draft economic plan.

April 26:   Explosion at the No. 4 reactor at Chernobyl' nuclear power plant, sixty miles north of Kiev, sets off a graphite fire in the most serious nuclear accident in history.

May 14:   Gorbachev, ending his silence on Chernobyl', proposes four-point program to strengthen cooperation within the International Atomic Energy Agency, criticizes the West for an "unrestrained anti-Soviet campaign," and extends Soviet moratorium on underground nuclear weapons testing until the August 6 anniversary of the 1945 bombing of Hiroshima. The United States welcomes four-point proposal but rejects proposals to join the testing moratorium and convene a summit meeting restricted to the nuclear testing issue.

November 19:   Supreme Soviet approves legislation, to take effect in May 1987, that will allow individual citizens to engage in private enterprise to manufacture certain consumer goods and provide basic services.

December 19:   Soviet government announces the ending of Andrei Sakharov's exile in the city of Gorky. Sakharov and Bonner return to Moscow December 23.

1987

January 27:   At Central Committee plenum, Gorbachev describes Party's administrative stagnation and systemic failures; advocates secret balloting and a choice of candidates in Party elections; says Soviet leadership is considering giving voters choice of candidates in general elections to local bodies.

May 1:   Legislation giving Soviet citizens the right to engage in limited private business activities takes effect, permitting citizens to obtain local licenses and sell their skills for profit in forty business categories.

November 2:   Gorbachev, launching celebration of seventieth anniversary of Bolshevik Revolution, denounces Stalin's historical legacy, acknowledges contributions of Party theoretician Nikolai Bukharin, criticizes Leon Trotsky. Gorbachev defends perestroika (restructuring) and proclaims intention to seek a strategic arms agreement with the United States.

November 11:   Moscow Party chief Boris Yeltsin is dismissed from post amid rumors he had angrily complained about slow pace of reform at Central Committee meeting. Yeltsin is named deputy director of State Committee for Construction.

December 7–10:   Reagan and Gorbachev sign treaty providing for destruction of 2,611 Soviet and American INF missiles and continuous mutual verification inspections of both countries' installations for thirteen years after treaty goes into effect. Reagan and Gorbachev discuss Soviet troop withdrawal from Afghanistan and proposed strategic nuclear forces reduction treaty.

1988

February 18:   Former Moscow Party Chief Boris Yeltsin removed as a candidate member of Politburo, by decision of a CPSU Central Committee plenum.

June 5–12:   With full support of Soviet government, Russian Orthodox Church marks millennium of introduction of Christianity into Russia.

June 28–July 1:   At nineteenth All-Union Conference of the Communist Party (the first such conference since 1941), Gorbachev proposes restructuring of Soviet government into system with a strong president to be chosen by a more representative national legislature that would replace Supreme Soviet. Gorbachev obtains approval for introducing fixed terms for high officials, vesting greater authority in local soviets, allowing multicandidate elections, and banning Party interference in economic matters.

October 1:   At a meeting of Supreme Soviet, Gorbachev is confirmed as new Soviet president, replacing Andrei Gromyko.

November 28–
December 1:   Supreme Soviet approves constitutional changes proposed by President Gorbachev that would transform unicameral Supreme Soviet into a standing bicameral body chosen by a new 2,250-member Congress of People's Deputies, with 1,500 to be elected at local and regional levels and 750 to represent established political and governmental organizations. Chairman of Presidium of the ruling council of the legislature (president) would assume authority over USSR's eco-

nomic, social, and foreign policies and be limited to serving two five-year terms.

December 7: An earthquake registering 6.9 on Richter scale strikes Soviet republic of Armenia, devastating cities of Leninakan and Kirovakan, almost completely destroying town of Spitak, and killing at least 25,000 people. USSR accepts offers of emergency aid from United States.

1989

March 26: Nationwide multicandidate elections are held in Soviet Union for 1,500 seats in 2,250-seat Congress of People's Deputies; in many districts, Communist Party regulars are defeated by populists, liberals, or ethnic nationalists. Yeltsin captures Moscow's at-large seat with 89 percent of vote.

May 25–June 9: New Soviet Congress of People's Deputies opens in Moscow. Approximately 85 percent of 2,250 deputies represent Communist Party; remainder represent unofficial opposition groups, including radical reformists and ethnic nationalists. Gorbachev is elected president with the augmented authority granted under the constitutional changes approved the previous November. In his acceptance speech, Gorbachev provides first official Soviet figures on defense spending: $128 billion for 1989. Prime Minister Nikolai Ryzhkov announces a government deficit of 6.2 percent of GNP, concedes that Afghanistan war cost approximately $70 billion.

July 10–26: Coal miners in western Siberian town of Mezhdurechensk go on strike in protest over poor wages, bad working, housing, and medical conditions, environmental pollution, and shortage of consumer goods. Strike spreads throughout Kuznetsk Basin. Siberian miners accept settlement with government, but strikes continue in Ukraine and elsewhere. In July 23 television interview, Gorbachev contends that although strikes are harmful to economy, strikers' demands are supportive of his reforms. Strikes wane after July 26.

July 27–30: Supreme Soviet votes to approve resolution supporting plans of Lithuania and Estonia to develop autonomous free-market economic systems. On July 30 approximately 300 dissident members of Congress of People's Deputies, including Yeltsin and Sakharov, form Inter-Regional Group of People's Deputies.

August 18:

Chairman of Central Committee International Policy Commission Aleksandr N. Yakovlev (after decades of official denials) admits existence of secret protocols to the 1939 Nazi-Soviet nonaggression pact that partitioned Poland and gave the USSR a free hand in Estonia, Latvia, and Lithuania. Four days later, Supreme Soviet of Lithuania declares that the Soviet annexation of the nation in 1940 was unlawful, as was the status of Lithuania as a republic of Soviet Union. A million-strong human chain of demonstrators stretching 400 miles from Tallinn through Riga to Vilnius protests the Molotov-Ribbentrop pact.

1990

February 3–7:

As a Central Committee plenum convenes, an estimated 300,000 prodemocracy demonstrators march through Moscow. Plenum votes to recommend to national legislature that Article 6 of the Soviet constitution, mandating Communist Party's monopoly of power in USSR, be deleted.

March 11:

By a 124–6 vote, Supreme Soviet of Lithuania declares independence from Soviet Union, while voting to retain Soviet laws temporarily. Landsbergis elected president of Lithuania. Gorbachev calls Lithuanian independence "illegitimate and invalid."

March 13–15:

Third Soviet Congress of People's Deputies votes (1,771–24, with 74 abstentions) to abrogate Article 6 and to create new office of executive president, with broad powers over foreign policy and conduct of military affairs; the first president to be chosen by itself, and subsequently by popular election. Gorbachev is elected to new presidency.

May 1:

Government for first time allows independent and unofficial organizations to participate in Moscow May Day parade; thousands of protesters among participants jeer President Gorbachev and other members of Soviet leadership standing atop Lenin's Mausoleum.

May 29:
Boris Yeltsin, running on platform of "real economic and political sovereignty" for Russia, is elected president of Russian Federation, ousting Gorbachev's choice, A.V. Vlasov.

June 12–14:
USSR Supreme Soviet approves legislation establishing freedom of press; votes to support, in principle, transition to market economy, calls on President Gorbachev to institute joint-stock companies and other reforms by presidential decree; approves corporate income tax, but rejects government plan to triple bread prices.

July 2–13:
At Twenty-eighth Congress of Communist Party of Soviet Union, Gorbachev admits that Party under his leadership has made "mistakes" and calls for a regulated market economy. Yeltsin calls for radical reform of Party. Congress approves Gorbachev's proposal to expand Party Politburo to include representatives from all Soviet republics. Gorbachev is reelected Party general secretary. Yeltsin, nominated for seat on Party Central Committee, stuns congress by announcing his resignation from Party; mayors of Moscow and Leningrad jointly resign from Party, congress adjourns after electing new 410-member Central Committee; Ligachev indicates he will retire. Central Committee elects new Politburo of twenty-four members, including only two holdovers from previous Politburo (Gorbachev and Ivashko); fifteen of twenty-two new members are Party leaders from each of Soviet Union's republics.

August 29– September 14:
Gorbachev meets in Moscow with Yeltsin to discuss radical 500-day plan for economic and political restructuring of Soviet Union developed by panel of their principal economic advisors headed by Stanislav S. Shatalin. At economic summit presided over by Gorbachev, Federation Council and Presidential Council approve "Shatalin Plan." Yeltsin demands resignation of Ryzhkov government. Ryzhkov denounces Shatalin Plan and threatens to resign if legislature adopts so radical a program. Gorbachev announces that he prefers Shatalin Plan to Ryzhkov's more moderate government proposal. Gorbachev offers Supreme Soviet "President's Plan," a more moderate version of Shatalin Plan that preserves central government authority over banking, taxation, and currency.

October 16:   Gorbachev presents to Supreme Soviet his formula for economic reform endorsing transition to market economy but excluding Shatalin Plan's 500-day timetable while preserving central government authority over economy; Yeltsin and Shatalin reject Gorbachev Plan. On October 19, Supreme Soviet approves Gorbachev Plan but on October 31 Parliament of Russian Federation votes to approve implementation of radical 500-day plan, beginning November 1.

October 20–21: "Democratic Russia," a coalition of opposition political groups in Russian Federation, holds first congress in Moscow, adjourns without reaching agreement on common platform.

October 26:   Using new emergency powers, Gorbachev issues decrees permitting foreigners to operate wholly-owned subsidiaries in USSR and to lease Soviet real estate, allowing Soviet citizens to invest in enterprises, and devaluing ruble as a step toward establishing convertibility and raising interest rates on bank savings. On November 2 he issues decree requiring that Soviet enterprises return 40 percent of their hard-currency earnings to central government.

November 23:   Gorbachev proposes new Union Treaty governing relationship between USSR central government and fifteen constituent republics. Under the treaty, which all republics must sign, central government would retain control of military and foreign policy while republics would gain "full authority" over their territory (including natural resources) and their economic systems. Central government laws would nonetheless take precedence over those of republics; USSR Council of Ministers and position of premier would be retained.

December 17–27: Addressing opening session of Fourth Congress of People's Deputies, Gorbachev demands that each Soviet republic hold a referendum on his proposed Union Treaty. On December 20, Soviet Foreign Minister Shevardnadze announces his resignation and warns that reactionary forces threaten Soviet Union with renewed dictatorship. On December 22, KGB chairman Vladimir A. Kriuchkov attacks Western economic involvement in USSR as masked attempt to gather strategic information. On December 24 Congress approves Gorbachev's proposed treaty on a looser Soviet federation; on December 25 votes to make cabinet secretaries directly subordinate to Soviet president, to create new post of vice-president, to reject Gorbachev's proposed Supreme State Inspectorate designed to enforce presidential decrees, and to include on Federation Council representatives of fifteen republics and several smaller ethnic groups. On December 27, Gennadii I. Yanaev, Gorbachev's nominee, is elected vice-president.

1991

January 13:   In a crackdown on pro-independence forces, Soviet army troops kill fifteen protesters in Vilnius. In address to Supreme Soviet the following day, Gorbachev denies giving the order for the army attack, contending that military chief in Lithuania, Maj. Gen. Vladimir Uskhochnik, carried out the attack on his own initiative and in response to pleas for help from republic's "National Salvation Committee." On January 13 Yeltsin signs a mutual-security pact with representatives of the three Baltic republics that calls for Baltic states and Russia to respect each other's sovereignty, to refrain from recognizing any nonelected government in any of the four republics, and to come to each other's defense should the central government attack. All four presidents issue a joint appeal for UN intervention in the Baltic region to prevent further bloodshed. Latvian parliament passes resolution condemning planned Soviet troop deployments as the start of a Soviet "invasion" of the Baltic region.

January 20:   In Moscow, an estimated 100,000 to 300,000 people march to Kremlin to protest repressive measures in Baltic states. Soviet "black beret" Interior Ministry troops storm the headquarters of the Latvian interior ministry in Riga, causing at least four deaths.

June 12:   Yeltsin, campaigning as a political independent, is elected to the newly created executive presidency of the Russian republic with 60 percent of vote. Col. Aleksandr V. Rutskoi is elected vice-president on Yeltsin's ticket. On July 10, in the Kremlin, Yeltsin is inaugurated as Russian president.

August 19–21:   TASS announces that Gorbachev, vacationing at his dacha in the Crimea, is incapacitated with an unspecified illness and is being replaced by Vice-President Yanaev and seven other officials calling themselves the State Committee for the State of Emergency. Hours later, military units, including hundreds of tanks, take up positions on key streets, intersections, and bridges in Moscow. The coup leaders declare state of emergency "in individual localities" of the USSR, prohibit large gatherings of people in certain localities, set curfews, and ban opposition political activity and the press. Western leaders condemn the coup. Yeltsin denounces the coup as unconstitutional, brands the Emergency Committee members traitors, telephones President Bush and British Prime Minister John Major and receives assurances that those governments will not recognize Emergency Committee as the legitimate Soviet leadership. On August 20 Yeltsin addresses an estimated 150,000 people at Russian parliament building and repeats his charge that Yanaev and his allies have seized power illegally. Pavlov abruptly resigns as premier and member of Emergency Committee, citing illness. On August 21 armored vehicles approaching Russian parliament clash with hundreds of civilians armed with "Molotov cocktails"; three people are killed and several are injured, but the military pulls back. Amid uncertainties over the degree of military support for the plotters, and with overwhelming opposition both inside and outside the country, the coup collapses. By late afternoon, Gorbachev is released and calls overthrow of the coup plot a "serious victory for the perestroika process"; lauds Yeltsin for standing up to conspirators and hails Soviet people for having the self-esteem to fight the takeover. Bush welcomes apparent end of coup and Gorbachev's return to power; German Chancellor Helmut Kohl and French President François Mitterrand urge the West to increase economic aid to the Soviet Union in order to preserve political stability.

August 23–
September 11:
Gorbachev, under pressure from Yeltsin, appoints air force Gen. Evgenii Shaposhnikov as defense minister, Vadim V. Bakatin as KGB chief, Gen. Vladimir Lobov as Soviet chief of staff. He names Viktor Barannikov as Soviet interior minister (replacing Boris Pugo, who committed suicide after participating in failed coup), fires Foreign Minister Bessmertnykh, and appoints Boris Pankin as foreign minister. On September 11 the Russian prosecutor's office discloses that ten of

the fourteen coup defendants pleaded not guilty to all counts of treason, that three pleaded guilty to some counts, and that one admitted guilt on all counts.

August 20–21:   Republics of Estonia and Latvia declare independence, Lithuania reaffirming 1990 declaration of independence. Latvian and Lithuanian communist parties are banned and their properties are expropriated in both republics (August 22–23). Yeltsin issues decrees recognizing Estonia and Latvia as independent states (August 24). The EC recognizes the three republics, and President Bush announces full U.S. diplomatic recognition. The Soviet State Council formally recognizes the independence of the Baltic republics on September 6 and declares Soviet support for their membership in the UN and in the Conference on Security and Cooperation in Europe (CSCE). The Union Treaty, which had been scheduled for signature August 20, is effectively killed (see entry for December 8).

August 24:   Gorbachev resigns as general secretary of Soviet Communist Party but not from the Party; issues series of decrees curbing the power and perquisites of the Party, including the dissolution of the Central Committee and the transfer of all Party property to the Soviet parliament's control. Gorbachev also dismisses the remaining members of the Cabinet of Ministers and replaces this body with a special committee headed by Russian Premier Ivan Silaev, who assumes the role of acting premier and replaces former USSR Premier Pavlov, one of the arrested conspirators.

Late August–
early September: The parliaments of Ukraine, Belarus, and Moldova vote to declare independence (August 25–27). On August 27, Gorbachev threatens to resign office if republics do not halt their stampede for independence and urges the republics to preserve military and economic unity. Parliaments of Azerbaijan, Uzbekistan, and Kyrghyzstan vote independence declarations (August 30–31). Parliament of the Crimea region votes declaration of independence from Ukraine (September 5). Parliament of Tadjikistan declares independence and calls for presidential elections (September 9).

September 6:   Leningrad citizens vote to adopt the city's prerevolutionary name of St. Petersburg.

November 1: Russian Congress of People's Deputies grants Yeltsin sweeping powers to initiate and direct radical economic reforms, including the removal of most price controls by the end of 1991; the immediate privatization of small and medium-sized state farms and state industries; the creation of a convertible Russian currency; the cutoff of Russia's funding of seventy Soviet central ministries; and the cessation of Russia's contribution to Soviet foreign aid programs.

December 1: Ukrainian voters elect Leonid M. Kravchuk president and approve a referendum to declare independence from the Soviet Union and create an independent nation. Russian republic recognizes Ukrainian independence (December 2).

December 8: The Presidents of Russia, Ukraine, and Belarus declare that the Soviet Union has ceased to exist and proclaim a new "Commonwealth of Independent States" that would be open to all Soviet republics. Yeltsin telephones President Bush to explain the accord, which puts free-market initiatives and military affairs under joint command of the three states and invalidates Soviet authority. Ukrainian, Belarusian, and Russian parliaments ratify commonwealth agreement (December 10–12) and thereby preempt Gorbachev's Union Treaty. Gorbachev had already rejected the right of leaders of the three republics to dissolve the Soviet Union. Bush administration states that although it is prepared to work with the new commonwealth, U.S. would not break relations with central Soviet government (December 10).

December 21: Eleven republics of Soviet Union formally constitute themselves as the Commonwealth of Independent States and sign an agreement that guarantees separate sovereignties but leaves unresolved such issues as mutually acceptable system of command for common military policy and nuclear weapons control. A council of state and government leaders, assisted by committees of republic ministers of foreign affairs, defense, and economics would be in charge, with operations to begin no later than January 15, 1992, following ratification by the eleven republics. (Armenia, Moldova, and Azerbaijan join the five Asian republics and the three founding republics, while the Baltic states and Georgia do not participate.)

Former Soviet republics decide to assign the permanent UN Security Council seat of the USSR to Russia.

December 25: Gorbachev resigns as president of Soviet Union, defends his seven years in office, and states that he cannot support the Commonwealth that is replacing the USSR. The Soviet red flag with hammer and sickle is lowered over Kremlin and the white-blue-red Russian flag hoisted in its stead. Yeltsin takes control of the Soviet nuclear arsenal. President Bush praises Gorbachev for his role in history and says the U.S. will recognize the former Soviet republics.

1992

January 2: As first stage of its radical economic reform program, the Russian government eliminates state subsidies on most goods and services, allowing prices to soar. Ukraine, Belarus, and Moldova also begin lifting price controls.

January 2: Ukrainian parliament declares the "creation of a sovereign state, the republic of Crimea," subject to voter approval in region-wide referendum. On May 21 the Russian Supreme Soviet votes to annul the 1954 transfer of the Crimea region to Ukraine from Russia.

May 23: The United States and the four other nuclear-armed CIS members—Russia, Ukraine, Belarus, and Kazakhstan—pledge to comply with START treaty.

July 25: Estonia and Latvia adopt citizenship laws that effectively curb legal and other civic rights of ethnic Russians.

July 27: Estonian troops in capital exchange shots with Russian soldiers as tensions grow over continued Russian presence in the Baltic. On August 8 Russia asks that the Baltic states pay $7.7 billion in exchange for withdrawing its troops from the region by 1994.

October 1: Russia begins issuing vouchers to its 150 million citizens in a program to privatize up to 70 percent of its state-owned factories.

November 23: Yeltsin reaches accord with his principal parliamentary critics on stopgap economic reforms. Although the plan includes compromises on both sides, it retains the main elements of government's economic program setting up guideposts for production, inflation, acceptable living standards, and ruble stabilization.

December 1: Russian Congress of People's Deputies convenes. Yeltsin calls for political ceasefire and declares that the nation is showing signs of economic recovery, but admits lowering of living standards; vows to boost government support for factories On December 3 fistfights break out in congress after acting Prime Minister Egor T. Gaidar appeals for centrist support to stop hard-line attacks on market reforms. In secret balloting the congress on December 5 narrowly rejects constitutional amendments to dilute Yeltsin's control over government and give new powers to a parliament that is dominated by hard-liners. By a vote of 486–467, with 22 abstentions, the parliament on December 9 rejects Yeltsin's nomination of Gaidar as prime minister. In compromise meeting Yeltsin and rival parliamentary leader, Ruslan I. Khasbulatov, agree to call for a referendum on new constitution in April. Congress suspends session December 11. On December 17 Yeltsin appoints Gaidar as presidential adviser on economic policy.

December 14: Yeltsin chooses Viktor Chernomyrdin as prime minister to replace Gaidar. Chernomyrdin pledges loyalty to free-market policies, but stresses that reforms must be achieved "without impoverishing our people." Yeltsin approves cabinet put together by Chernomyrdin (December 23).

1993

March 10–13: Russian Congress of People's Deputies meets in special session, votes to limit the powers granted to President Yeltsin in the December 1992 compromise, and cancels the referendum scheduled for April that would have asked Russian people to decide on the relationship between presidential and congressional power. On March 20 Yeltsin claims special emergency powers and confirms April 25 as date for popular vote of confidence in him and his vice-president, Aleksandr Rutskoi. Supreme Soviet in emergency meeting passes resolution declaring Yeltsin's measures to be "an attempt on the constitutional foundations of Russia's statehood" and asks Constitutional Court to rule on their legality. Constitutional Court rules that Yeltsin's actions violated nine constitutional provisions and number of provisions of Russian Federation treaty, but does not call for president's impeachment. On March 28 Yeltsin narrowly survives a vote for impeachment, but congress passes measures terminating Yeltsin's powers to rule by decree and his claims of executive branch primacy over the legislature.

April 25: Yeltsin's policies receive solid if not ringing endorsement when 53 percent of voters participating in nationwide referendum say they approve of the president's social and economic policies.

May 1: Rioting breaks out during May Day demonstrations in Moscow, despite government order not to march; 570 people wounded.

July 12: Russian constitutional conference, convened to draw up new charter, approves draft providing for presidential republic with bicameral legislature and strong provincial autonomy.

September 1: Yeltsin suspends Vice-President Rutskoi from office, citing damaging allegations of corruption against him. On September 3 parliament votes by large majority to halt implementation of Yeltsin's decree suspending Rutskoi as a violation of the Constitution.

September 21: Yeltsin dissolves congress by decree and orders that elections will be held December 12 for a new legislative body. Parliament declares Yeltsin's actions to be coup d'état; votes to depose him and swears in Vice-President Rutskoi as acting president; turns the parliament building (the White House) into armed camp. On September 23 Constitutional Court upholds decision to unseat Yeltsin; defense ministry says that army will observe "strict political neutrality." Most regional leaders seem to support Yeltsin's actions. Western governments, including the United States, endorse Yeltsin's actions.

October 3–4: Around 5,000 Russian conservative, communist, and monarchist protestors sympathetic to deputies and their leaders break through lines of riot police to White House; Rutskoi and Khasbulatov urge mob to seize mayor's office, the Kremlin, and main Moscow broadcast center at Ostankino; violence erupts between police and demonstrators. Yeltsin declares state of emergency and imposes curfew; Russian soldiers take back parliament building; after severe fighting, large numbers of unarmed defenders surrender, including Rutskoi and Khasbulatov, who are arrested along with 158 suspects; 187 people, including 76 noncombatants, are announced to have been killed. On October 8 Yeltsin moves to concentrate administrative authority; suspends publication of communist newspapers and some extreme nationalist publications as well as several of the more centrist news media; bans several militant communist organizations; dismantles local soviets, staffed for the most part by officials from the communist era; reaffirms that elections to a new national legislature and a referendum on the new constitution will be held on December 12.

December 12: Nationalists and former communists make a surprisingly strong showing in elections to Russia's new parliament, the Duma. Nationalist Vladimir Zhirinovskii and his Liberal Democratic Party win 22.79 percent of votes; Russia's Choice, the pro-Yeltsin party led by Egor Gaidar, receives 15.38 percent; revived Communist Party led by Gennadii Ziuganov wins 12.35 percent; other blocs that clear the 5 percent hurdle for representation include pro-reform bloc, the Women of Russia, the conservative Agrarian Party, and the centrist Democratic Party. Voters approve the new Russian Constitution, which grants the president extensive powers to issue decrees, appoint the government, and overrule the legislature. On December 15 President Clinton discounts the significance of Zhirinovskii's strong showing and expresses continued support for President Yeltsin and his reform policies. Vice-President Gore, during a visit to Moscow December 20, signs a number of cooperative agreements relating to economic assistance and outer space research.

Biographical Notes

Persons Mentioned in the Text

Akhmadulina, Bella Akhatovna (b. 1937), a prominent, contemporary poet. Her surrealistic poems, lyrically evocative of the historical past, are often characterized by a sense of alienation from, or entrapment in, what Soviet society defined as normal.

Akhmatova, Anna Andreevna (pseudonym of Anna Gorenko, 1889–1966), preeminent Russian poet and translator. Her creative career falls into three periods: the period of her association with the symbolists and acmeists (1910–22); the period following her expulsion from the Writers' Union, which deprived her of the right to publish (1922–40); and the late period, when wartime relaxation of government controls, her son's release from prison, and the "thaw" permitted her to publish again. International recognition brought her the Taormina Prize for Poetry in Italy (1964) and an honorary degree from Oxford University (1965). Notable among her poems are "Requiem," "The Course of Time," and "Poem Without a Hero."

Aksyonov, Vassily Pavlovich (b. 1932), prose writer. His short novel *Ticket to the Stars* caught the qualities of post-Stalin youth (uninhibited, independent-minded, attracted to Western culture), and his later works, including *The Island Crimea* (1981), dealt with such phenomena as agonizing encounters between former political prisoners and their former jailers. These works reflected the unfulfilled expectations of the "men of the sixties." In 1980 he was exiled after the appearnace of *Metropol,* a collection of anti-Communist works published without official authorization. He lives in the Washington, D.C., area. His most recent novel, *Seasons of Winter,* was published in 1994.

Andreev, Leonid Nikolaevich (1871–1919), one of Russia's most popular writers, dramatists, and publicists of the early twentieth century. He was nearly as

307

famous in his time as Anton Chekhov and Maxim Gorky were in theirs'. He actively opposed the Bolshevik Revolution in October 1917.

Antonov, A.S., a Socialist Revolutionary leader of a peasant anti-Bolshevik revolt of 1920–21. —V.I.

Askol'dov, Sergei (pseudonym of Sergei Alekseevich Alekseev, 1871–1945), philosopher, literary critic, and poet. Askol'dov spent many years in prison and in exile after being removed in 1922 from his position as professor of philosophy at Petrograd University. Captured by the Germans when Novgorod fell in 1941, Askol'dov died abroad in 1945 after being liberated by Soviet forces and by a fortunate KGB error set free.

Astaf'ev, Viktor (b. 1924), a leading prose writer associated with the Village Prose movement. Astaf'ev's Siberian peasant background is reflected in his use of dialects and folk imagery. Among his major works are *The King Fish* (1976) and *The Sad Detective* (1986).

Bakhtin, Mikhail Mikhailovich (1895–1975), the most widely known Russian thinker and literary scholar of this century, an author of books on the dialogical aspects of Dostoevsky (*Problems of Dostoevsky's Poetics*, Minneapolis: University of Minnesota Press, 1984), Rabelais and the carnival culture (*Rabelais and His World*, 2d ed., Bloomington: Indiana University Press, 1968), problems of cultural anthropology (*The Dialogical Imagination*, Austin: University of Texas Press, 1981; and *Art and Answerability: Early Philosophical Essays* (Austin: University of Texas Press, 1990). Some of his books were published under the names of his friends and students. He was arrested in 1929 and spent most of his life far from the principal cities of Russia. Fame came to him not long before his death from a chronic illness caused by the loss of one leg when he was in exile in Kazakhstan. Bakhtin is among the most influential thinkers in modern cultural studies in Russia and elsewhere (see The *Bakhtin Newsletter*, 1993, no. 4). —V.I.

Bakunin, Mikhail Aleksandrovich (1814–1876), a Russian political thinker and politician and one of the founders of modern anarchism. Bakunin participated in the European revolutionary movements of 1848–49, was arrested by the Austrian police, and was put into a Russian jail, from which he was transferred to Siberian exile. He fled and participated in the new European revolutionary movement, also opposing Karl Marx. —V.I.

Barkashov, Aleksandr, the head of the avowedly fascist Russian National Unity Party. Barkashov escaped from the White House during the events of October

3–4, 1993, using an underground sewer, and remains at large. He has subsequently organized armed formations for service in the Bosnian war on the Serbian side.

Barkov, Ivan (1732–1768), a Russian poet and translator famous for his erotic verses. —C.A.F.

Bednyi, Dem'ian (pseudonym of Efim Alekseevich Pridvorov, 1883–1945), a Russian poet and satirist and one of the most active and effective Communist Party propagandists. He was a favorite of V.I. Lenin and Leon Trotsky, survived a period of disgrace (including expulsion from the Party), and, unlike other old Bolsheviks, lived a productive life through World War II.

Belinskii, Vissarion Grigor'evich (1811–1848), renowned Russian literary critic and one of the founders of modern Russian literature. In the beginning of his career, he lived in utter poverty, suffering from tuberculosis. —V.I.

Berberova, Nina Nikolaevna (1901–1993), a poet, prose writer, and critic who left Russia in 1922 with the poet Vladislav Khodasevich. For many years she taught Russian literature at Princeton University. She contributed to *Sovremennye zapiski, Novyi zhurnal, Vozrozhdenie, Opyty, Grani, Zveno,* and other journals of the Russian emigration.

Berdiaev, Nikolai Aleksandrovich (1875–1948), eminent Russian religious thinker and a contributor to the 1909 *Vekhi* (Landmarks) essays. Berdiaev was exiled from Russia in 1922 because of his strong religious views; he lived the remainder of his life in France. Among his most important works are *The Meaning of History, The Destiny of Man, Freedom and the Spirit, The Origin of Russian Communism,* and *The Russian Idea.*

Blok, Aleksandr Aleksandrovich (1880–1921), considered to be the most accomplished Russian symbolist poet. He was a follower of Vladimir Solov'ev in his early writings. His essays address important problems of modern Russian history. He was close to the left wing of the Socialist Revolutionaries and accepted their vision of the Revolution. He was arrested after their expulsion from the first Soviet government, and although he was set free owing to the intervention of Maxim Gorky and other important figures, he completely lost faith in the Revolution. *V.I.*

Bogdanov, Aleksandr Aleksandrovich (pseudonym of Aleksandr Aleksandrovich Malinovskii, 1873–1928), a philosopher of Marxism, a literary activist and writer, and an early associate of V.I. Lenin. Under the influence of the Viennese philosopher Ernst Mach, he developed the system of philosophical views known as empiriomonism (1906), which Lenin attacked in his *Materialism and Empiriocriticism* (1909). Bogdanov, a medical doctor by profession, founded the Institute for Blood Transfusion in Moscow; his death occurred as the result of an experiment performed upon himself.

Briusov, Valerii Iakovlevich (1873–1924), a poet, novelist, short story writer, essayist, literary historian, and translator. Briusov was a teacher of some of the major poets of the twentieth century, including Andrei Belyi and Aleksandr Blok. The true birth of the Russian symbolist movement can be dated from March 1894, when Briusov published the anthology *The Russian Symbolists.* After the Revolution he joined the Communist Party and was a manager of Narkompros (Department of Public Education); he later organized its literary division, LITO.

Bulgakov, Sergei (1871–1944), prominent Russian intellectual. Bulgakov contributed to the 1909 *Vekhi* (Landmarks) essays and edited, with Nikolai Berdiaev, the periodical *Novyi put'.* He later took orders as an Orthodox priest and became one of the most controversial Orthodox theologians of this century.

Bunin, Ivan Alekseevich (1870–1953), the first Russian writer awarded the Nobel Prize (1933). He viewed the Bolshevik Revolution with contempt and emigrated to Paris. Notable among his stories are *Sunstroke, Dark Avenues, Mitya's Love,* and *Dry Valley.*

Chaadaev, Petr Iakovlevich (1793–1856), eminent Russian philosopher, persecuted by the government after he published his *Philosophical Letters* (complete English edition by R.T. McNally, *The Major Works,* London, 1969). Chaadaev's later works were rediscovered after the Revolution, but have been published in Russia only recently. —V.I.

Chernyshevskii, Nikolai Gavrilovich (1828–1856), influential Russian political thinker, writer, and scholar. For his radical political activity, he was arrested in the time of the reforms of Alexander II and kept in jail, then exiled to Siberia and later to the Volga region. He was extraordinarily popular with all the leftist intellectuals and deeply hated by the members of the other movements (as may be seen, for instance, in Vladimir Nabokov's novel *The Gift*). —V.I.

Chizhevskii, Aleksandr Leonidovich (1897–1964), a Russian scientist and the founder of a new field of study investigating the influence of physical events in cosmic space on the earth. Chizhevskii surmised that the cycles in the world history he studied were caused by the influence of the activity of the sun (heliobiology) and other cosmic objects. —V.I.

Danilevskii, Nikolai (1822–1885), a pan-Slavist theorist whose best-known work, *Russia and Europe*, was published in 1869. In his youth he was a member of the Petrashevskii circle; he later became a naturalist and an expert on Darwinism.

Esenin, Sergei Aleksandrovich (1895–1925), renowned Russian poet whose poetic career lasted only ten years. Lauded as a "people's poet," his long poems *Anna Snegina* and *Pugachev*, as well as his prose, are not as successful as his brief lyric poetry, which captured the imagination of the average Russian. Esenin's suicide in 1925 came to symbolize the disillusionment of many Russian intellectuals with early revolutionary ideals.

Fedorov, Nikolai Fedorovich (1828–1903), eminent Russian religious philosopher who suggested a project on the physical resurrection of the dead as the "common cause" of the science of the future. —V.I.

Fedotov, Georgii Petrovich (1886–1951), historian, essayist, and religious thinker. Emigrating to France in 1925, he was professor of church history at the Russian Theological School in Paris from 1926 to 1940. In 1941 he went to the United States and taught at St. Vladimir's Theological Seminary until his death. His great work, *The Russian Religious Mind* (2 vols., 1946–66), is considered indispensable for students of Russian culture and literature.

Filatov, Sergei (b. 1926), President Boris Yeltsin's chief of staff and frequent spokesman. He played a key role in drafting the Constitution.

Florenskii, Pavel Aleksandrovich (1882–1943), a scholar, religious philosopher, folklorist, and poet. In his chief work, *The Pillar and Foundation of Truth*, Florenskii attempted a universal theodicy in which he brought to bear his great scientific, historical, literary, and linguistic knowledge in defense of Orthodox dogma against Solov'evian all-unity. Subsequently, he departed from dogmatic Orthodoxy and turned increasingly toward Vladimir Solov'ev's Platonism and the aesthetic theories of symbolist poet Viacheslav Ivanov. Florenskii was repeatedly arrested and died in exile.

Frank, Semen (1877–1950), a Russian religious philosopher, political economist, sociologist, critic, publicist, and educator. He contributed essays to the collections *Problemy idealizma* (Problems of Idealism, 1902), *Vekhi* (Landmarks,

1909), and *Iz glubiny* (From the Depths, 1918). Following his expulsion from Russia in 1922, Frank lived in Germany, France, and England.

Galich, Aleksandr (pseudonym of Aleksandr Ginzburg, 1918–1977), a Russian poet who sang his work, accompanying himself on a guitar, and who became famous as one of Russia's unauthorized "bards." In 1972 he was expelled from the Writers' Union at the insistence of Dmitrii Polianskii, a member of the Politburo. He emigrated in 1974 and died in Paris.

Gippius, Zinaïda Nikolaevna (1869–1945), a poet, writer, and critic. Her creative work emphasized the values of universal culture and the mysteries of aesthetic beauty and harmony, focusing on the love of God and Christian ethics. She left Russia in 1924 with her husband, Dmitrii Merezhkovskii. They eventually settled in Paris, where they founded the famous Green Lamp literary and philosophical society.

Gogol, Nikolai (1809–1852), preeminent Russian prose writer. In his early work, the folk mythology of his native Ukraine is complemented by his own imagination. —V.I.

Goncharov, Ivan Aleksandrovich (1812–1891), a writer who also worked as an official in the Russian government censorship agency. His accusation of plagiarism against Ivan Turgenev caused a scandal. After the hostile critical reception of *The Precipice* he wrote little and lived out his last years in seclusion. His most famous novels are *A Common Story, Oblomov, The Frigate Pallas,* and *The Precipice.*

Griboedov, Aleksandr Sergeevich (1795–1829), accomplished Russian playwright, diplomat, and poet. In his comedy, *Woe from Wit; or, The Misfortune of Being Clever,* he depicted a hostile, old-fashioned social environment that proclaimed a modern young man to be crazy. While serving as an ambassador in Persia, he was killed by a fanatical mob. —V.I.

Gumilev, Lev Nikolaevich (1912–1993), eminent Russian ethnologist, author of many works on the steppe peoples, including *Searches for an Imaginary Kingdom: The Legacy of the Kingdom of Presbyter John* (Cambridge: Cambridge University Press, 1987); and *Ethnogenesis and Biosphere* (Moscow: Progress Publishing House, 1990). The son of two great poets, Nikolai Gumilev and Anna Akhmatova, he was twice arrested and kept in jail and forced labor camps for many years. —V.I.

Gumilev, Nikolai Stepanovich (1886–1921), influential Russian poet and the founder of the acmeist school of poetry. He was executed in 1921 as a supposed participant in anti-Soviet activity. —V.I.

Il'in, Ivan Aleksandrovich (1883–1954), religious philosopher, jurist, and political scientist; also a historian and critic of literature and the arts. After being expelled from Russia in 1922 (he was an active foe of Bolshevism), he taught at the Russian Scientific Institute in Berlin until the Nazis removed him from that position in 1934. From 1938 until his death he lived in Zurich. His literary legacy includes several hundred articles and more than thirty books on philosophy and religion, law and political science, literature and the arts, and Russian and Soviet studies.

Ivanov, Viacheslav Ivanovich (1866–1949), a poet, translator, critic, and scholar, who made major contributions to the interpretation of Aleksandr Pushkin, Nikolai Gogol, and Fyodor Dostoevsky. Ivanov became one of the leaders of the symbolist movement and soon its principal theorist. He established a brilliant literary salon in St. Petersburg, the famous Bashnia (tower), in 1905. In 1924 he emigrated from Russia and spent the rest of his life in Italy, where he held a professorship of Russian literature at the University of Pavia from 1926 to 1934.

Kharms, Daniil Ivanovich (pseudonym of Daniil Ivanovich Iuvachev, 1905–1942), a poet and writer who participated in the avante-garde group of poets and artists Oberiut (Association for Real Art). During the 1920s, Kharms indulged widely in theatrical behavior—both on and off stage—and was imprisoned on charges of distracting people from the tasks of construction with his "transense" poetry. After his release in 1932, Kharms worked in various genres of children's literature. He was arrested again in 1941 and died of starvation in the camps.

Khlebnikov, Velemir (Viktor Vladimirovich) (1885–1921), accomplished Russian futurist poet. He studied mathematical equations through which he wanted to describe repetitions of similar and opposite events in world history (*The King of Time*, Cambridge: Harvard University Press, 1990). —V.I.

Khodasevich, Vladislav Felitsianovich (1886–1939), a symbolist poet and literary critic. He began publishing poems in symbolist almanacs and journals in 1905. After leaving Russia in 1922 and living in Berlin, Prague, Rome, and Sorrento, he made his home in Paris. He wrote for the émigré press (*Volia Rossii, Sovremennye zapiski, Vozrozhdenie*). Among his most famous works are the collections of poems *Molodost'* (Youth, 1908), *Shchastlivyi domik* (The Happy Little House, 1914), *Putem zerna* (By Way of a Grain of Corn, 1920), *Tiazhelaia lira* (A Heavy Lyre, 1922), and the cycle *Evropeiskaia noch'* (European Night) and his *Literaturnye stat'i i vospominaniia* (Literary Articles and Memoirs, 1954).

Kliuchevskii, Vasilii Osipovich (1941–1911), one of the greatest Russian historians, the author of a famous course in Russian history. —V.I.

Kliuev, Nikolai Alekseevich (1887–1937), the most talented of the so-called peasant poets in Russia, who moved away from earlier symbolist models to emphasize his origins as a "people's poet," making broad use of dialect and folk imagery and combining Russian nationalism, eroticism, and deep religiosity. He was exiled to the Narym area of Siberia, and the circumstances of his death are unknown.

Kondrat'ev, Nikolai Dmitrievich (1892–1938), eminent Russian economist who discovered the so-called Kondrat'ev's waves determining cycles of the economic recession until the end of the century. He was a director of the Institute of the Economic State of the Market (1920–28) and worked out the first plan for the development of Russian villages and forests (1923–28). He was executed in Josef Stalin's time, and many people connected with what was called Kondrat'ev's Heresy (Kondrat'evshchina) were arrested. —V.I.

Korolev, Sergei Pavlovich (1906/1907–1966), the main constructor of the Soviet spaceships. He spent part of his life in a Soviet jail and a labor camp, after which he continued his work on rockets. —V.I.

Kropotkin, Petr Alekseevich, Prince (1842–1921), Russian scholar and political thinker, one of the founders of modern anarchism. He spent most of his life in emigration, returned in 1918 and met Lenin, but refused to work with the Bolsheviks. In Moscow, several places have borne his name since the time of his death, but his works were not reprinted until recent years. —V.I.

Kuprin, Aleksandr Ivanovich (1870–1938), influential Russian writer, who was, along with Maxim Gorky, Ivan Bunin, and Leonard Andreev, a prominent figure in the so-called Znanie [Knowledge] group of writers. He emigrated to France after the Revolution but returned to the Soviet Union in 1937 and died a year later in Leningrad.

Kuzmin, Mikhail Alekseevich (1875–1941), a Russian poet, prose writer, playwright, and critic who was associated with symbolist circles and then a member of the acmeist school. His article "On Beautiful Clarity" (1910) was perceived by the literary world as one of the manifestos of acmeism.

Leont'ev, Konstantin (1831–1891), a writer, critic, playwright, philosopher, and publicist. His work, including his brilliant literary criticism, attracted little attention during his lifetime. Leont'ev took monastic vows in 1891 and lived in Trinity–St. Sergius Monastery until his death later that year.

Ligachev, Egor Kuz'mich (b. 1920), Soviet Party official. Ligachev rose through Party ranks to prominent positions in the Politburo under Yuri Andropov. Initially a conditional ally of Mikhail Gorbachev and second secretary of the Party, Ligachev became a strong opponent of reform, eventually losing his post as Central Committee secretary for personnel and ideology in 1988. He resigned from the Politburo in 1990 and has recently been active in the Russian Federation Communist Party.

Lomonosov, Mikhail Vasil'evich (1711–1765), renowned Russian scholar who successfully united different fields of research (chemistry, philology, and so forth), a court poet, and one of the founders of modern Russian versification. —V.I.

Losskii, Nikolai Onufrievich (1870–1965), a philosopher and metaphysician of the Russian Silver Age. He left Russia in 1922 and during the 1920s and 1930s taught philosophy at the Free Russian University in Prague. He moved to New York in 1947 and taught at the Russian Theological Academy. After 1952 he lived in Los Angeles and Paris. In addition to his works on epistemology (or "intuitivism," as he called it), Losskii is known for his literary criticism (articles on Leo Tolstoy and the book *Dostoevskii i ego khristianskoe miroponimanie* (Dostoevsky and His Christian Understanding of the World, 1953) and his two-volume *History of Russian Philosophy*, which was originally published in English translation in 1951.

Lubarskii, Kronid (b. 1934), a former political prisoner and long-time editor of human rights bulletins in exile, who returned to Russia in the early 1990s to edit a parliamentary bulletin on human rights. —C.A.F.

Lukianov, Anatolii (b. 1930), the former speaker of the Soviet parliament. He was charged as one of the plotters of the August 1991 coup, was released, and allegedly supported the October 1993 rebellion of the Russian parliament. —C.A.F.

Makanin, Vladimir Semenovich (b. 1937), prominent modern Russian writer, author of novels, short stories, and essays. His long essay "Quasi" (1993) contains a discussion of the Bolshevik ideology as a substitute for religion. —V.I.

Makashov, Albert (b. 1938), a general and leader of the anti-Yeltsin insurrectionists in the White House. He was arrested after the failure of the coup.

Mandelstam, Osip Emil'evich (1891–1938), preeminent Russian poet and essayist of the twentieth century. His poetry divides into two major periods, the published collections (poems of 1908–25) and the unpublished notebooks (poems of 1930–37), preserved by his wife, Nadezhda Mandelstam, until they could be printed abroad. After his second arrest on May 1, 1938, he perished in the camps; the date given for his death is December 27, 1938.

Merezhkovskii, Dmitrii Sergeevich (1865–1941), a Russian writer, religious philosopher, and a translator from several languages, including Greek. He was a popularizer of French symbolism in the 1890s, chief advocate of the "new religious consciousness" after 1900, and prophet of a religious revolution after 1905. He died in Paris, a bitter opponent of Bolshevism to the very end.

Miliukov, Pavel Nikolaevich (1859–1943), a historian and liberal leader. He was a founding member of the Constitutional Democratic Party and a harsh critic of the incompetence of Nicholas II and his government, especially their management of Russia's war effort. Miliukov served as foreign minister in the Provisional Government. He was subsequently one of the organizers of the Volunteer Army and left Russia after the defeat of the Whites to spend the rest of his life in France.

Neizvestnyi, Ernst (b. 1926), a Russian sculptor now living in New York. He is best known for creating the monument for Nikita Khrushchev's grave in Novodevichyi Cemetery in Moscow, which Khrushchev commissioned despite his censure of the sculptor's work.

Odoevtseva, Irina Vladimirovna (1901–1990), a Russian poet and novelist who emigrated from Russia in 1923 with her husband, the poet Georgii Ivanov. She returned to Leningrad shortly before her death.

Platonov, Andrei Platonovich (1899–1951), an engineer, a writer, war correspondent, and critic. His first book, *Electrification*, appeared in 1921, followed by a book of verse entitled *Light-Blue Depth.* Many of his subsequent works, including *The Foundation Pit* and most of the novel *Chevengur*, were originally published in the West after his death. Persecuted by Josef Stalin and forbidden to publish under his own name for many years, Platonov spent the last years of his life working at the Detskaia Literatura publishing house, where he rewrote folktales. He died of tuberculosis, which he contracted from his son, who had caught the disease in the camps.

Pobedonostsev, Konstantin (1827–1907), Russian state figure, jurist, and chief procurator of the Synod. He held the Chair of Civil Law at Moscow University from 1860 to 1865 and later served as a senator, a member of the State Council, and chief procurator of the Synod. Pobedonostsev taught jurisprudence to the grand dukes, who later became Alexander III and Nicholas II, over whom he, an arch-conservative, had great influence. As chief procurator of the Synod, Pobedonostsev promoted Russian Orthodox Church schools while repressing those operated by the *zemstvos*.

Prokhanov, Aleksandr (b. 1938), the editor-in-chief of the right-wing newspaper *Zavtra* (formerly *Den'*). —C.A.F.

Rozanov, Vasilii Vasil'evich (1856–1919), writer, critic, philosopher, and journalist. Rozanov is considered one of the finest nonfiction stylists in the Russian language and is credited with drawing critical attention to the significance of "The Legend of the Grand Inquisitor" in Dostoevsky's *Brothers Karamazov*.

Saltykov-Shchedrin, Mikhail Evgrafovich (pseudonym, N. Shchedrin, 1826–1889), accomplished Russian writer who is now considered the greatest satirist of nineteenth-century Russia.

Shakhrai, Sergei (b. 1925), reformist political leader and a close ally of Boris Yeltsin. He has been first deputy premier and (until May 1994) minister for nationalities.

Shestov (pseudonym of Lev Isaakovich Shvartsman, 1866–1938), critic and philosopher. After 1919, he and his family left Russia to reside in France, where he gained an international reputation as a philosopher of existentialism, teaching at the Sorbonne. A writer known for his brilliant philosophical prose, Shestov also made substantial contributions to Russian literary criticism.

Simonov, Konstantin (Kirill) Mikhailovich (1915–1979), Soviet prose writer, dramatist, and poet. He worked as a correspondent for *Krasnaia zvezda* during World War II and later served as editor-in-chief of *Novyi mir* and editor of *Literaturnaia gazeta*. In addition to the wartime love poems "Wait for Me and I'll Return" and "With You and Without You," his most popular works are his war novels *Comrade in Arms*, *Days and Nights*, *The Living and the Dead*, and *Soldiers Are Not Born*.

Siniavskii, Andrei (b. 1925), a brilliant literary critic and essayist who, with Iulii Daniel, became a symbol of intellectual opposition during a 1965 trial for having circulated (under the pseudonym of Abram Tertz) mordant *samizdat* essays, including "Fantastic Tales," "The Trial Begins," and "What Is Socialist

Realism?" Now living in Paris, Siniavskii excoriated Boris Yeltsin for his actions during the September–October 1993 crisis of government.

Sologub, Fedor Kuzmich (1863–1927), a symbolist poet, short story writer, novelist, and dramatist. After his wife's suicide he renounced his intention to emigrate but was unable to publish original works after 1923 because their idealistic philosophy and fantasies ran counter to socialist realism. Sologub died in penury in Leningrad.

Solov'ev, Vladimir Sergeevich (1853–1900), eminent Russian religious philosopher, mystic, poet, and essayist. —V.I.

Stolypin, Petr Arkad'evich (1862–1911), a Russian right-wing politician who initiated the agrarian reform. He was killed by a socialist revolutionary terrorist (a subjective version of the story is given by Aleksandr Solzhenitsyn in *August 1914*). Stolypin became very popular in the time of Mikhail Gorbachev's reforms. —V.I.

Suvorov, Aleksandr Vasil'evich (1830–1800), redoubtable Russian general who fought against Napoleon. —V.I.

Tiutchev, Fedor Ivanovich (1803–1873), one of Russia's greatest lyric poets. The son of a noble family, Tiutchev studied in Moscow and St. Petersburg before entering the diplomatic service. From 1822 to 1844, he spent most of his time in Western Europe, sporadically publishing his verse in Russia. His first major success came with the publication in Pushkin's journal *Sovremennik* of a group of sixteen poems entitled "Poems Sent from Germany." Tiutchev lived in Russia from 1844 until his death in 1873, publishing the first collection of his verse in 1854 under Turgenev's editorship.

Tolstoy, Aleksei Nikolaevich (1883–1945), prominent Soviet Russian writer. A nobleman by birth, Tolstoy was one of the most authoritative apologists for Josef Stalin's regime. Tolstoy's literary career extended from symbolism to realism, from stories and novels about gentry life to fantastic tales, and then to historical novels. His death in 1945 was considered a great loss to Soviet letters and culture, second only to the death of Maxim Gorky in 1936. His most famous novels are his trilogy on the Revolution, *The Road to Calvary, Peter the First*, and *Aelita*.

Trubetskoi, Nikolai Sergeevich, Prince (1890–1938), a great Russian émigré linguist, the founder of modern phonology and some other fields of modern linguistics. His works on the Eurasian version of the philosophy of Russian history are published in English in *The Legacy of Genghis Khan and Other Essays on Russian Identity*, edited by A. Liberman, preface by Vyacheslav Ivanov (Michigan Slavic Publications, Ann Arbor, 1991). —V.I.

Tsiolkovskii, Konstantin Eduardovich (1857–1935), eminent Russian scientist and philosopher, the founder of the Russian technology of rockets and space-ships, the discoverer of the calculations that made space travel possible. Having become almost completely deaf in his childhood, he could not attend school. He was educated by Nikolai Fedorov, who also paid him from his own salary. Later, Tsiolkovskii served as a provincial school teacher. He published some of his fundamental works at his own expense in a provincial typography that had no Latin type fonts (in his equations they are substituted by Cyrillic letters). Some of his important works, including mystical notes, are still unpublished. —V.I.

Tsvetaeva, Marina Ivanovna (1892–1941), a Russian poet, essayist, and critic. She belongs to the quartet of Russia's greatest twentieth-century poets along with Anna Akhmatova, Osip Mandelstam, and Boris Pasternak. Tsvetaeva's work won early praise from Valerii Briusov, Maksimilian Voloshin, and Osip Mandelstam, and she is currently one of the poets most admired abroad, as much for her life as for her work. Tsvetaeva left Russia in 1922 to join her husband, who had emigrated after fighting with the Whites in Crimea. Her years in exile were marked by poverty and isolation, especially after her husband's role as a Soviet agent became public. She returned to the Soviet Union in 1939, where she committed suicide in 1941 following the German invasion and her evacuation from Moscow to Elabuga.

Tukhachevskii, Mikhail Nikolaevich (1893–1937), a famous Russian general executed by Josef Stalin. —V.I.

Vavilov, Nikolai Ivanovich (1887–1943), geneticist, agronomist, geographer, and academician. A champion of objective scientific research at a time when the charlatan geneticist Trofim Lysenko was propagating fraudulent agricul-tural schemes at Stalin's behest, Vavilov led numerous botanical expeditions throughout the world from 1920 to 1940 and promoted farming of Russia's underdeveloped northern, semidesert, and high mountain regions.

Voloshin, Maksimilian Aleksandrovich (1877–1932), a Russian poet, translator of French poetry, and artist. He was a contributor to the symbolist journals *Vesy* and *Zolotoe runo* and later to the acmeist periodical *Apollon*. He depicted the sufferings of Russia as a nation, invoked its dismal history, and expressed his belief in its Christian essence and mission. His literary criticism is contained in his most famous prose work, *Liki tvorchestva* (Masks of Creation).

Vvedenskii, Aleksandr Ivanovich (1904–1941), a poet and writer. Vvedenskii is best known for his participation, with Daniil Kharms, N.Z. Zabolotskii, and others, in the Obeirut (Association for Real Art) group active from 1928 to 1930. Vvedenskii read his controversial poems at the stage shows produced by the Obeiruts, which included dramas, film, poetry, and music. After 1930, he wrote numerous books for children and published in the journals *Ezh* and *Chizh*. (Most of Vvedenskii's work for adults was not published during his lifetime.) Vvedenskii moved from Leningrad to Kharkov in 1936, was arrested in 1941, and died later that year during the evacuation. The circumstances of his death are not clear.

Witte, Sergei Iulievich, Count (1849–1915), a skillful politician, and author of several important reforms, including the agrarian reform associated with Stolypin. As described in his extremely valuable memoirs, he tried without much success to find support for the government among the leaders of the new capitalist class. —V.I.

Zhvanetskii, Mikhail (b. 1934), a contemporary satirist, writer, and social humorist. The actor Arkadii Raikin made Zhvanetskii famous through stage performances of his short pieces critical of the Soviet way of life and socialist traditions.

Ziuganov, Gennadii (b. 1944), head of the new Russian Communist Party, which competed in the December 1993 elections. —C.A.F.

Index